PROBLEMS OF THE MODERN ECONOMY

The Goal of Economic Growth

PROBLEMS OF THE MODERN ECONOMY

General Editor: EDMUND S. PHELPS, *University of Pennsylvania*

Each volume in this series presents prominent positions in the debate of an important issue of economic policy

---

The Goal of
Economic Growth

Edited with an introduction by

EDMUND S. PHELPS

UNIVERSITY OF PENNSYLVANIA

REVISED EDITION

NEW YORK

W · W · NORTON & COMPANY · INC ·

Growth Through Taxation, by James Tobin. From *The New Republic* (July 25, 1960). Reprinted by permission of *The New Republic*.

The Costs of Economic Growth from *The Costs of Economic Growth* by Ezra J. Mishan (1967). Reprinted by permission of Frederick A. Praeger, Inc., and Staples Press.

What Price Economic Growth? from *Papers on Welfare and Growth* by Tibor Scitovsky. Reprinted with the permission of the publishers, Stanford University Press, and George Allen & Unwin Ltd. © 1964 by Tibor Scitovsky.

Economic Growth as a National Goal, originally published as "High Employment and Growth in the American Economy," by Herbert Stein and Edward F. Denison, from the Report of the President's Commission on National Goals in *Goals for Americans* by The American Assembly, Columbia University, copyright 1960. Reprinted by permission of Prentice-Hall, Inc.

Public Responsibility for Growth and Stability (final paragraph) from *Economics: An Introductory Analysis* by Paul A. Samuelson. Copyright 1961 by McGraw-Hill Book Company, Inc. Used by permission.

Governmental "Neutralism" and "Activism" in Growth Decisions, by Edmund S. Phelps. Drawn in part from material in *Fiscal Neutrality Toward Economic Growth*, McGraw-Hill Book Company. Reprinted with permission.

Fixed Investment and Economic Growth by Robert Solow. From *Perspectives on Economic Growth*, Walter W. Heller (ed.). © Copyright 1968 by Walter W. Heller. Reprinted by permission of Random House, Inc.

Investment in Human Capital, by Theodore W. Schultz. From the *American Economic Review* (March 1961). Reprinted by permission of the author and the American Economic Association.

Underinvestment in College Education? by Gary S. Becker. From the *American Economic Review* (May 1960). Reprinted by permission of the author and the American Economic Association.

Research and Economic Growth: The Role of Public Policy, by Benton F. Massell and Richard R. Nelson. From the *California Management Review* (Winter 1962). Reprinted by permission of the *California Management Review*.

Can There Be Too Much Research? by Fritz Machlup. From *Science* (November 28, 1958). Reprinted by permission of the author and *Science*.

Technological Change and Industrial Research from *The Economics of Technological Change* by Edwin Mansfield. Reprinted by permission of W. W. Norton & Company, Inc. Copyright © 1968 by W. W. Norton & Company, Inc.

Economic Growth: The Last Hundred Years, by Deborah C. Paige, with F. T. Blackaby and S. Freund. From the *National Institute Economic Review* (July 1961). Reprinted by permission of the National Institute of Economic and Social Research, 2 Dean Trench Street, London, S.W.1.

The Pattern of U.S. Economic Growth, by Simon Kuznets. From *The Nation's Economic Objectives*, Edgar O. Edwards (ed.), a Rice University Semicentennial Publication 1964). Reprinted by permission.

Postindustrial America in the Year 2000, reprinted with permission of The Macmillan Company from *The Year 2000* by Herman Kahn and Anthony J. Wiener. Copyright © The Hudson Institute 1967.

Acknowledgments

My thanks to Steven Salop, Penn's white hope, for bibliographic and editorial assistance in this extensive revision, and to Carole Horwell, Southampton's vivacious solution to deadlines.   E. S. P.

Contents

1494272

Introduction

THE ECONOMIC GROWTH of this country was, until recently, a matter of little popular concern. There was continual concern over the growth of *market demand* in relation to the growth of productive capacity: inflation was feared if demand grew too rapidly, unemployment was feared if demand grew too slowly. But the growth of *productive capacity* itself was not a source of worry. The nation's capacity to produce grew steadily decade after decade. The adequacy of the rate of growth, which had made this nation the most prosperous in the world, was not questioned.

The lack of popular concern over growth was reflected in government policy. We had no public policy toward the rate of growth. Many government activities, especially investments in the public sector, made a vital contribution to growth. Yet no branch of government ever took measures explicitly to alter the growth of the private economy where the great bulk of the goods and services are produced. Our public policies sought mainly to make the private economy efficient, equitable, and stable. Clearly an economy can achieve all these goals and yet not grow; pursuit of these goals did not necessarily stimulate growth. If the legislation, expenditures, taxes, and monetary operations by which government pursued these goals sometimes affected the rate of growth, this effect was typically a by-product. Government policies expressly designed to alter the growth of the private economy were not contemplated.

Around 1960 attitudes and public policy gave signs of changing. After a brief postwar spurt ending about 1952, capacity grew at an average annual rate of 3.6 percent. This was a respectable rate by our historical standards; it exceeded slightly our growth rate between 1900 and 1929, and it was far better than the dismal years of the Great Depression and World War II. (See Table 1.) But many people were no longer content with our average peacetime growth rate. They called growth a public responsibility.

Government measures to raise the rate of growth were proposed. President Kennedy declared 4½ percent annual growth in the 1960's a goal of public policy.

Yet the idea of accelerating our economic growth has, quite properly, raised many questions and controversies. Recently, a mood of Anti-Growth has been detectable in some quarters. Do we, the richest nation in the world, need to be richer? What benefits could faster growth confer that we cannot have now through better use of our existing resources? Does growth bring true progress? Can government avoid affecting the rate of growth? These questions are taken up in Part One of this volume.

TABLE 1. *The Growth of Productive Capacity in the United States Economy 1900–1967.*

Total Annual Capacity Output in Selected Years
(1967 prices in billions of dollars)

1900	1929	1947	1952	1957	1962	1967
90	241	373	465	551	666	786

Annual Rates of Growth of Total Capacity Output
(In percent)

| Terminal Year | Initial Year | | | | | |
	1900	1929	1947	1952	1957	1962
1929	3.5					
1947	3.1	2.5				
1952	3.2	2.9	4.5			
1957	3.2	3.0	4.0	3.5		
1962	3.3	3.1	3.9	3.7	3.8	
1967	3.3	3.2	3.8	3.6	3.6	3.4

NOTES: The growth rates are compounded annual rates of change of Total Capacity Output. Capacity Output—sometimes called Potential GNP—is the Gross National Product (in 1967 prices) obtainable through full utilization of the economy's existing resources. GNP is the market value of all final goods and services produced. For purposes of calculation, full utilization is defined as a 97.5% employment rate.

In estimating the level of GNP that an employment rate of 97.5% would have produced, it was assumed that a decline of the unemployment rate by one percentage point would raise actual GNP as a percentage of potential GNP by 3 points (in the postwar years and 2 points in the two prewar years).

Actual GNP data are from the U. S. Department of Commerce, with the exception of GNP in 1900, which is from the Kendrick-Kuznets series published in John W. Kendrick, *Productivity Trends in the United States* (Princeton, 1961).

Part Two considers the means of economic growth. Which are best? This section examines what economists have learned about how to grow and what is being done to implement this knowledge. Finally, Part Three looks at the past growth record and peers into the future.

GROWTH: A NEW GOAL OF PUBLIC POLICY?

The first essay, by James Tobin, exemplifies the mood of many liberal economists around 1960. The comparatively rapid growth of the Soviet Union and of Western Europe in the decade then just ended produced dissatisfaction with America's growth rate. The Rockefeller Brothers Fund report of 1958, for example, saw in faster growth the most practicable way to provide the public services, including the envisioned defense outlays, that it expected to be desirable ten years hence. The answer, according to these economists, was to raise taxes, or to check the round of tax cuts, so as to restrain for a while the rise of consumption and thus to leave a greater volume of resources available for investments in tangible capital, education and technological research.

Since one of the impulses behind the plea for faster American growth was competition with the Soviet Union, it may be of some interest to consider the arithmetic of international growth rate differences. Table 2 tabulates the time it would take the Soviet Union to reach the American level of GNP on various growth rate assumptions if the Soviet GNP is two thirds of ours.[1] On the top row are hypothetical U.S. future growth rates and

TABLE 2. *Years Until USSR Overtakes the U.S. GNP*

USSR Growth Rate	U.S. Growth Rate		
	3%	4%	5%
5%	20	41	—
6%	14	20	41
7%	10	14	20
8%	8	10	14

1. When we add up the Russians' heterogeneous outputs and compare it to the menu of goods produced here, we have to put price tags on the corn, caviar and machine tools which we and they produce. It makes a difference whose price tags are chosen.

in the lefthand column are hypothetical Soviet growth rates. The table shows the catch-up time for each pair of growth rates.[2] (Observe that the lapse of time before the economic "lead" changes hands depends only on the difference between the two countries' growth rates.)

The Anti-Growth reaction to the call for faster growth is exemplified in the selection by Ezra Mishan. He argues that economic growth has ceased effectively to expand our choices: As the carpet of "increased choice" is being unrolled before us by the foot, it is simultaneously being rolled up behind us by the yard. The essay by Tibor and Anne Scitovsky points to the damaging side-effects of rising wage rates and specialization upon the cultural and intellectual quality of life when public institutions are unable or unwilling to remedy these effects.

Herbert Stein and Edward Denison also question much of the enthusiasm for faster growth. They believe that the need for faster growth has not always been well reasoned. If we are going without public services which are needed *now*, then the most rational response would seem to be simply to supply them. Should inflation threaten, we can cut back less badly needed public or private expenditures. It ought to be the least needed goods and services for which we must wait until the capacity of our economy is able to meet them.

To validate the unmet-social-needs argument, Stein and Denison suggest, it must be assumed that we are the victims of a system which has "locked" government expenditure at some fixed proportion of national income. If we cannot change the share of resources committed to the public sector, then we shall have to make GNP grow exactly as fast as we want the public sector to grow.

Yet growth facilitates a change in the share of national resources allocated to the satisfaction of unmet public needs. Could we afford present government programs without our past growth? By raising the productivity of private industry we can meet the demand for private goods in our economy with fewer workers. Rising productivity in the private sector will release resources

2. Simple GNP comparisons do not capture differences in population size and hence in consumption per capita and the possible differences in the efficiency with which the two economies meet consumer preferences.

for public use *with no loss of private output*. Similarly, if we could find a way to raise the productivity of the public sector—and automation is beginning to play a role in both military and civilian agencies—resources there would be released for use in the private sector or in new uses in the public sector. In any case, the growth of productivity expands the opportunities of the economy.

Stein and Denison touch on another issue which is raised in subsequent essays in Part One. They call it a "real and serious issue" whether the government should take deliberate steps to alter the national rate of growth. They cite the "alternative view" that the "desirable rate of growth and the correct means to achieve it are those that would emerge from private decisions." Just such a view seems to be taken by W. Allen Wallis.

Wallis feels, first of all, that many proposals to accelerate economic growth threaten individual freedom. The "modern mercantilists" wish to "force" growth on the economy. Their approach involves compelling people to consume less either through taxes or through inflation, in order to free resources for investment and other growth-producing uses. He opposes "depressed" levels of consumption except in "dire emergency," and he sees none now. In view of this country's substantial lead over the Soviet Union and the rate at which we are already satisfying public needs, Wallis wishes to let growth emerge as the natural by-product of an economy in which the government's task is to strengthen equality of opportunity, individual initiative, and economic stability and to provide public services with "realism and restraint."

Wallis concludes that the "right" rate of growth in a free and efficient economy is "that rate which conforms to the voluntary choices of the people" rather than a rate obtained by "coercion."

Paul Samuelson's essay relates to this issue. He contends first that the government *can* control the level of investment in the economy—private investment as well as public investment—by the way it chooses among various monetary and fiscal instruments in its efforts to control the level of employment in the economy. For example, a "tight" money policy and a compensating "easy" fiscal policy boosts consumption, reduces investment, and hence reduces the rate of growth. He believes the range of choice among these policy instruments is sufficiently wide that we can have whatever level of employment *and* rate of growth that our society wishes to have.

Samuelson points out that every modern economy necessarily follows certain monetary and fiscal policies. Every society *must choose* how to use its policy instruments. Therefore, the government *does* control investment and growth and cannot avoid doing so.

Samuelson's view has important implications for Wallis' position. If it is true that the government is confronted with such choices, then is the present rate of growth necessarily the "right" one? Personal consumption expenditures are typically made in a voluntary manner; but if the level of voluntary consumption is partly the product of government decisions about taxes and so forth, can we be sure we happen to have the right level? The principle of voluntarism appears to validate any aggregate consumption level, whence any rate of aggregate investment and growth.

Stein and Denison recognize that "the rate of growth emerging from private decisions is inevitably affected by the action of the government in discharging its important functions." Yet they question, without committing themselves, whether these functions should be extended to include "the explicit determination" of the rate of growth. But what if Samuelson is right that the government must choose among more than one way to discharge important functions like maintaining high employment: then how can the government (and the people who elect it) escape responsibility for the effect of its decisions on the rate of growth?

Still, one should consider whether the government could exercise its responsibility in a way that makes it "neutral" toward the rate of growth. In the essay by Edmund Phelps, a concept of fiscal neutrality toward growth is introduced. Under certain conditions, private markets would operate to give consumers and savers the rate of growth they want if tax policy were neutral. Whether one should opt for an "activist" policy toward growth, by which the government decides the growth rate on behalf of the citizenry, or instead opt for a "neutralist" policy, depends upon how one assesses the failure of the economy to meet these conditions.

THREE WAYS TO GROW

Our rate of growth depends on how we use our inputs. Like consumer demands, public needs, or any economic want, growth requires the expenditure of scarce resources. What are the principal means of growth? Which instruments of growth are the most effective, which the "best buy"? This is an important area in economic policy.

As Tobin suggested, we can increase our future capacity in three principal ways: we can devote our resources to increasing our stock of *capital goods;* we can employ resources in *research;* and we can allocate resources to the *education* of the population. Alternatively, if we would rather not grow, we can let our resources lie idle—unemployment frequently makes a large claim on our resources—or we can use them to provide the consumer goods and leisure which constitute a country's standard of living.

In making such growth-producing expenditures, we are giving up potential (if not actual) consumption. It would be correct to say therefore that all three means of growth constitute forms of investment. The effectiveness of these three kinds of investment in increasing our productive capacity, the manner in which they contribute to growth, are the concern of Part Two.

Tobin attaches great importance to investment in tangible capital. After the early 1950's, annual private expenditures for plant and equipment increased relatively little; private fixed investment even dipped below 10 percent of GNP. This could provide part of the explanation for the detectable retardation of the economy in the middle and late 1950's.

In the first essay of Part Two, Robert Solow discusses the impact of tangible investment on growth. Solow focusses particular attention on fixed tangible investment, that is, on the production of plant and equipment.

Without investment, productivity would not grow at all. Clearly we have to renew and reshape old capital if we are to take advantage of the technological advances which account for so much of our growth. Thus investment is needed to modernize the capital stock as well as to maintain or enlarge it. One implication of this new view of investment is that the net rate of return on business investment may be substantially higher than had been thought before. (This will shortly be elaborated.) Still the major sources of growth seem to lie elsewhere.

Theodore Schultz believes the secret of growth is education. Schultz finds that the capital stock has not been keeping up with output. We seem to need less and less tangible capital. One explanation of this, Schultz acknowledges, is increasing returns to scale: our productivity per man-hour and per unit capital may benefit from the increase in the size of the economy. But the more important explanation, Schultz believes, is that "human capital" has been growing very rapidly—faster than tangible capital and faster even than output—and that this human capital is replacing tangible capital. While tangible capital was about four times larger in 1956 than 1900, the "stock of education"—the value of the resources devoted to the education of the population —rose about eight times in the same period. If we want to grow rapidly in the future, we dare not neglect investment in education.

Schultz goes farther and suggests that there may be "substantial underinvestment" in human beings at the present time. Schultz may very well feel that we have too little of all kinds of capital; however by "underinvestment" he means that we have invested too little in "human capital" *relative* to our enormous investment in tangible capital. He is suggesting that had we invested less in the latter and more in the former, we would have a higher level of productivity.

Gary Becker questions this hypothesis. Presumably most of the benefits of education are reflected in the greater incomes that educated persons in the labor force can earn. But Becker estimates that college students earn a rate of return on their "investment" in a college education of only 9 percent or so (before taxes). Is this better than the rate of return earned by businesses on their tangible capital? Becker estimates that businesses in the early 1950's earned at least 8 percent on their capital (before taxes). But when the superior efficiency of modern investments is taken into account, the rate of return on business capital may be as high or higher (at high levels of capacity utilization). So there is still no strong case for the "underinvestment" hypothesis, although the matter is not settled yet.

One kind of calculation of the *private* rate of return to investment in tangible capital is the following. The gross earnings (before taxes and depreciation) in the U.S. business sector, which excludes government production and a variety of nonprofit enterprises, would have been about $100 billion had the level of business activity been normal that year. The gross earning *rate* on capital depends upon the replacement cost of the tangible capital employed by the business sector that year. This cost has been estimated at about $650 billion in 1954 on the basis of a depreciation rate of 4 percent. (See Row 1 in Table 3.) This gives a net rate of return on capital of about 11 percent. This conventional estimate neglects the possibility of a quality differential between old and new capital goods of the same real historical cost: It assumes that a 1930 truck that cost as much in terms of consumption goods as a 1954 truck can do as much work as the newer one. But if the new truck can do the work of two 1930 trucks, the reproduction cost of a 1930 truck is only half the cost of a new truck. Row 2 of the table shows a recalculation of the true replacement cost when there is a 2 percent improvement per annum in the efficiency of investments. The replacement cost is of course smaller than in Row 1. The corresponding gross earnings rate is higher, but the *net* rate of return is less for we must deduct the obsolescence rate caused by 2 percent improvement.[3]

TABLE 3. *Potential Net Rate of Return on 1954 Business Investment*

Assumed improvement rate	*Replacement cost of business capital*	*Gross earnings rate*	*Rate of depreciation*	*Rate of obsolescence*	*Net rate of return*
$\iota = 0\%$	$650 billion	15.4%	4%	0%	11.4%
$\iota = 2\%$	510 billion	19.6%	4%	2%	13.6%
$\iota = 3\%$	470 billion	21.3%	4%	3%	14.3%

NOTE: Potential gross business earnings in 1954 in the business sector are assumed to be $100 billion.

3. The student may wonder whether the improvement rate should be deducted from the gross earnings rate in calculating the *social* rate of return. This deduction is appropriate. It reflects the attraction to society of waiting to invest (hastening consumption) in order to take advantage of the future cheapening of capacity increases in terms of consumption goods.

For an advanced discussion of social return estimation, see E. S. Phelps, "The New View of Investment," *Quarterly Journal of Economics*, November 1962.

The third kind of investment discussed in Part Two is "investment in technology." Presumably research makes a great contribution to technical change. But what kind of research do we need? What is the most efficient allocation of our research personnel? Benton Massell and Richard Nelson look at this question.

They see no need to subsidize or otherwise stimulate industrial research and development. So long as the benefits of industrial research accrue only to the firms that undertake it, we can count on these firms to make correct research decisions.

The core of the policy recommended by Massell and Nelson concerns fundamental or basic research. Here the incentives of private firms are much weaker. Basic research, by its very nature, has a payoff which is difficult to estimate. Characteristically, the benefits of fundamental research, even when successful, are apt to accrue significantly to a large segment of the economy, not simply to the firm undertaking the research. So there is some presumption that private firms, on the whole, neglect basic research from the standpoint of its total social benefits. This justifies government promotion of basic research.

Fritz Machlup ties together some of the ideas of Part Two. Machlup defines certain departments of economic activities. First, there is the *capital goods* department; and second is the department of *knowledge*—that is, education, basic research, and applied research. Given the level of consumption we want to have, the choice is between "knowledge" and "equipment."

Machlup points out that it is one thing to stress the importance of knowledge in providing the rate of growth we already have. But it is another thing to suggest that technological research should have first claim on *additional* resources. The allocation problem is especially treacherous in the knowledge department. The hugh increase in industrial research and development in the past twenty or thirty years, Machlup reasons, has been largely at the cost of basic research and of education.

Edwin Mansfield's essay discusses several topics in the economics of technological progress and research, including his own recent estimates of the private rates of return to industrial research, basic plus applied, in selected American industries. While the range of these rates of return is enormous, their mean value apparently is at least as great as the probable rate of return from investment in tangible capital and in human capital.

THE LONG VIEW

In Part Three, the study by Deborah Paige and colleagues at the National Institute shows that the rapid postwar growth rates posted by so many countries have ample historical precedent. But these exceptional periods typically have some special explanation, like the recovery of the capital stock to a normal relation to output following a war.

Simon Kuznets is impressed by the relative constancy of the rate of growth of output per head. Indeed, his data suggest that the United States has maintained a fairly constant distance, in terms of income per head, between itself and the major European countries ever since 1840.

If per capita growth in this country continues at its customary pace, what will be its effects on society in the future? Keynes, writing in 1930, thought the "economic problem" would be solved within a hundred years. He wrote hopefully of the kind of social and cultural changes this would permit, though he expressed some worry that these developments would not occur. Herman Kahn and Anthony Wiener take a darker view. According to their "standard scenario," which portrays a continuation of historical trends and a substantial increase of leisure, continued growth at past rates until the year 2000 will produce problems of alienation on an unprecedented scale. The principal task of social science and politics may very well be to bring an adjustment by society to these impending economic developments.

PROBLEMS OF THE MODERN ECONOMY

The Goal of Economic Growth

PROLOGUE

Perspective on Economic Growth

EDMUND S. PHELPS

The author is Professor of Economics at the University of Pennsylvania. This brief look at American growth, past and future, was broadcast over the Voice of America in 1966 as a part of the Forum Lectures on American economics. The lectures were published the following year in the volume The Changing American Economy, *edited by J. R. Coleman.*

THE RAPID GROWTH of the American economy over more than a hundred years presents many puzzles for the economist and the economic historian. The prospects for American economic growth in the future and the manner in which the federal government ought to influence future growth are equally open to question.

By the "growth rate" is usually meant the proportionate rate of increase per year of *national product* or *national income*. This concept of national product is an aggregate measure of the market value of the consumption goods (including services) produced and sold to households, of plant and equipment produced and sold to business firms and of goods produced and supplied to the community by federal, state, and local governments. (Another way to arrive at national product is to add the wages and salaries earned by households to the profits received by businesses.) To be more precise, the economist means by the growth rate the rate of increase of *real* national product—i.e., the money value of national income adjusted for inflation. Unfortunately it is hard to make this adjustment accurately because of quality improvements in goods which justify price increases; this is increasingly a problem as the American economy becomes more and more a service-producing rather than a commodity-producing economy. Finally,

1

the purist in these matters, the academic economist, means by the growth rate the rate of increase of *potential* or *capacity* real national product. This concept can only be estimated, not measured. It is a measure of the real national product that would have been produced in a given year had the economy been employing its resources fully in that year. The "growth economist" is not directly concerned with those cyclical fluctuations in real national product which are caused by variations in the degree to which the labor supply and existing capital goods are utilized.

In addition, the economist is interested in the rate of increase of "productivity," as measured by national product per person employed or per manhour worked.

THE GROWTH STORY

Now a brief look at the record. In 1840 the United States was already at a high economic level, ranking fourth among nations in income per head, below England, France, and Germany. But at about this time there began rapid and fairly continuous growth. By 1870 the United States had surpassed Germany and France.

Between 1871 and 1913 American real national product grew at the very high rate of 4.5 percent per year. This was by far the highest growth rate of that period. Much of this growth was due to immigration, of course, but even real national product per person employed grew very fast—at the rate of 2.2 percent per year. This was higher than the rate for all the major industrial countries of the world except Sweden and Japan, which were growing from a much lower initial level. By 1913, and even before, the United States had the highest income per head in the world.

In the years between 1913 and 1959 real national product grew at only 3 percent per year and the growth rate of national product per employed person was only 1.8 percent per year. But, with the exception of Japan, this was still a bit above the rate for the other major industrial countries. Thus the United States slightly strengthened its industrial lead over most countries in the twentieth century even though its growth was slower than it had been earlier.

A reason for this slowdown in American growth between 1913

and 1959 is not hard to find: the Great Depression of the 1930's led to a drastic reduction of investment-goods expenditures; as a consequence, the capital stock grew very slowly. In addition, industrial research and development activities of U.S. firms were reduced. During World War II, when the American economy operated at full capacity, investment-goods production that could be used for postwar civilian purposes was still below the normal peacetime level. Therefore the relatively slow pace of American growth over the period 1913–1959 is entirely reasonable.

The American economy made up for some of this lost growth in the postwar period. Between 1947 and 1957 potential real national product grew at the rate of 3.9 percent, well above the twentieth-century average. The rate of increase of output per employed person was very high as well: about 2.5 percent. This transition from an extraordinarily low to an extraordinarily high growth rate can also be explained by the war and the preceding depression: those events had reduced the capital-output ratio, which made it easy to have rapid proportionate growth of the capital stock in the postwar period. In addition, the capital stock had grown old and obsolete by the end of World War II, so that the postwar investments had a great effect in modernizing the economy's capital stock.

Before turning attention to future growth prospects, let us ask what can be said to explain America's rapid growth over this long period from 1840. There is considerable agreement by economists that an important part of the explanation was America's quickness to develop new techniques of production and new products from theoretical scientific advances then occurring and to put these new techniques and products into industrial practice. This quickness must have been due, in part, to scientific expertise, especially in industrial management, to a well-educated population, to an adequate amount of competition and incentive, as well as to a host of other noneconomic influences. Though the details of this mechanism are not yet known, and may never be, it is especially agreed that America's tendency over most of these years to invest about 15 percent of national product in tangible capital goods—plant and equipment—has not been the prime mover in its economic growth. For without continued technological progress, the persistent investment of a constant fraction of national product would lead eventually to a constant level of national product per head. It is true that some small portion of the difference between national income per head in America and national income per head in the other major industrial countries is due to a higher capital stock per head in the U.S. But this difference in capital per head is largely due to America's higher income per head and hence to its past technological progressiveness, not to its greater propensity to invest in capital hardware.

WHAT OF THE FUTURE?

I come now to America's prospects for growth in the future. Undoubtedly, American economic growth over the far future will depend in large measure upon the underlying advances in science that are going to take place. It is probably safer to predict America's growth rate over, say, the next fifteen years. But even that prediction is fraught with difficulties.

In making such predictions, economists usually assume that there will be no war nor any prolonged "depression" during this period. Frequently, they further assume that America will continue to invest about 15 percent of its national product each year in new tangible capital goods. Making these assumptions, it might be argued (and has been argued) that the rate of increase of productivity—of real national product per employee—will be about 2.2 percent per year. This was the rate experienced in the pre-World War I period and approximately the rate experienced in the period 1900–1929 before the Depression, World War II, and the postwar recovery. In addition, the labor force is expected to grow at about 1.8 percent per year until 1975, perhaps until 1980. Adding together these two rates, we obtain a growth rate of real national product of approximately 4 percent per year.

There is a more optimistic school which argues that our growth rate will be nearer to 4.5 percent per year, thanks to a faster rise in productivity. This school puts much more weight on the unusually rapid increase in productivity during the postwar period. Pointing to the ever enlarging expenditures on technological research and development by both private business and the federal government, it stresses the steady advance of technology.

Whichever school is right—the pessimists or the optimists—we can expect the gap between per capita income in America and that in several of the other industrial countries to be somewhat narrowed over the next fifteen years. Certainly Japan and probably the Soviet Union, West Germany, France, and Italy, to mention a few, will catch up with America to some degree. These countries have enjoyed more rapid growth of potential national product than has America since the war, including the past few years, but as they approach American technological practice they may find it increasingly difficult to close the remaining gap.

GOVERNMENT AND THE RATE OF GROWTH

The possibility that America may lose its relative economic position has led some American economists to urge governmental action to increase America's rate of growth. This has raised many questions. What is the most efficient way to increase growth: By increased investment in tangible capital goods? By increased research? or by increased education? And how expensive would it be in terms of consumption goods—in terms of present enjoyment —to increase America's rate of growth by one percentage point over the next fifteen years? Is faster economic growth worth the necessary sacrifices?

Actually the question of how much growth concerns even the majority of economists who are not worried about America's relative position. Since economics is largely the study of the allocation of scarce resources to satisfy competing ends, it is natural that economists would be concerned about the division of resources between those uses that satisfy current wants and those uses that contribute to growth and hence to satisfying future wants. Yet this concern about the "right" rate of growth is only some ten years old in the United States.

The late eighteenth- and nineteenth-century English political economists, who are intellectual ancestors of American economists, realized that the central government could reduce economic growth by running a "budgetary deficit"—by taxing less than enough to cover expenditures; this would stimulate consumption and choke off investment. But these classical economists considered budgetary deficits (and surpluses) to be immoral and hence put an end to any discussion of the best rate of investment or the best rate of growth.

John Maynard Keynes, the great English economist of this century, produced a revolution against classical thinking. His argument was that a budgetary deficit or surpus will usually be needed to maintain full employment. Keynes appeared to believe that, usually, there would be just one budgetary deficit consistent with full employment, not a whole range of deficits each one having different consequences for growth.

American economists have interpreted Keynes's view of the economic system somewhat differently. Many of them believe that full employment can be achieved by a budgetary deficit (low taxes) and "tight money" (high interest rates) *or* by a budgetary surplus (high taxes) and "easy money" (low interest rates). If the government chooses high taxes and low interest rates, consumption expenditures by the heavily taxed households will be small while the low interest rates will stimulate large investment expenditures and hence produce a high rate of growth. Tangible investment expenditures as well as expenditures for research and for education may be stimulated.

In addition to these general controls, the federal government is recognized to have specific controls over research, tangible capital expenditures, and education. It carries out and subsidizes a great deal of "basic" scientific research and allows private business firms to treat research-and-development outlays as a current expense to be deducted from taxable profits; recently it instituted a "tax credit" on business expenditures for capital equipment. The federal government has also been giving increasing stimulus to education, which was once almost exclusively the province of the state governments and of private colleges and universities.

Thus it is now widely felt by American economists that the government can bring about the desired level of employment and at the same time control the division of resources between consumption and growth-producing investments and even to control the broad division of resources among tangible investment, technological research, and education. In view of these government controls, American economists are now very much interested in two questions: "How fast should America seek to grow?"—i.e., how much present consumption goods should we sacrifice in return for growth and future consumption? And, second, "What is the least expensive, most efficient way to grow at a specified rate?" That is, what is the best "mixture" of research, education, and tangible capital formation?

How Much Growth Is Best? · There is no agreement on the part of American economists on the first question, "How much growth?" One minority school argues that the question itself is a bad one. These people, who include some economists, argue that it is not a proper function of the government to decide—or for the American electorate to decide through the polls—how fast the economy ought to grow. They contend that the government should pursue a "neutral" policy toward growth, leaving it to the private marketplace to determine the amount of investment and consumption, hence to determine the rate of growth. Unfortunately, there are so many imperfections in the private marketplace that a neutral policy would not be ideal; indeed, even if markets were perfect, there probably would exist government policies that would make the presently living population better off than would a neutral policy.

The discussion of "How much growth?" raises the fundamental question of what should we *mean* by "optimal" growth or the "right" rate of growth? How should the "growth optimum" be defined? Many mathematical economists in America and abroad have explored the concept of a growth optimum which involves assigning certain weights to the consumption or to the enjoyment of the consumers living at the present time and assumed to be living at each year in the future. But it is not indicated how these weights are to be chosen—whether dictatorially or through some improbable ethical consensus. Further, it may be unrealistic to expect future generations to behave as is assumed in this approach: future generations may pursue their own self-interests. Nevertheless these mathematical exercises may sometime prove to have been useful in the development of a concept of a growth optimum.

While the academic economists reflect, the government continues to make decisions about the use of its controls, conscious or unconscious of the consequences of these decisions for America's future growth. What consequences have these decisions had for growth? The Kennedy administration and the Johnson administration saw their principal economic problem as the task of reducing the large volume of unemployment that plagued the American economy in the first half of this decade. To reduce unemployment, the government could have stimulated mainly investment expenditures by means of low interest rates and tax measures, or the government could have stimulated mainly consumption expenditures by the reduction of personal income tax rates. In fact, the government chose a combination of measures which may have stimulated consumption a little more, percentagewise, than investment. But, of course, the resulting increase in capacity utilization and business profits induced a substantial rise in investment expenditures.

What measures did the government take to reduce unemployment? There was a substantial reduction of personal income tax rates, which increased consumption expenditures. To stimulate investment, the government took a number of steps: it introduced the new fiscal device of a tax credit (or tax reduction) given to certain businesses making investment expenditures; it liberalized the depreciation schedules which businesses could use in figuring their profits for tax purposes; and it reduced tax rates on corporate profits. The total reduction of business income taxation, taking these measures together, was about equal proportionately to the reduction of taxation on the personal income of households. But probably consumption responded more strongly to these tax reductions than investment did.

The American government did not reduce interest rate and ease credit to stimulate investment. America's balance-of-payments troubles played a role here. Although the Johnson administration might have liked to have lower interest rates, the Federal Reserve System—the nation's central bank, which can operate independently of the Executive Branch of the government— chose high interest rates to prevent an outflow of short-term capital abroad. There is some question, however, whether this policy of high interest rates has been very effective. When the Federal Reserve System raised interest rates during America's emergence from the situation of low employment and depressed business conditions, foreign central banks were free to raise their interest rates in response, so as to nullify the effect of America's action. The end result may largely have been an all-round rise of interest rates in America, Europe, and other financial centers, with the main consequence being a reduction of growth in many countries and little alteration of the international payments imbalances.

The second question of interest is how to grow efficiently, at minimum cost. Given the total amount that is being spent on investments of all kinds, should we have more research and less plant and equipment expenditure? More education and less research? What is the right combination? To this question, at least, economists have some theoretical and conceptual answers. In a laissez-faire economy there is a presumption that there will be too little research relative to investment in tangible capital goods because research is risky and because it rewards society more than it rewards the individual business firm that undertakes it. But the American economy is not laissez-faire; the government already gives much support to research and to education—more support than to plant and equipment expenditures. Whether the federal government should tip the scales even more in favor of research or education is an open question. Economists are trying to answer this question by statistical analysis of "rates of return," but it is a formidable task.

It is clear, then, that America is a long way from finding answers to these perplexing questions of economic growth. But there is new and increasing interest in these questions and it may be that we will have tolerably good answers to them before this century has passed.

PART ONE   How Much Growth?

Growth Through Taxation

JAMES TOBIN

James Tobin, Sterling Professor of Economics at Yale University, wrote this essay in 1960 for The New Republic *shortly before becoming a member of the Council of Economic Advisers under President Kennedy. In the recent collection of his popular essays,* National Economic Policy, *published in 1966, he states that this piece does not entirely reflect his present views.*

THE OVERRIDING ISSUE of political economy in the 1960's is how to allocate the national output. How much to private consumption? How much for private investment in plant and equipment? For government investment and public services? For national defense? For foreign aid and overseas investment? Though our productive capacity is great and is growing, the demands upon it seem to be growing even faster.

The allocation of resources among competing uses is *the* central and classical theoretical problem of economics. Likewise it is the inescapable central practical problem of a Soviet-type planned economy, or of any economy under the forced draft of total war. Only recently has allocation of the output of the peacetime American economy begun to emerge from economics texts into the political arena, as a challenge and opportunity for democratic decision and governmental action. Public economic policy and debate have long been dominated by other concerns: unemployment, inflation, inequality. The composition of national output has been an unintended byproduct rather than a conscious objective of economic policy.

The importance of accelerating economic growth brings the question of allocation to the fore. Can we as a nation, by political decision and governmental action, increase our rate of growth? Or must the rate of growth be regarded fatalistically, the result of uncoordinated decisions and habits of millions of consumers, businessmen, and governments, uncontrollable in our kind of society except by exhortation and prayer? The communists are telling the world that they alone know how to mobilize economic resources for rapid growth. The appeal of free institutions in the underdeveloped world, and perhaps even their survival in the West, may depend on whether the communists are right. We cannot, we need not leave the outcome to chance.

USING OUR CAPACITY FOR GROWTH

How can an increase in the rate of growth of national output be achieved? The answer is straightforward and painful. We must devote more of our current capacity to uses that increase our future capacity, and correspondingly less to other uses. The uses of current capacity that build up future productive capacity are of three major types: (1) *Investment:* replacement and expansion of the country's stock of productive capital—factories, machines, roads, trucks, school buildings, hospitals, power dams, pipelines, etc. (2) *Research,* both in basic science and in industrial application, by government, private industry, and non-profit institutions, leading sooner or later to more efficient processes and new products. (3) *Education* of all kinds augmenting the skill of the future labor force. The competing uses of current capacity are: (1) *Unemployment:* failure to employ current capacity to the full, letting potential production be lost through unemployment. (2) *Consumption,* where most of our resources are engaged, providing us with the goods, services, and leisure that constitute the most luxurious standard of living the world has known.

. . . A society geared to the objective of growth should keep the average unemployment rate down to 3 percent. Reduction of unemployment to this level could increase Gross National Product from the current labor force and capital stock by about 20 billion dollars. But this increase in output will contribute to economic growth only if it is used in substantial part for investment, research, and education; it will make no contribution if it is all consumed.

To stimulate growth we must somehow engineer two shifts in the composition of actual and potential national output. One is from private consumption to the public sector, federal, state, and local. Domestic economic growth is, of course, not the only reason for such a shift. Increased defense, increased foreign aid, increased public consumption are possibly equally urgent reasons.

The second shift of resources that must be engineered is from private consumption to private investment. About three quarters of Gross National Product is produced with the help of business plant and equipment. Faster growth of output requires a more rapidly expanding and more up-to-date stock of plant and equipment. . . .

Between 1953 and 1959 potential GNP rose from 365 to an estimated 500 billion dollars. Some of the potential increase went to waste in unemployment. Of the realized increase, 69 percent went into consumption, 13 percent into government activity, and 18 percent into investment. . . .

POLICY MEASURES FOR GROWTH

Policy to accelerate growth must be double-edged. On the one hand, it must stimulate the desired government and private expenditures. On the other hand, it must discourage consumption. Here are some major constituents of a program for growth:

1. Increased expenditure by federal, state, and local governments for education, basic and applied research, urban redevelopment, resource conservation and development, transportation and other public facilities.

2. Stimulus to private investment expenditures by:

(a) Federal Reserve and Treasury policy to create and maintain "easy money" conditions, with credit readily available and interest rates low, especially in long-term capital markets.

(b) Improvements of averaging and loss-offset provisions in taxation of corporate income, in order to increase the degree to which the tax collector shares the risk of investment as well as the reward.

(c) The privilege of deducting from corporate net income for tax purposes a certain percentage of a corporation's outlays for plant and equipment to the extent that these outlays exceed a specified minimum.[1] The specified minimum would be the sum of depreciation and (on the assumption that the tax rate is 52 percent) 48 percent of net income before tax. To qualify for the tax concession, a corporation would have to be investing more than its normal gross profits after tax. The concession, and the minimum requirement for eligibility for it, are designed to encourage greater corporate saving, the full investment of internal funds, and, most important, the undertaking of investment financed by outside saving obtained from the capital market. An analogous proposal to encourage non-corporate saving and investment is suggested below.

If these measures were adopted, a reduction in the basic corporate income tax rate, advocated by many as essential to growth, would be neither necessary nor equitable. Indeed the strength of these measures might be greater if the rate were increased.

3. Restriction of consumption, by:

(a) Increase in personal income tax at all levels, accompanied by permission to deduct a certain amount of saving from income subject to tax. Like present deductions for charity, medical care, etc., the saving deduction would be claimed at the taxpayer's option, with the burden of proof on him. A schedule of "normal" saving for taxpayers of various incomes and family circumstances would be established, and only saving in excess of a taxpayer's "normal" would be eligible for deduction. A scheme of this kind seems to be the most feasible equitable way to use the tax instrument to favor saving at the expense of consumption.

(b) Improvements in the social security system—e.g., raising retirement benefits and relating their amount, above a common minimum, to cumulated covered earnings—should be introduced on a quasi-contributory basis. Since the payroll tax contributions then precede the benefits, the funds accumulate and can be an important channel of national saving.

1. [The investment tax credit bill passed by Congress in 1963, and suspended in 1967, is similar but omits the minimum.—*Editor.*]

(c) Increases in state and local taxes—property or sales or income as the case may be—to keep pace with the share of these governments in the necessary expansion of the public sector.

(d) Limitation, to a reasonable proportion of sales, of the privilege of deducting advertising and promotional expenses from corporate income subject to tax. No observer of the American scene doubts that advertising is excessive. From the economic point of view, it absorbs too large a share of the nation's resources itself, and at the same time it generates synthetic pressures for ever-higher consumption.

RESTRAINING THE INCREASE OF CONSUMPTION

Increased taxation is the price of growth. We must tax ourselves not only to finance the necessary increase in public expenditures but also to finance, indirectly, the expansion of private investment. A federal budget surplus is a method by which we as a nation can expand the volume of saving available for private investment beyond the current saving of individuals and corporations. The surplus must, to be sure, be coupled with measures to stimulate investment, so that the national resolution to save actually leads to capital formation and is not wasted in unemployment and unrequited loss of consumption. It is only superficially paradoxical to combine anti-inflationary fiscal policy with an expansionary monetary policy. The policies outlined above must be combined in the right proportions, so that aggregate demand is high enough to maintain a 3 percent unemployment rate but not higher. There are several mixtures which can do that job; of them we must choose the one that gives the desired composition of aggregate demand. If the overwhelming problem of democratic capitalism in the '30's and even the '50's was to bring the business cycle under social control, the challenge of the '60's is to bring under public decision the broad allocation of national output. Fortunately the means are at hand. They are techniques well within the peacetime scope of government. We can do the job without the direct controls of wartime—priorities, rationing, price and wage controls.

The means are at hand; to use them we will need to muster

more wisdom, maturity, leadership, and sense of national purpose than we displayed in the '50's. . . . Our communist competitors have an advantage. Since they do not pay out increases in output as personal incomes in the first place, they do not have the problem of recapturing them in taxes or saving. That problem we cannot escape in a free society. Unless we master it, we shall not fare well in the competition for economic growth and national survival.

The Costs of Economic Growth

EZRA J. MISHAN

Ezra J. Mishan is Reader in Economics at the London School of Economics and a specialist in welfare economics. His book, The Costs of Economic Growth, *from which this selection is taken, had a significant impact on British political opinion when it appeared in 1967.*

REVOLUTIONS from below break out not when material circumstances are oppressive but, according to a popular historical generalization, when they are improving and hope of a better life is in the air. So long as toil and hardship was the rule for the mass of people over countless centuries, so long as economic activity was viewed as a daily struggle against the niggardliness of nature, men were resigned to eke out a living by the sweat of their brows untroubled by visions of ease and plenty. And although economic growth was not unheard of before this century—certainly the eighteenth century economists had a lively awarness of the opportunities for economic expansion, through innovation, through trade and through the division of labour—it was not until the recent post-war recovery turned into a period of sustained economic advance for the West, and the latest products of technological innovation were everywhere visible, and audible, that countries rich and poor became aware of a new phenomenon in the calendar of events, since watched everywhere with intentness and anxiety, the growth index. While his father thought himself fortunate to be decently employed, the European worker today expresses resentment if his attention is drawn to any lag of his earnings behind those of other occupations. If, before the war, the nation was thankful for a prosperous year, today we are urged to chafe and fret on discovering that other nations have done perhaps better yet. . . .

If the country was ever uncertain of the ends it should pursue, that day has passed. There may be doubts among philosophers

and heart-searchings among poets, but to the multitude the kingdom of God is to be realized here, and now, on this earth; and it
is to be realized via technological innovation, and at an exponential rate. Its universal appeal exceeds that of the brotherhood of
man, indeed it comprehends it. For as we become richer, surely we
shall remedy all social evils; heal the sick, comfort the aged and
exhilarate the young. One has only to think with sublime credulity
of the opportunities to be opened to us by the harvest of increasing
wealth: universal adult education, free art and entertainment, fre-
quent visits to the moon, a domesticated robot in every home and,
therefore, woman forever freed from drudgery; for the common
man, a lifetime of leisure to pursue culture and pleasure (or,
rather, to absorb them from the TV screen); for the scientists,
ample funds to devise increasingly powerful and ingenious computers so that we may have yet more time for culture and pleasure
and scientific discovery. Here, then, is the panacea to be held with
a fervour, indeed with a piety, that silences thought. What conceivable alternative could there be to economic growth? . . .

But to be tediously logical about it, there is an alternative to the
postwar growth-rush as an overriding objective of economic policy: the simple alternative, that is, of not rushing for growth.
The alternative is intended to be taken seriously. One may concede
the importance of economic growth in an indigent society, in a
country with an outsize population wherein the mass of people
struggle for bare subsistence. But despite ministerial twaddle
about the efforts we must make to "survive in a competitive world,"
Britain is just not that sort of country. Irrespective of its "disap-
pointing" rate of growth, or the present position of the gold reserves, it may be reasonably regarded, in view of its productive
capacity and skills, as one of the more affluent societies of the
West, a country with a wide margin of choice in its policy objectives. And it is palpably absurd to continue talking, and acting, as
if our survival—or our "economic health"—depended upon that
extra one or two percent growth. At the risk of offending financial
journalists and other fastidious scrutinizers of economic statistics,
whose spirits have been trained to soar or sink on detecting a half
percent swing in any index, I must voice the view that the near-
exclusive concern with industrial growth is, in the present condition of Britain, unimaginative and unworthy.

The reader, however, may be more inclined to concede this point and to ponder on a more discriminating criterion of economic policy if he is reminded of some of the less laudable consequences of economic growth over the last twenty years. . . .

For today's generation in particular, it is a fact of experience that within the span of a few years the unlimited marketing of new technological products can result in a cumulative reduction of the pleasure once freely enjoyed by the citizen. If there is one clear policy alternative to pressing on regardless, it is the policy of seeking immediate remedies against the rapid spread of disamenities that now beset the daily lives of ordinary people. More positively, there is the alternative policy of transferring resources from industrial production to the more urgent task of transforming the physical environment in which we live into something less fit for machines, perhaps, but more fit for human beings.

It is impossible not to dwell for a moment on the most notorious by-product of industrialization the world has even known: the appalling traffic congestion in our towns, cities and suburbs. It is at this phenomenon that our political leaders should look for a really outstanding example of post-war growth. Our consequence is that the pleasures of strolling along the streets of a city are more of a memory than a current pastime. Lorries, motor-cycles and taxis belching fumes, filth and stench, snarling engines and unabating visual disturbance have compounded to make movement through the city an ordeal for the pedestrian at the same time as the mutual strangulation of the traffic makes it a purgatory for motorists. The formula of mend-and-make-do followed by successive transport ministers is culminating in a maze of one-way streets, peppered with parking meters, with massive signs, detours, and wierdly shaped junctions and circuses across which traffic pours from several directions, while penned-in pedestrians jostle each other along narrow pavements. Towns and cities have been rapidly transmogrified into roaring workshops, the authorities watching anxiously as the traffic builds up with no policy other than that of spreading the rash of parking meters to discourage the traffic on the one hand, and, on the other, to accommodate it by road-widening, tunnelling, bridging, and patching up here and there; perverting every principle of amenity a city can offer in the attempt to force through it the growing traffic. This "policy"—apparently justified by reckoning as social benefits any increase in the volume of traffic and any increase in its average speed—would, if it were pursued more ruthlessly, result inevitably in a Los Angeles-type solution in which the greater part of the metropolis is converted to road space; in effect a city buried under roads and freeways. . . . The radical solution of prohibiting private traffic from town and city centres, resorts, and places of recreation, can be confidently expected to meet with the organized hostility of the motoring interests and "friends of freedom." Yet, short of dismembering our towns and cities, there is no feasible alternative to increasing constraints on the freedom of private vehicles.

Other disagreeable features may be mentioned in passing, many of them the result either of wide-eyed enterprise or of myopic municipalities, such as the postwar "development" blight, the erosion of the countryside, the "uglification" of coastal towns, the pollution of the air and of rivers with chemical wastes, the accumulation of thick oils on our coastal waters, the sewage poisoning our beaches, the destruction of wild life by indiscriminate use of pesticides, the changeover from animal farming to animal factories, and, visible to all who have eyes to see, a rich heritage of natural beauty being wantonly and systematically destroyed—a heritage that cannot be restored in our lifetime.

To preserve what little is left will require major legislation and strong powers of enforcement. But one cannot hope for these without a complete break with the parochial school of economics that has paralysed the mind of all governing authorities since the industrial revolution. It will require a new vision of the purposes of life to stand up to the inevitable protests of commerce, of industry, and of the financial journalists, protests that employment, expansion, exports—key words in the vocabulary of the parochial school—will be jeopardized if enterprise is not permitted to develop where profits are highest.

Our political leaders, all of them, have visited the United States, and all of them seem to have learned the wrong things. They have been impressed by the efficient organization of industry, the high productivity, the extent of automation, and the new one-plane, two yacht, three-car, four-television-set family. The spreading suburban wilderness, the near traffic paralysis, the mixture of pandemonium and desolation in the cities, a sense of spiritual despair scarcely concealed by the frantic pace of life—such phenomena, not being readily quantifiable, and having no discernible impact on the gold reserves, are obviously not regarded as agenda.

Indeed, the jockeying among party leaders for recognition as the agents of modernization, of the new, the bigger and better, is one of the sadder facts of the postwar world, in particular as their claim to the title rests almost wholly on a propensity to keep their eyes glued to the speedometer without regard to the direction taken. Our environment is sinking fast into a welter of disamenities, yet the most vocal part of the community cannot raise their eyes from the trade figures to remark the painful event. Too many of us try not to notice it, or if occasionally we feel sick or exasperated we tend to shrug in resignation. We hear a lot about the "cost of progress," and since the productivity figures over the years tend to rise we assume that on balance, and in some sense, we must be better off.

In the endeavor to arrest this mass flight from reality into statistics, I hope to persuade the reader that the chief sources of social welfare are not to be found in economic growth *per se,* but in a far more selective form of development which must include a radical reshaping of our physical environment with the needs of pleasant living, and not the needs of traffic or industry, foremost in mind. Indeed, the social process by which technological advance is accommodated is, in any case, almost certain to reduce our sources of gratification in life. . . .

SOME PRETEXTS FOR RAPID GROWTH

Though no economist who has studied the relation between economics and social welfare would endorse a policy of economic growth without an embarrassing amount of qualification, the profession as a whole behaves as if, on balance, it was a good thing. This attitude may spring from an impatience with quasi-philosophical inquiries that unavoidably call into question the usefulness of much of the highly skilled economic research currently undertaken. But there is room also for rationalization. One of the more obvious pretexts for pressing on regardless is the existence of poverty in the greater part of the world: in Asia, in Africa, and in large parts of South America. There are pockets of degrading poverty even within the wealthy countries though, as indicated earlier, their continuation may be attributed ultimately to political prejudices, not to economic necessity.

Now if the rich countries, in response to a moral challenge, sought to convert themselves into an arsenal to provision the hungry areas of Asia and Africa, a case could be made for retaining economic growth as the chief goal of economic policy for some considerable time. But though magniloquence on the foreign aid theme marks all fitting occasions, the scale of such aid to poor countries in the postwar period is more suggestive of "conscience money" than of moral commitment. When we bear in mind that the total aid given to poor countries by the largest donor, the United States, a country that is struggling continuously with problems of near-surfeit, does not amount to as much as one percent of its Gross National Product, one has no choice but to reject this justification out of hand.

The belief that only a faster economic growth will enable any country to "pay its way in the world," or that faster growth generates more exports, hardly stands up to analysis. . . . Neither does the view that our ability to survive a military attack depends on our rate of economic growth carry conviction. If it were felt that the country's chance of repelling an enemy attack in the foreseeable future would be distinctly improved by augmenting our weapons supply and by improving our war technology, we could achieve these things more directly by shifting a large proportion of our national resources into the production of weapons and into more intensive scientific research for defense. It is, of course, possible to believe that a change in the growth rate from between 2 and 2½ percent to between 3 and 3½ percent would have the incidental effect of enabling us better to withstand enemy attacks. But no one surely would be rash enough to argue that the goal of faster growth is justified solely, or even largely, by defense considerations.

We fall back then on the more popular and explicit belief that a *per capita* rise in real income is a good thing in itself; that in expanding the range of opportunities for ordinary people it increases their welfare. It will not, however, be difficult to uncover serious weaknesses in this common presumption, enough at any rate to warrant a conclusion that economic growth *per se* is a component of policy on which the least emphasis should be placed if we are interested primarily in social welfare.

Indices of economic growth may measure, in a rough sort of way, the increase in a country's gross productive power. But no provision is made in such indices for the "negative goods" that are also being increased; that is, for the increasing burden of disamenities in the country. Nor can they reveal certain imponderable but none the less crucial consequences associated with the indiscriminate pursuit of technological progress. Indeed, the adoption of economic growth as a primary aim of policy, whether it is urged upon us as a moral duty to the rest of the world or as a duty to posterity, or as a condition of survival, seems on reflection as likely to add, at least, as much "ill-fare" as welfare to society. Certainly there can be no purely economic justification for a policy of growth *per se*. The simple view that it "enriches" society, or that it expands the range of choice open to mankind, stands up neither to argument nor to the facts of common experience—unless, of course, words such as "enrich" or "expanding choices" are made to carry the same meaning an an increase of productive potential which is, roughly, what the index of productivity seeks to measure. If, however, we are concerned with social welfare in the ordinary sense, the only legitimate procedure is to consider consequences of each and every economic reorganization entailed by the growth process, in the endeavour to determine which, on balance, are beneficial and which are not.

Indeed, we might go so far as to suggest that economic growth *per se* should be jettisoned as an independent goal of policy. For if we are concerned primarily with social welfare, those forms of economic growth that meet our welfare criteria will in any case be approved and adopted, the remainder being rejected: thus, sources of "worthwhile" economic growth will continue to be sought after. . . .

THE MYTH OF CONSUMERS' SOVEREIGNTY

A basic assumption frequently invoked to vindicate economic growth is that any extension of the *effective* range of opportunities facing a person (whatever presented to him through the market or directly by the Government) contributes to an increase in his welfare. Similarly any reduction in the effective range of opportunities contributes to a diminution of his welfare.

However, even a market economy in which government intervention is at a minimum, there is one important opportunity that is denied to the customers; that of selecting the range of alternatives that will face him on the market. He can choose only from what is presented to him by the market—and a range of alternative physical environments is not the only thing that the market fails to provide. For one thing, the so-called extension of opportunities is not necessarily *effective*, in the sense defined. When new kinds of goods or new models of goods appear on the market the older goods or models are not always simultaneously available. They are withdrawn from production at the discretion of industry.

The argument purporting to show how consumers' wants ultimately control the output produced is facile enough: for it is, on the one hand, admittedly profitable to be first to discover and cater to a new want, while, on the other hand, it would seem unprofitable to withdraw from the market any good for which the demand continues undiminished. It would not be hard, therefore, to lay down conditions under which the wants of consumers tend quickly to influence the sorts of goods produced. But, unless the wants of consumers exist *independently* of the products created by industrial concerns it is not correct to speak of the market as acting to adapt the given resources of the economy to meet the material requirements of society. In fact, not only do producers determine the range of market goods from which consumers must take their choice, they also seek continuously to persuade consumers to choose that which is being produced today and to "unchoose" that which was being produced yesterday. Therefore to continue to regard the market, in an affluent and growing economy, as primarily a "want-satisfying" mechanism is to close one's eyes to the more important fact, that is has become a want-*creating* mechanism.

This fact would be too obvious to mention, except that its implications are seldom faced. Over time, an unchanged pattern of wants would hardly suffice to absorb the rapid growth in the flow of consumer goods coming on to the markets of rich countries, the U.S. in particular, without the pressure afforded by sustained advertising. In its absence, leisure, one suspects, would be increasing faster than it is. National resources continue to be used to create new wants. These new wants may be deemed imaginary or they may be alleged to be as "real" as the original set of wants. What cannot be gainsaid, however, is that the foundation necessary to enable economists to infer and measure increases in individual or social welfare crumbles up in these circumstances. Only as given wants remain constant and productive activity serves to narrow the margin of discontent between appetites and their gratifications are we justified in talking of an increase of welfare. And one may reasonably conjecture that unremitting efforts directed towards stimulating aspirations and enlarging appetites may cause them to grow faster than the possibilities for their gratification, so increasing over time the margin of social discontent.

Be that as it may, in high consumption economies such as the United States, the trend is for more goods, including hardware, to become fashion goods. Manufacturers strive to create an atmosphere which simultaneously glorifies the "pace-setter" and derides the fashion laggards. As productivity increases without a commensurate increase in leisure the accent shifts ever more stridently to boost consumption—not least to boost automobile sales although cities and suburbs are near-strangled with traffic—in order, apparently, to maintain output and employment. The economic order is accommodating itself to an indigestible flow of consumer gadgetry by inverting the rationale of its existence: "scarce wants" have somehow to be created and brought into relation with rising industrial capacity.

Under such perverse conditions growthmen may continue, if they choose, to so juggle with words as to equate growth with "enrichment," or "civilization," or any other blessed word. But it is just not possible for the economist to establish a positive relationship between economic growth and social welfare.

INSTITUTIONAL CONSTRAINTS ON CHOICE

Since economists make rather free with word 'choice', the reader may excuse some rather obvious remarks that serve to remind us how existing institutional restrictions influence and, indeed, reduce effective choice.

Over the decision most vital of all to his well-being, the epoch and society wherein he lives, the individual alas is unable to exercise any choice whatsoever. Born into a certain social and physical *milieu,* born into a certain home, much of the pattern of his life follows as a matter of course. Many of the consequences that arise from nature and nurture, from inherited natural endowments and from upbringing, he will be powerless to influence. Within limits determined by these consequences he is, later, free to choose an occupation but, having adopted it, the material choices that he exercises through the market are thereafter somewhat narrowly conscribed. If, for example, he becomes a stockbroker or bank manager in the City, his choice of clothes, car, residence, even his choice of food and entertainment, will not differ markedly from that of his colleagues. The conventions followed by friends, associates, and customers will continually weigh with him unless he is ready to forfeit their good opinion of his character and soundness upon which his success depends. . . .

Let us turn to the restrictions placed on a man's choice of occupation by existing technology and institutions. In seeking to establish the optimal properties of a perfectly competitive economy the traditional liberal economist would argue that just as the individual chooses, as consumer, to buy various amounts of the goods offered by the market, so also, as the owner of productive services, he is guided by market prices in offering various amounts of his services in different occupations. This symmetry is obviously forced on the analysis in the interests of elegance and mathematical convenience. It may be that in some imaginary economy a person could spread his work among a variety of occupations on the familiar equimarginal principle in the same way as he is deemed to spread his income among the goods offered to him by the market. But modern industry is not so accommodating, and for the superficially good reason that if a man were allowed to choose in this way—choosing each day to put a few hours in this occupation and a few hours in that—the productivity of the economy could not be maintained. The employee has therefore to choose his work subject, for the most part, to the condition that he conform exactly to the working week of the firm.

In the narrow growth sense, one in which social welfare is measured directly by output, such a constraint on working hours may appear necessary. But if the economist is interested in social welfare rather than in physical output he must concern himself with the burden of this constraint on the worker's choice in a modern economy that is almost wholly consumer oriented—and, indeed, the private enterprise system is generally vindicated by reference to the individual's satisfaction *qua* consumer while neglecting his satisfaction *qua* worker. It is, of course, easy to forget that the individual may have occupational wants independent of technical progress since, over time, he is seen to adapt himself to whatever technological means are available. Though we suppose him, at any moment of time, to have a set of preferences among existing occupational opportunities, there is no use in comparing his preferences between newly adopted and obsolete methods inasmuch as he is rapidly deprived of any choice of the latter. The economist has no means of discovering what changes in welfare, if any, result from a change-over from one technology to another.

Yet something may be said. The tedium of repetitive work in modern industry, even that of watching a screen and turning knobs, is easy to underestimate by those fortunate to escape such tasks. One has only to reflect on the efforts and the expenditure incurred by large numbers of people in combating the monotony of their daily occupation, their growing eagerness to engage in all manner of hobbies in their spare time, their desire to recapture a feeling of craftsmanship or creativity—one has only to reflect on these things to discern opportunities for social gain in making existing industrial arrangements more flexible. Nor need one contemplate a clear choice between the existing highly organized system of production and the extreme alternative of uninhibited choice in respect of hours of work and variety. One need only admit the clear possibility of social gain, after full allowance has been made for the consequent reduction in physical output, of extending to people of all ages a much wider choice in the hours of work, a wider geographical choice in the location of smaller units of industry and, above all, a wider choice in the methods of production. Experiment on such lines is obviously inconsistent with any criterion of technical efficiency: some material remuneration would have to be sacrificed in the conscious pursuit of ways and means of deriving positive enjoyment, stimulation, and companionship in one's daily occupation. Indeed, this proposal may be recognized as an instance of the separate facilities concept for promoting welfare. Not everyone would wish to sacrifice efficiency, and therefore earnings, in exchange for more of these other desirable factors. But there should be enough people capable of enriching their lives by such arrangements to justify the experiment.

Measured by the conventional index of finished goods, the implementation of such proposals may well involve negative economic growth. That an increase in social welfare—an increase in the range of effective choice—may be brought about by negative economic growth may appear paradoxical, if not infuriating, to some growthmen. But that is because they are interested in social welfare only insofar as it seems to justify economic growth, and not the other way about, as they sometimes pretend.

WEAKNESS OF THE LINK BETWEEN CHOICE AND WELFARE

We have assumed, provisionally, a positive connection to exist between effective choice and welfare, and confined ourselves to revealing some of the limitations on effective choice under existing institutions. We also drew attention to the difficulty of detecting and measuring changes of welfare over time in an economy devoted to altering people's tastes. However, even if tastes remained unaltered over time the connection between effective choice and welfare is by no means self-evident—at least, not in the affluent society.

In the first place, although the whole range of consumer goods is growing, one of its chief manifestations is the multiplication of brands and models of already popular goods. The task of choosing in a rational way, on each occasion, one brand or model from a bewildering and, indeed, ever-changing array of such goods— that is, to weigh up the relative merits of quality, taste, appearance, performance, longevity, and other characteristics with respect to the range of prices of some several score objects all purporting to serve the same need—would be too time-consuming and too exhausting an occupation even if the entire staff of a Consumers' Advisory Board were placed at the customer's disposal. In the event, there are many things a person buys from habit and much that is bought on the impulse. Nevertheless, in all that involves fairly large expenditures on durable goods, the process of choosing is itself a time-consuming business, one that is not made easier by the trend towards more rapid obsolescence of existing models, and by variations in price at different times and in different places. It may seem, on a superficial reflection, that no person need inconvenience himself if he does not wish to; he can always reach out and take the first thing that catches his eye or he can adhere to his customary brand—if it remains available. One can call this a rational solution if he wishes, but it is one that affords little consolation. As the pace of fashion accelerates, as goods become technically more complex and their variety proliferates, the plain fact is that ordinary people do become apprehensive about the increasing possibilities of choosing the wrong thing. If, therefore, an independent panel were given the task of radically reducing the existing prolific variety of goods on the market to a few clearly differentiated types of each good, one could reasonably anticipate a saving of time and some elimination of anxiety, to say nothing of a potential decline of manufacturing costs arising from the resulting standardization of products.

If the link between choice and welfare does not already appear tenuous, we can go further. The political philosophy of John Stuart Mill may suggest to some that if a man has a mind to drink himself to death no intervention other than that of persuasion is called for. It is thought better (in some political sense) that a man act unwisely of his own free will—provided, always, his action harms no other persons—than that he be coerced into a wiser course of action. Without taking issue with this doctrine as a political maxim it should nonetheless be transparent that in many circumstances some measures of constraint on a man's choice can increase his welfare. To illustrate with a homely example, the concept of "consumer's rent" may be employed by the economist to measure the *additional* benefit a man enjoys in choosing to smoke two packets of cigarettes a day for the rest of his life compared with a situation in which, say, no tobacco at all were available. Any restraint imposed by government edict, or any shortage that reduced his ration—directly or through higher prices —below two packages must necessarily appear as a reduction in his welfare. Yet it is far from impossible that if there were a tobacco famine, or if he were conscripted into some task-force which was sent to a place where tobacco could not be had, the craving for the weed might vanish over time, and the man live to bless the event. He would continue his life in better health, and pocket, than before, and assert roundly that his welfare had been vastly improved by these initially frustrating circumstances. This kind of event may be discussed with a great deal of political sophistication, but whatever is concluded it cannot be denied that a welfare economics based exclusively on free choice within institutional constraints does not recognize the ample opportunities for increasing social welfare by initial departures from the free-choice path. If, for example, television or cinema audiences were deprived for a longish period of the shallow entertainment they have habitually succumbed to, many of them might be expected, after a period of tedium, to develop a taste for more sophisticated programs, so that if the old shabby fare became available again it would be rejected out of hand. . . .

A final weakness of the link between expanding output and social welfare is revealed by consideration of what economists are wont to call "the relative income hypothesis"—the hypothesis that what matters more to a person in a high consumption society is not his absolute real income, his command over material goods, but his position in the income structure of society. In its purest form, the thesis asserts that, given the choice, the high-consumption society citizen would choose, for example, a 5 percent increase in his own income, all other incomes constant, to, say, a 25 percent increase in his income as part of a 25 percent increase in everybody's real income. The evidence in favor of the hypothesis in its purest form is not conclusive but it is far from being implausible, and in a more modified form it is hardly to be controverted. Our satisfaction with many objects depends upon their publicly recognized scarcity irrespective of their utility to us. It is not difficult to imagine the gratification experienced by a person living in a country in which all the other inhabitants are aware of his being the sole possessor of a radio, high-fi recorder, washing machine and other durables. Nor is it difficult to imagine his great satisfaction, arising from the knowledge of his being the sole possessor of these things, melting away as they become common household appurtenances; indeed, of his gradual dissatisfaction with them as he learns that his neighbours now possess far more advanced models than his own. However, the more truth there is in this relative income hypothesis—and one can hardly deny the increasing emphasis on status and income-position in the affluent society—the more futile as a means of increasing social welfare is the official policy of economic growth.

In sum, facile generalizations about the connection between expanding choice and social welfare which serve to quieten misgivings about the single-minded pursuit of economic growth are here rejected. The fact that what matters most to affluent-society man is not the increase of purchasing power *per se* but his relative status, his position in the income hierarchy, robs the policy of industrial growth of much of its conventional economic rationale. In part, this attitude of affluent-society man is to be explained by this central thesis: that beginning from the norms of postwar affluence economic growth has failed to provide men with additional choices significant to his welfare; that, indeed, it has incidentally destroyed some cardinal sources of welfare hitherto available. The bewildering assortment of gadgetry and fashion goods offers the sort of expansion that is as likely to subtract from than to add to his welfare. As producer, affluent-man has little choice but to adapt himself to the prevailing technology; no provision is made by industry enabling him, if he chooses, to forgo something in the way of earnings for more creative and enjoyable work. Nor, as citizen, has he yet been presented with the vital choice of quieter and more human environments, free of the ravages of unrestrained traffic.

What Price Economic Growth?

TIBOR AND ANNE SCITOVSKY

Tibor Scitovsky is Professor of Economics at Yale University. This essay, written with Anne Scitovsky, appeared in The Yale Review *and in his* Papers on Welfare and Growth *published in 1964.*

THE OPTIMISTIC PHILOSOPHERS of the eighteenth and nineteenth centuries expected economic progress to accomplish many wonderful things. It was going to bring about "the greatest possible abundance of objects suitable to our enjoyment, and the greatest liberty to profit by them";[1] it was expected to free man increasingly from daily toil and thus to provide him with more time to cultivate his mind. In short, they hoped that progress would turn more and more people into philosophers in their own image, engaged in the leisurely and philosophical contemplation of the world and its wonders.

In a material sense, and measured in terms of output per manhour or income per head, economic progress in the West has achieved or surpassed these men's wildest hopes. The consequent rise in our standard of living is a genuine and substantial gain; but the potentialities it offers we certainly employ very differently from the way they envisaged. What was wrong with their vision; or, to turn the question around, what is wrong with us that we do not measure up to their hopes? In the following pages we shall give a partial answer to this question and show that economic progress itself influences and changes man's aspirations. We shall argue that economic progress in our society has wrought cultural and social changes that divert time and energy from intellectual pursuits and "idle" speculation, lower the prestige of learning, and diminish the availability of channels for intellectual discussion and the dissemination of new ideas. These and some related conse-

1. Mercier de la Rivière in *L'Ordre Naturel et Essentiel des Sociétés Politiques* (1767), quoted and translated by J. B. Bury, *The Idea of Progress.*

quences are part of the price we pay for economic progress in our society.

From a purely materialistic point of view, the price of economic progress is the cost of the resources invested in plant, equipment, scientific research, training, and whatever else contributes to expanding and improving productive capacity. These are direct and easily quantifiable costs. The undesirable social and cultural effects of progress are costs additional to these, indirect, intangible, less easily quantifiable, but no less real.

Many of these social and cultural effects are identical with those features of modern American life and society that have for some time occupied the attention of sociologists and social psychologists in this country. In discussing these effects therefore, we shall be dealing with well-known and much discussed phenomena; but we hope to offer something new by tracing them back to economic progress as one of their causes.

The people most aware of the existence of a causal relation between economic progress and certain cultural features of modern society are perhaps those European intellectuals to whom economic progress means Americanization and who fear that Americanization in the economic sphere would bring with it some of those elements of American culture and civilization that they dislike. America to them means not only a high standard of living but also excessive conformity, a hectic life, an atmosphere unfavorable to intellectual and cultural pursuits; and they feel in a vague way that one cannot have one side of the American coin without also having the other. We propose to show that these fears are indeed justified to some extent and, to the extent that they are justified, they imply that these undesirable cultural elements are characteristic, not so much of America, as of the advanced economy. They are the price of economic progress. . . .

Two features of the advanced economy have important cultural and social implications. One is the high cost of labor, the other large-scale organization and extreme specialization.

THE IMPLICATIONS OF THE HIGH COST OF LABOR

Economic progress consists mainly in the rising productivity of labor and consequent growth of national income. Market forces in our economy cause the earnings of labor to rise more or less in proportion with its productivity; and the consequent rise in labor's standard of living is among the main achievements of economic progress. But a rise in labor's earnings is, from another point of view, a rise in its cost. Parallel rises in labor cost and labor productivity have mutually offsetting effects on costs of production; and this is what we observe when we look at the economy taken as a whole. When one looks closer, however, one becomes aware of differences in the rate at which productivity rises in different industries and fields of activity, and also of differences in the rate at which earnings rise in different occupations. The two sets of differences do not always run parallel: now the rise in productivity, now the rise in earnings prevails, causing costs of production to fall in some fields and to rise in others. The resulting distortion in the structure of costs, prices, earnings and profitabilities is a normal manifestation of economic life; but it has some undesirable cultural consequences often overlooked. These appear most often in industries and fields of activity whose productivity lags behind, which are generally the ones that suffer the growing pains of the economy.

For the laggard sectors of the economy are usually in competition with the more progressive ones; and it is the pressure of this competition that causes the trouble. If they compete with the more progressive industries mainly in the labor market, they face rising costs and are forced to raise prices; if they compete mainly in the product market, they experience lower earnings and are forced to pay lower wages; if they compete in both labor and product markets, their profits diminish, which puts them under pressure to raise their productivity. Each of these three cases has important cultural implications.

The Shift in Relative Prices · Every tourist is aware of differences in relative prices that economic development brings about, and each has his pet grievance concerning the high American price of some commodity that is more accessible in less developed countries. But the commodities whose prices have been raised the most by the rising cost of labor are leisure and personal services. For the price of leisure, being the income sacrificed in taking one's leisure, *is* the cost of labor looked at from the seller's (worker's) point of view, so it necessarily rises with the cost of labor. As to personal services, such as domestic service, household repairs, hairdressers' services, etc., their prices have risen in (or almost in) proportion with the cost of labor, because productivity in rendering these services has risen hardly or not at all. One would expect the rise in these prices (relative to the prices of material goods) to have induced the consuming public to buy less leisure and fewer personal services, except to the extent that the rise in real incomes enables people to buy more of everything, including leisure and personal services.

What is the evidence? When one contrasts the regular, routinized, and contractually regulated employment of labor in the developed economies against the seasonal, intermittent, and patriarchically controlled farm labor with its many forms of disguised unemployment in the underdeveloped countries, then it seems obvious that the former have more work and less leisure than the latter. The major increase in work and diminution in leisure, however, seems to have occurred during the early stages of industrialization. More recently, the dominant force would seem to be the shortening of the working week. . . .

This trend, let it be noted, need not indicate an increased *desire* for leisure. For one thing, fifty years ago, when unions were in their infancy, the length of the working week may have been the result more of employers' demands than of workers' wishes. For another, there is some evidence that the present short working week is not entirely to the workers' liking. It is a matter of union strategy to demand, not higher wages, but shorter hours with the same take-home pay, thus asking for higher wages only by implication; and there are signs of increasing dissatisfaction with this policy on the part of workers, many of whom would prefer to work longer hours for higher pay.

But whether or not it is wanted, the shorter working week is here. The question is whether it implies correspondingly more leisure; and there are reasons for thinking that it does not. To begin with, the percentage of married women working has risen, from 5½ percent in 1900 to 30.2 percent in 1956. Secondly, the number of workers who hold more than one job is also increasing. In 1956, 6.9 percent of employed men and 5.5 percent of the entire labor force had more than one job; this is double the percentage of multiple job holders in 1943, the earliest date for which these data are available. 1494272

These two factors already offset two-thirds of the gain in leisure due to the shorter working week; and they are not the only ones. Until recently, the continuing shift of labor from farming into the service industries was probably another factor, although by today, the diversification of agriculture has greatly reduced the seasonal fluctuations and increased the total amount of the work performed by farmers and farm-workers. The total amount of work performed may still have diminished and the amount of leisure available increased in the American economy over the last half-a-century, but not by much, certainly by much less than the shortening of the working week would suggest.

More important perhaps has been the change in the distribution of leisure among social classes and income groups, and the change in people's *use* of leisure. Statistics of the length of the working week by occupation suggest that the main beneficiaries of the shorter working week are the manual and lesser clerical workers; it is doubtful if businessmen, managers, officials and professional people have benefited at all. And these latter groups are virtually certain to have lost in terms of leisure time if the effect of the rising cost of personal services is also taken into account.

We have mentioned already that the higher relative price of personal services could be expected to discourage demand; and this expectation is fully borne out by the evidence. The number of (full- and part-time) domestic servants in the United States, while stable in absolute terms, has declined relatively, from 94.3 servants per 1,000 families in 1900 to 35.3 servants per 1,000 families in 1950. These figures understate the decline by about 10–20 percent, because the definition of domestic servant used in 1950 is more inclusive than that used in 1900.

The significance of this decline is that it implies an increase in the amount of services people perform for themselves, since they achieve the saving on personal services largely at the cost of their own leisure. It is true that labor-saving innovations have greatly eased the burden of householding; and that families that in 1900 would have had servants, today have smaller houses. On the other hand, the introduction of automatic household appliances seems to have raised both standards of householding and the number of tasks performed within the household. . . .

It would be misleading, however, either to add to a national total or to distribute evenly over all households this loss of leisure, which is suffered not by all families but only by those who formerly, with the relative price of domestic service lower, would have employed domestic servants. Distributed over this smaller group, which comprises the professional classes and others in the middle-income range, the loss of leisure per family becomes very much greater. At the same time, it also becomes apparent that people in the lower income groups, who would not have employed domestic help even at a lower relative price, have gained on balance, since they too have benfited by the increased productivity of modern household appliances.

Domestic service is not the only personal service whose price has been raised by the rising cost of labor. The same is also true of household repair services of all kinds; and the effect of the rise in their prices on the distribution of leisure is very similar. The great expansion of the industry that provides the tools for the do-it-yourself man and the greatly increased percentage of household paints sold to the non-professional painter amply demonstrate the increasing tendency for household repairs to be done by the householder himself. Equally suggestive is a questionnaire survey, according to which the average American husband spends three hours per week as a home handyman, two hours as a garage mechanic, and three hours as a gardener. We have no corresponding estimates for earlier years with which to compare the above and establish the nature of the trend over time; but the main conclusions seem obvious enough. The higher price of house repair and maintenance has caused the professional classes and middle-income groups to do by themselves work that in an earlier age they would have had done by others; and this means an equivalent reduction in their leisure time. People in the lower income groups on the other hand have probably always done their own household repair; and they are likely therefore to have gained in terms of leisure, since they benefit by the technical improvements that render this type of work easier and quicker.

Needless to add, some of the activities referred to here as encroachments on leisure are far from unpleasant and are regarded by many people as forms of leisure. Indeed, when increasing specialization renders most factory and office jobs increasingly monotonous, exchanging part of such a job for the greater challenge and variety of improving or embellishing one's home is bound to be attractive. But our concern here is with leisure time available for intellectual and cultural activities. However enjoyable do-it-yourself activities may be, they do divert time and energy from intellectual pursuits.

We conclude therefore that the rise in the relative cost of personal services has greatly contributed to the redistribution of leisure (or rather of the part of it available for intellectual pursuits) from professional and middle-income groups to the working classes. Yet another factor that pulls in the same direction is the move of the middle-income groups to suburbia, since the time they spend in commuting also encroaches upon their leisure.

This trend towards "leisure for the masses, toil for the classes" is welcome from the point of view of social justice; but it is not conducive to the further progress of society. Leisurely contemplation and "idle" speculation seem to be necessary conditions of creative intellectual activity. The professional classes, being the best educated, are the best able to make intellectual use of their leisure; and this is attested by the fact that most of the political, cultural and technical progress of the past has been their achievement. A diminution in the amount of leisure available to them must therefore be regarded as undesirable from society's point of view. This judgment, however, does not necessarily imply that professional people are the step-children of economic progress in our society. For that is a matter which has to do with the distribution not of leisure but of income—a subject we shall take up in the next section. Here we are concerned solely with the availability and distribution of leisure; and if professional people obtain less leisure today than they used to, and devote less of it to intellectual pursuits, the reason need not be that they can afford less leisure than before, it may simply be that, facing a different structure of relative prices, this is the way they have chosen to allocate their expenditures and organize their lives.

We turn now to the changing *use* of leisure time. The high productivity and consequent high cost of labor have made people increasingly conscious of the fact that time is money; and this seems to have engendered the belief that time should be fully and efficiently utilized both in work and in leisure—although the efficient utilization of leisure is, of course, a contradiction in terms.

It is only natural that the pace of work should be speeded up and working time better utilized as the cost of labor rises; and there is every indication that this is what has happened in the United States, the country with the highest cost of labor. As to the pace of leisure and leisure activities, it is speeded up both directly, by the high cost of labor, and indirectly, through transference of the pace and habits of work. The high cost of labor renders the European coffeehouse, with its leisurely and often intellectual atmosphere, an unprofitable business proposition in the United States; and it puts pressure upon restaurants to speed up their turnover through quick service, large-scale operation, overcrowding, and other means of hurrying the customer. Indirectly, the habits and pace of work are carried over into leisure activities owing simply to man's inability to change at short notice his ingrained habits and accustomed pace. Hence the tendency to attend machines, such as TV, radio or movies, and let them set the pace; hence the preference for organized leisure, for doing things; and the attitude of regarding idle conversation and leisurely contemplation as a waste of time—even of leisure time.

Leisure, however, and personal services are merely extreme examples of goods whose relative prices have risen. Other services that have become relatively more expensive owing to the lagging productivity of the labor rendering them are urban public transportation, postal and telegraphic communication, and most of the administrative services rendered by government. Whether the scope for raising labor productivity in these fields is genuinely limited, or whether the inducement to raise productivity is lacking in the public domain, is irrelevant from our point of view. Whatever the reason, these services have become dearer compared to other goods; and this fact, combined with the public's reluctance to spend more on them, has occasionally led to the reduction in their supply or worsening of their quality. Hence the paradox that sometimes the richest countries seem the least able to afford these services.

The Shift in Relative Earnings · The second category of effects of the high and rising cost of labor is the change in relative earnings brought about by the uneven rate of progress in different industries and fields of activity. The main fields in which lagging productivity has caused relative earnings to fall are the learned professions. Their productivity can be increased relatively little; and their life is sufficiently different from that of other people for a fall in their relative earnings to have no short-run effect on the numbers entering the professions. Indeed, hand-in-hand with the fall in the relative earnings of teachers, academic people, civil servants, lawyers, etc., their relative numbers have increased— presumably owing to the lesser cost of acquiring the education needed to enter these professions.

Two sets of statistics show that economic progress lowers the earnings of professional people in relation to those of others. First of all, an international comparison of thirty-eight countries has shown a much greater disparity between the earnings of professional people and of manual workers in underdeveloped than in developed countries. . . .

Essentially the same picture is shown also by the statistics of the trend of earnings over time. The decline of the economic position of professional people and intellectuals in the United States is too well known to need comment here; but it is worth mentioning that this trend seems to extend to all the economically developed countries. For example, in Canada the income of professional people rose only one quarter as fast as the income of industrial workers over the period 1911–51. . . .

This is a sad state of affairs for the professional people themselves; but what is the significance of their declining economic position from society's point of view? Let us note first of all that professional people are among the few groups whose working week has not been reduced over time. On the contrary, under pressure of the fall in their incomes, many professional people have tried to increase or supplement their incomes by additional work. Also, they are among those hardest hit by the rising cost of personal services. Hence the redistribution of leisure already mentioned, with professional people suffering the most drastic curtailment of their free time—and they are the group the best able to use leisure time for intellectual and cultural activities. For many professional people have functions going beyond those that, in a narrow sense, they are paid for. These additional functions are often the most important and the most creative; and they can be so erratic, their nature and usefulness so unpredictable, that they cannot be contracted for but must be performed in what, by other people's standards, is considered leisure time.

Secondly, the smaller share of professional people in the national income has diminished their share in consumers' demand and hence diminished the weight allotted to their tastes and preferences in the allocation of resources and the planning of production. If we regard professional people as cultural leaders of our society, then their loss of influence over production decisions must be considered a loss to society. . . .

A third effect of the declining economic status of the professions is a corresponding decline in their prestige—and in the prestige of learning itself. This is especially so in the United States, with its tendency of expressing all values in terms of money and hence of valuing everything according to its price. The low price, then, that society puts on learning and the learned may have much to do with anti-intellectualism, with the neglect of basic research and basic science as against problem-oriented research; and perhaps also with the neglect of general education in favor of vocational training. . . .

THE PRESSURE TO MASS PRODUCE

Having dealt with some of the implications of the changes in relative prices and relative earnings, we proceed to discuss some consequences of the change in relative profitabilities.

Economic progress in our age is closely linked with mass production, because the lowering of costs usually depends on economies of scale. At first sight there seems nothing wrong with this. Indeed, to bring within reach of the many what before was accessible only to the few is among the noblest achievements of economic progress. Very often, however, the advantages of mass production are obtained at the sacrifice of quality and variety.

In fact, the low cost of mass production often hinges on a restriction of variety and lowering of quality. In addition, the sale of many products cannot be raised significantly by price reduction alone; changes in quality may also be needed to make them appeal to a wider public and its less educated taste. Finally, and this is the main point, mass production does not remain confined to the fields that provide the greatest scope for it, competition imposes it in other fields too. When some firms in some fields engage in mass production at lower costs, they divert demand from and raise costs against competing firms in related fields; and the combination of falling demand and rising costs puts pressure on these other firms to adopt mass-production methods too. When such pressure stimulates technical advance, well and good; but in fields where the scope for technical improvements is limited, the pressure of dwindling profits merely lowers standards, restricts variety, and worsens quality. There are many examples of this; paramount among those involving cultural standards [is] the theatre.

The first means of mass producing theatrical entertainment was the cinema; and it will serve to exemplify the effects also of the radio and television. The economics of the mass market are such that it is almost always more profitable to cater to the tastes of the unsophisticated majority than to those of the sophisticated minority, however saturated the former and unsatisfied the latter segment of the market may be. Thus, the cinema, catering to a mass audience, provides entertainment designed to appeal to a large and hence unsophisticated public.

There remains, of course, the legitimate theatre to perform serious drama; but it, too, has suffered from the competition of the movies, the radio and television; and it has become less willing to perform its traditional function as a result. The decline of the theatre due to increased competition has been serious enough. From 1927–28 to 1952–53, the number of New York theatres open declined by 69 percent. . . . More serious, however, than the decline in the number of theatres open and companies operating was the 77 percent decline in the number of plays produced, from 280 to 65 over the same period. This implies an increase in the average run of a play; and indeed, there is independent evidence of a very great increase in the number and proportion of so-called long runs. Actors' Equity regards this as the one bright spot in their otherwise gloomy sky; but from the cultural point of view it is undesirable, because it implies that producers, facing a decline in demand and rise in costs, are maintaining profits by shunning the more controversial plays and concentrating on the production of the safer and more popular ones. Needless to say, our concern is not with the displacement of sophisticated comedy by musicals but with the decline of serious drama. After all, the theatre has for a long time been an important forum in which to present serious social, psychological and political problems for discussion and analysis by the intelligent public; and the narrowing of this forum must be considered a loss to society. . . .

THE IMPLICATIONS OF EXTREME
SPECIALIZATION AND HIGH COMPLEXITY

So far we were concerned with some implications of the rising cost of labor; and we now propose to deal with a few of the consequences of the high degree of specialization and technical complexity that characterize the advanced economy.

The Political Implications · The political implications of extreme specialization are perhaps the best known and most obvious. Let us recall that democracy is rule by dilettantes—a dilettante government controlled by a dilettante Congress, itself controlled by a dilettante electorate; dilettantes not in a pejorative sense but in the sense of not being experts in the various fields in which they have to pass judgment. With increasing specialization, however, and with the increasing technical complexity of each field of specialization, dilettante rule becomes both more difficult and more dangerous—a trend that seems so obvious at the present time that we will not elaborate on it any further.

One aspect, though, may be worth mentioning. Increased specialization of knowledge tends to turn professional people from intellectuals into technicians. This means that as each of them gets to know more and more about less and less, he becomes not only more of an authority in his own field but also more willing to accept the authority of others on matters outside his own field. In other words, specialization renders the professional classes not only a better tool of authority but also a more pliable one, and makes them abdicate to an increasing extent their traditional rôle of upholders of political liberties.

A Psychological Effect · Further well-known implications of mass production and extreme specialization are psychological; they often have been described by more competent observers, but we shall mention them here nevertheless, for completeness' sake. They have to do with man's increasing isolation, partly from his environment, and partly from his fellow human beings.

A rudimentary understanding of man's use and control of nature, of the nature and origin of the objects around him, and of the way in which different tasks are performed and divided among different people, seems a good in itself, perhaps even a psychological necessity. Not so long ago, most people acquired understanding by just looking around and exercising their natural curiosity. They knew the provenance of the foods, materials and tools they used daily; and the division of labor was simple enough to be explained in terms of the butcher, the baker, the candlestickmaker.

Today, in the age of push-button appliances, ready-mix foods, plastics, and synthetic fabrics, this is becoming increasingly difficult. We use many materials of whose provenance we know next to nothing; we are surrounded by household implements we know how to operate but whose working principles we ignore; and we are more and more at a loss when trying to answer the simplest questions of our children concerning the nature of the everyday objects around them. This applies not only to the atom but even to the shirts on our backs. Hence man's feeling today of the utter dependence of his everyday life on a complex technical and social organization about whose working, outside his own narrow sphere, he is largely in the dark; and this, too, contributes to his feeling of impotence in relation to organized society. . . .

Another Psychological Effect · Let us now deal with another psychological effect of an advanced economy: man's increasing alienation from his fellow men. With the growing size of the economic unit, the average person no longer deals with his employer, his grocer, his banker; instead, he has dealings with firms that are forever growing larger and more impersonal, more bureaucratic and more rigid, and hence more inhuman and frightening. They are represented by employees whose very blandness and polite-ness render the organization they represent all the more remote and inaccessible. This situation, the frightening aspect of man's being surrounded by giant organizations, the frustration of there being no particular human being to be angry at or hold responsible for the occasional cruelty, rigidity and administrative inefficiency of these giant organizations—all this has been amply described and analysed by Erich Fromm and other members of the Ameri-can neo-Freudian school of psychologists. Added to this is the fact that even the few human contacts remaining have been rendered less human and personal by the rising cost of labor and the increasing economy of its use. Our relations with the corner grocer, the elevator man, the waiters in our favorite restaurant and the family doctor used to be fairly close and friendly. Today, in the age of medical groups, of cafeterias and supermarkets, of vending machines and automatic elevators, and of various other forms of self-service, such human contacts have become fewer, shorter, and very much less personal. Even in factories, automation is thinning out the number of workers to such an extent as to create isolation. If one adds to this the move to the suburbs and the decline of metropolitan public transportation, both of which force people to spend a large part of their time sitting alone in the gilded cage of their automobile, then one has a fairly complete picture of how, thanks to his rising standard of living, modern man is increasingly left alone—not, indeed, with his thoughts, but with his gadgets.

Now what does man do when he finds himself increasingly cut off from personal contact with his fellow man? He tries to estab-lish closer contacts with woman. Here again, one finds the in-stinctive desire to compensate for the loss of human contacts out-side the family by seeking earlier and stronger contacts within the family. As is well known, the median age of marriage is steadily declining in all the advanced countries. . . . Also, the median age of marriage is lower in the United States than in any of the West-ern European countries; although there, too, it is declining over time.

There are, of course, several reasons for early marriage in the United States. One is, probably, that being better off, Americans can afford to marry early. Another one may be the stricter sexual morality of the United States. It is very likely, however, that a further and important reason is the scarcity of human contacts and people's greater loneliness outside marriage and the family circle. The high cost of personal services may also be a factor.

The trend towards earlier marriage is being welcomed by many people and from many different points of view. From the cultural and intellectual point of view, however, it is probably a bad thing. For the time between a person's emancipation from his parents and the establishment of his own family is among the intellectually most fertile periods of his life. It is then that people are the most anxious and the most able to explore new fields and avenues of knowledge and to think and argue about intellectual problems. Early marriage, with its family obligations, tends to cut short this period of life. Indeed, the ever-increasing percentage of married couples among university students may well dampen the spirit of intellectual inquisitiveness and adventure that is so essential a part of university life.

We have discussed above a few of the consequences of economic progress that seem to have contributed to changing its direction and diverting its path from the course envisaged by the eighteenth-century believers in progress. We want to stress once again that the great rise in the standard of living and the decline in its inequalities brought about by economic progress are real benefits, well worth paying a price for. The purpose of this discussion was to point out that there is a price and to analyze its nature. The question we wish to raise in closing is not whether the price is too high but whether it has to be paid, and be paid in full.

Some of the undesirable features of the advanced economy are probably here to stay. The technical complexity of our civilization and the organization of society and the economy into very large administrative units seem to be unavoidable; and so are, in all probability, many of their political and psychological effects. Those consequences, however, of economic progress that have to do with the changing structure of relative prices, earnings and profitabilities are peculiar to economies where market forces are given free rein; and they can be mitigated or avoided by subsidizing certain activities and services or by taking them out of the realm of the market altogether. . . . The need for the State or for non-profit organizations to modify, supplement or supplant the market mechanism in certain areas has always been recognized in our society. We have tried to show that economic progress renders this need ever greater and widens the areas where it arises.

Economic Growth as a National Goal

HERBERT STEIN AND EDWARD F. DENISON

Herbert Stein is Director of the research staff of the Committee for Economic Development. Edward F. Denison is an economist at the Brookings Institution. Both organizations sponsor research on current economic problems. This essay was part of a longer contribution to the American Assembly symposium on American goals in the 1960's.

THE AMERICAN ECONOMY works well. It produces the highest income per capita ever known, and a rate of growth that raises real income per capita by half from one generation to the next. This income, and its increase, are widely distributed. Economic advance has produced a revolutionary reduction in the hours and burdens of work. Americans have great freedom to use their resources and incomes as they choose. The system is highly responsive to the demands of the people, producing with exceptional efficiency, inventiveness and adaptability the particular goods and services for which a private or public demand is expressed. Unemployment remains a problem, but one so reduced in magnitude since the 1930's as to be qualitatively different.

America and the civilization to which it belongs stand at an historic turning point. They confront a critical danger and inspiring opportunities. The danger is indicated by the phrase "cold war." Among the opportunities are to help the billion people of the under-developed world realize their aspirations, to reduce nationalist and racialist limitations upon man's freedom and horizons, and to push back the frontiers of human knowledge in many directions. Neither avoidance of the danger nor realization of the opportunities *requires* that the American economy work better, although better economic performance would make both objectives easier to attain. Insofar as movement toward

47

these more important goals depends upon the availability of economic resources, the American economy as it is and is likely to be can provide them. It would be tragic if the United States should fall prey to the danger or fail to grasp the opportunities because of preoccupation with the idea that it is not rich enough and needs to become richer faster.

NATIONAL PRODUCTION AND NATIONAL NEEDS

From 1929 to 1957 the total production of goods and services in the United States increased at an average rate of 2.93 per cent per annum. We estimate that if unemployment is kept to about 4 per cent of the labor force, the annual rate of growth from 1957 to 1970 would be 3.27 per cent, and from 1957 to 1980 would be 3.24 per cent. At the estimated rate of growth GNP would be about $709 billion in 1970 and $972 billion in 1980 [at 1957 prices].

This estimate of future growth assumes that no special measures are taken to accelerate growth other than the reduction of unemployment. It is based on an analysis of the probable contribution to growth that will be made by several factors—the number, hours of work, educational attainment and age-sex composition of the labor force, the stock of capital, the increase of knowledge, and others. It assumes, among other things, that the 1970 labor force will be about 19 per cent larger and average annual full-time working hours about 5 per cent shorter than in 1960; that the educational attainment of the labor force will increase sharply; that the capital stock will grow at about the rate indicated by past ratios of saving to national product under prosperous conditions.

Estimates of future growth under conditions of high employment have been made by other students. Some project growth rates similar to ours, others project higher rates. The difference generally lies in the weight given to the relations observed in the long period 1929–57 as compared with a shorter more recent period, especially 1947–1950 or the postwar period inclusive of those dates. This shorter period may be interpreted as evidence that a "New Era" began after the war, in which various factors, notably the advance of technology, will hereafter generate a more rapid rate of growth than previously experienced. Alternatively, since this short period was one of quite low unemployment, it may be interpreted as evidence that high employment by itself makes a very large contribution to the growth rate.

In the space available here we cannot discuss and defend the points of difference between our estimates and others. We would only say that we believe the longer period to be more reliable than a selected shorter period, in the absence of clearer evidence than now exists of a persistent change in some relationship.

The most obvious question to ask about the projected rate of growth is: Will it be enough? In one sense of course the answer is No. The growth of production is the source from which desires for goods and services are satisfied. These desires appear limitless. However fast production may grow, some desires will be left unsatisfied, and many will wish that growth were faster.

However, the rate of growth will not be increased by wishing. Steps will have to be taken to increase it. By and large these steps will involve some cost to someone—otherwise we could assume that they would already have been taken. (Remember that we are discussing the problem of raising the rate of growth above that which would otherwise result at high employment—whatever that rate may be.) The question then is not whether faster growth is desirable but whether it is sufficiently desirable to justify any particular step that might be taken to achieve it.

This question may be concretely illustrated as follows. We estimate that if annual hours of work were to remain at their 1957 level, rather than to decline at the rate we project, our annual rate of growth from 1957 to 1970 would be 3.6 per cent instead of 3.3 per cent. Faster growth is a good thing and reduction of hours of work is a good thing. The question is whether increasing the rate of growth is more important than reducing hours of work. Similar questions can be asked about increasing immigration, or employment of women, or expenditures for education, or taxes for public investment, or tax changes to promote private investment, or expenditures for research.

When the question is put in this way it becomes obvious that the authors of this paper cannot responsibly pretend to answer it. We can try to illuminate the benefits of more rapid growth and indicate the costs of achieving it. But whether the benefits are worth the costs can be answered only by those affected or by those making the decisions. The costs and benefits are not reducible to any common terms that permit their objective measurement and comparison. In the end the decision will have to reflect subjective judgments, and insofar as they are collective decisions they will have to reflect some concensus of subjective judgments.

Whether a collective decision about the rate of growth should be made, through government, is in our opinion a real and serious question. The alternative view is that the desirable rate of growth and the correct means to achieve it are those that would emerge from private decisions. These would inevitably be affected by the action of government in discharging its important functions. But these functions do not include the explicit determination of the rate of growth. We believe that there is much to be said for this position, and we trust that it will receive due weight in public discussion of growth. We do not examine this position here only because it seems more fruitful to use our limited space to indicate what choices are available in the economic system if collective choices are to be made.

How much is growth worth? · If our economy grows at the rate we project, 3.3 per cent per annum, total output (Gross National Product) will be about $710 billion in 1970. If it grows at 4 per cent per annum, GNP in 1970 will be about $780 billion. The value of the higher rate of growth is $70 billion of output in 1970 and corresponding amounts in other years.

How much is this $70 billion worth? Obviously, the answer will depend upon what the $70 billion consists of and what wants it satisfies. If it includes critical defense expenditures, the caloric intake necessary for sustaining the population, the capital assistance that would set the underdeveloped world on the road to growth, then the $70 billion will be of the utmost importance. But anyone can think of possible uses of $70 billion that would be of little importance.

One can conceive of all possible uses of output being ranked in an endless descending series from the most important to the less important, to those of no importance at all, to those of negative value. Ideally, with $710 billion of GNP we would go down from the top of this list through the $710 billion most important uses. If we had another $70 billion of GNP we would take the next most important $70 billion of uses, all of which would be less valuable than any of the first $710 billion. The value of the additional $70 billion would be much less than 10 per cent of the value of the first $710 billion.

It may be that the actual American selection of uses of output does not conform to this pattern. Possibly we select more or less at random from the most important, less important, and unimportant uses. In this case the additional $70 billion of output might be as valuable, dollar for dollar, as the first $710 billion.

There might even be a systematic bias in the process, which causes the less important needs to be satisfied before the more important. If so, the needs satisfied by the additional $70 billion of output would be much more important, on the average, than those satisfied by the first $710 billion.

The importance of more rapid growth depends critically upon how well we allocate our output among our needs. This simply means that if we can count on devoting our expected output to satisfying our most urgent needs, additional output will be only as valuable as the satisfaction of our less urgent needs.

As the authors see it, the key current question about the allocation of output relates to the division between private and public uses. There may be limits upon the amount of public expenditure that keep critical public needs from being met, even though much less important private needs are met. Suppose, for example, that we cannot or will not spend more than 20 per cent of the gross national product for public purposes. If the gross national product in 1970 is $710 billion we can have only $142 billion of public expenditures, even though this may leave unmet many public needs more important than the needs satisfied by some of the $568 billion of private expenditures. The value of raising the GNP would then lie in the additional public expenditures it would permit.

It should be understood that in this paper we have made no evaluation of the need for additional public expenditure. Here we are concerned only to explore the implications for economic growth on the hypothesis that a very large increase of public expenditure is necessary.

There are two main possibilities to be considered. One is that we cannot raise tax rates above their present levels, at least without serious effects upon economic growth. The other is that we *will* not raise tax rates. In either case the yield of the existing tax rates sets a limit to public expenditure, and the only way to raise that expenditure would be to increase the yield of the existing tax rates by increasing the rate of economic growth.

Granted a willingness to raise tax rates, it must be recognized that certain patterns of tax increase might tend to retard the rate of growth. But substantial additions to revenue can be obtained without such an effect. This might involve some combination of (a) increases in the beginning rate of individual income tax (now 20 per cent), (b) a broadening of the income tax base by reduction of exemptions and exclusions and (c) increased taxation of consumption. Such taxation would be burdensome, but this burden is simply that which is implicit in any decision to sacrifice private consumption for public expenditures.

Whether higher public expenditures financed by higher taxes will retard the rate of economic growth depends not only on the character of the taxes but also on the character of the expenditures. If the expenditure increase is heavily weighted with public investment, research, education, and defense programs with a large research content, and if the taxation impinges almost entirely on private consumption, the net effect may be a higher rate of growth.

Even if taxes can be increased without adverse effects upon growth the public and its government representatives may be unwilling to impose the additional taxes. In this case a higher rate of growth would be needed to permit more public expenditures by increasing the yield of the existing tax system.

The authors believe that there are unnecessary obstacles to an increase or decrease of federal taxes. Sharp disagreement over the proper distribution of tax burdens, exaggerated impressions of the consequences of the level and structure of taxes, the complexity of the tax system—all these make a tax increase or decrease excessively difficult. As a result, government expenditures tend to be adjusted to the yield of the existing tax system, even though the best level of expenditure might be higher or lower.

Too much should not be made of this point. At least in this century, no President has been unable to get an increase of taxes when he asked for it to finance expenditures that he described as essential to a vital national interest. Nevertheless, the tendency to regard the yield of the existing tax system as a limit to public expenditures is, we believe, a potentially dangerous obstacle to sound public policy. No law of history assures us that we can get safely through the twentieth century with the yield of the tax system we inherited from the Revenue Acts of 1950 and 1954. The American people should recognize this.

A more rapid rate of economic growth would reduce the importance of this obstacle. But we are doubtful of the possibility of circumventing this obstacle by raising the rate of growth. Many of the steps that might be taken to increase the rate of growth would themselves require higher taxes. Is it likely that, being unable to raise taxes to pay for important public expenditures, we would be able to raise taxes to stimulate growth so that we could pay for these same expenditures? We think not, but we are not experts on what the American people can be persuaded to do. In any case we believe it would be a serious mistake to leave the American people with the impression that the rate of economic growth can be raised to whatever figure is necessary to make the yield of the existing tax system cover all desired public expenditures.

The argument to this point may be summarized as follows: If the national product is wisely used, the contribution of a higher rate of economic growth would be the satisfaction of less critical needs, not of the most critical needs. But the less critical needs are still worth satisfying, and should not be disregarded. They motivate a large part of the work done in this country.

If this country does not allocate its output to the most important uses, it cannot be sure that any specified rate of growth or level of output will satisfy its critical needs. In this case there are two possibilities. One is to increase the rate of growth, which would probably increase the likelihood that important needs would be met. The other is to become more intelligent in recognizing and responding to vital needs. The latter is essential whatever is done about the former. If we are not wise in the use of our resources, we cannot expect the abundance of our resources always to compensate.

The Competition of Soviet Growth · Up to this point we have been discussing the value of more rapid growth as a means of satisfying private or public needs for goods and services. In the present state of the world, rapid growth of the American economy may have an additional value.

Let us postulate this situation. The Soviet economy is now growing at a percentage rate higher than ours. If this should continue, the absolute annual growth of the Soviet economy will overtake our growth (it may already have done so). Although there are strong reasons to believe that the Soviet Union will be unable to maintain a growth rate faster than ours once it has achieved a comparable level of technical efficiency, let us nonetheless assume that it will do so. Suppose further that, despite this, the United States is able to maintain an adequate military establishment, provide for necessary public services and sustain a rate of growth of private income that is satisfactory to the American people individually. Would we then regard our rate of growth as adequate?

This is an extremely difficult question to answer. It requires us to project our imaginations into a totally new economic, political and psychological situation. We, our allies, neutral nations, and the Soviet bloc are all deeply affected by the vision of the United States as by far the world's richest and economically strongest country. It is hard to conceive a world in which this would not be true.

But it seems possible that a change to a situation in which the Soviet economy is generally recognized to be growing faster than ours, not only in percentages but also absolutely, not in spurts but steadily, and is approaching ours in total size, could have profound consequences. It could greatly strengthen the confidence of the Russians in their own system, increase the attraction of the Communist system for the independent, underdeveloped countries, worry our allies about their reliance upon us, and weaken our own morale.

These consequences might not follow. Certainly they are paradoxical on their face. They imply that in order to increase the attraction of our system to populations with average per capita incomes of $100 we, with per capita incomes of $2,000, must become still richer faster. They imply that even though we fully discharge our real obligations to our allies, they will lose confidence in us because we do not choose to raise our personal consumption more rapidly. They imply that the rest of the world will not evaluate us by the standards we choose for ourselves but will compel us to be measured by standards made in Moscow.

Moreover no one really knows what the standards are in the production race upon which world opinion is said to hinge. We do not know whether the Soviet GNP is now one-third of ours or two-thirds of ours, because the composition of their GNP is so different from ours. And it is not clear whether the race is in GNP at all, or in steel production, or in butter consumption per capita. Each side presumably wants to race on its own track and to persuade the world that it is the right track. The outcome may depend as much on the persuasion as on the running.

Nevertheless the possibility described cannot be ignored. Accelerating our pace in the production race is probably a positive factor for our national security. How important a factor it is, the authors cannot pretend to say. This is a question the American people will have to decide on the advice of people more expert than we in the politics and psychology of the cold war. If they should decide that it is important, this would, in our opinion, be the strongest reason for a collective decision to increase the rate of growth.

The costs of accelerating growth must also be considered. We do not do *everything* that might promote our national security. Especially, we want to promote our national security in the most efficient way. Somehow we must judge whether a cost of x spent in accelerating growth will yield more in national security than the same cost spent for weapons, or for foreign aid, or for space exploration, or for many other things that affect our military, political and psychological position in the cold war. Again this is a question that the authors cannot answer. . . .

CHOOSING AMONG GOALS

Economic growth is a good thing, and it is tempting to elevate any good thing to the state of a goal of national policy. The main point of our paper is that the establishment of such a goal is wise only if the benefits of the "good thing" are worth its costs. We have neither invented nor discovered the costs. In fact, we suppose that consciousness of these costs has weighed in the decisions not to undertake the measures that might have given us more rapid growth in the past.

We should refer here to one kind of benefit and one kind of cost that we have not mentioned but that may be very important. There may be value in having a "national goal" aside from the benefits of achieving any particular goal and almost without regard to what the goal is. The goal may be inspiring, give "point" to life, and serve as a common bond holding the society together. This may be a benefit even though at the present stage of history our psychological need would be better served by a goal less materialistic and less parochial than the growth of the American economy.

There is a limit to the number of goals that the American people or any people can pursue, the number of crusades they can engage in. There is a limit to our supply of leadership for "pointing the way" and to the supply of attention and followership. In this sense, any goal is proposed at the expense of others that are or might have been advanced, and the cost of elevating accelerated economic growth to the front rank of goals is that something else is deprived of that position. The number of goals calling for our attention is large—to help set the under-developed world on the path of economic progress, to reduce the barriers of nationalism and racialism, to strengthen our national security, to improve the lives we lead with our immense flow of goods and services, to set a floor of economic security and welfare for all. We need not feel guilty of negativism or passivity if we decide that accelerating growth is not one of our most critical needs.

In closing, the authors repeat what was said at the outset. We do not, in this paper, attempt to decide what the public attitude toward the rate of growth should be. This is a question that the people must decide, referring to the kinds of considerations discussed here but also in the end expressing their own values, their own views of what is worth what.

United States Growth: What, Why, How

W. ALLEN WALLIS

W. Allen Wallis, formerly Professor of Economics and Statistics at the University of Chicago, is now President of the University of Rochester. He presented this statement at the Third Annual Loeb Dinner for Economic and Business Journalists in June, 1960. At that time he was Special Assistant to President Eisenhower.

WHAT IS ECONOMIC GROWTH?

GENERALLY, PEOPLE think of economic growth as an increasing supply of goods and services. This is all right as far as it goes, but it doesn't go very far. As population increases, a larger supply of goods and services is needed to maintain a constant level of output. An economy may get bigger—or "grow" in an absolute sense, perhaps even as a world power—without adding to individual welfare. Obviously, growth must involve rising levels of *per capita* output if it is to mean increased welfare.

But this is not all. Growth in any meaningful sense must mean not just more things, but more things that are useful and that people want. Today we produce such things as automobiles, television sets, and missiles, instead of surreys, stereopticons, and cannon balls. Evolution in the composition of output is as much a part of economic growth as is expansion of the volume of output. Similarly, if growth is to be meaningful the output must be well distributed among all the people.

In our economy, changes in the composition of output reflect the free choices of the people, and the valuation of the output reflects the values placed on goods and services through voluntary purchases and sales. Private output conforms to choices made in the market, and public output to choices made through political processes by freely elected representatives. In a centralized economy, both private and public output reflect the

57

choices and values of the authorities, and the values placed on goods and services also represent authoritarian decisions. There is no valid criterion of the extent to which the nominal "growth" achieved by a centralized economy is meaningful growth in terms of the aspirations and desires of the people. Furthermore, with centralized economic authority the benefits of growth need not be distributed widely. Total and per capita output can rise, while the living levels of the masses are rising little or not at all.

Clearly, true growth must refer to economic welfare. This means we must consider not only goods and services but non-material aspects of growth. As our productive capacities have risen, we have chosen to take part of our growth in the form of leisure and improved working conditions. In fact, an economy could be growing even though output per capita were stable, if at the same time the amount of time and effort needed to produce that output were declining.

If the concept of growth is complex and elusive, as I have been trying to indicate that it is, the problem of measuring growth is fearsome. Not only do we lack adequate data, but the qualitative and non-material aspects of growth are impossible to quantify. A confession of St. Augustine more than 1500 years ago about the concept of time ought to be repeated daily by all who purport to measure economic growth: "For so it is, oh Lord my God, I measure it; but what it is that I measure I do not know."

Six of the most common gauges of economic growth are the percentage rates of increase in

(1) real Gross National Product, that is, GNP adjusted for price changes;
(2) real GNP per capita;
(3) industrial production;
(4) output per man-hour worked;
(5) output per unit of labor and capital combined; and
(6) real disposable personal income per capita.

Before considering what each of these gauges appears to show, let us consider certain major shortcomings that seriously limit what any of them really show. These ubiquitous flaws, which create troubles for anyone trying to compare growth rates between countries or between times for a given country, are:

(1) deficiencies of data,
(2) vagaries of valuation,
(3) aberrations of averages, and
(4) treacheries of timing.

About the deficiencies of data I will say little, except that the basic figures on GNP or industrial production even for this country—and ours are the best in the world—involve liberal use of estimation and guesstimation, of interpolation and extrapolation, of approximation and adjustment. With respect to Russian data, it is hardly better than conjecture at many crucial points.

The valuation problem I have already alluded to. The list of things produced includes such heterogeneous products as apples, nuts, bolts, cloth, appendectomies, tractors, missiles, financial writing, and speeches. To measure the list by a single number it is necessary to put a value on each item. In a market economy, we can value most things by prices people voluntarily pay and accept. Even in our economy, however, a large and increasing share of output is governmental, and can be valued only in terms of things used up. But just using up something by no means guarantees that an equal value is created; sometimes it is more, too often it is less.

U.S.–U.S.S.R. Comparisons · The magnitude of the valuation problem is shown by the comparatively simple problem of comparing Russian GNP with ours. The two lists of products must be valued by the same prices, otherwise the comparison will reflect differences in prices, not just differences in GNP. If Russian prices are applied to their output and to ours, our GNP is nearly four times theirs. If American prices are applied to the outputs of both countries, we are only twice their size. Russian GNP for 1955 is commonly described as 40 per cent of ours. This results from splitting the difference, but the difference that is split is not between two and four, which would give three, but between 27 per cent and 53 per cent, which are the two estimates of Russian GNP as a percentage of ours.

Averages can be tricky, and every one of the growth measures is an average of divergent rates of growth prevailing in different parts of the economy. It is possible, for example, for the overall average to go up even if every separate part is constant or even declining. To see that this is possible, suppose that a country has half its economy in agriculture, and that growth is slower in agriculture than in the other half of the economy (both these things are true of Russia). The average rate of growth for the whole economy will be half-way between the rate for agriculture and the rate for nonagriculture. Now suppose that the economy changes, and the nonagricultural segment is larger than the agricultural. Even if the rate of growth stays the same in both agriculture and nonagriculture, the new average rate of growth for the whole economy will be nearer the nonagricultural than the agricultural rate, and therefore higher than before. This kind of thing is in fact happening in Russia. In the United States, on the other hand, the opposite is happening. Agriculture here has an extraordinarily large rate of growth, so we are able to shift resources into things like services where growth is slower; and this pulls down the figures on our average rate of growth, even though the change is obviously a good thing. It would be possible for our rate of growth to be higher than the Russian rate in every part of the economy, yet for our average rate to be less than theirs.

Another affliction of our measures of growth is the problem of a proper time-span, whatever criterion is used. Like every kind of growth, economic growth proceeds at an uneven pace. Measurements must be made at times far enough apart to average out seasonal, cyclical, and erratic fluctuations. A fictitiously high rate will result if we start at a cyclical trough and end at a peak, or a fictitiously low rate if we go from a peak to a trough. For similar reasons, the periods used for measuring growth must not begin or end at the peak of a war boom or at the trough of a post-war reconversion.

The treacheries of timing are especially hazardous in comparing growth rates of different countries. For the United States, 1948 to 1957 is a valid peak-to-peak period for measuring growth. For some other country, however, it may be a peak-to-trough or a trough-to-peak period. Comparisons covering the same period for two countries may, therefore, be misleading,

THE HISTORICAL RECORD

All these difficulties mean, not that measurements of growth are futile and fruitless, but that to interpret them requires considerable care, skill, judgment, objectivity, and sophistication about both economics and statistics. Let us proceed to survey the principal measures of growth, paying particular attention to the recent record in relation to the long term record.

Real Gross National Product from 1909 to 1957 grew at an annual compound rate of 2.9 per cent per year. The long-run growth trend has been fairly stable in spite of large departures above and below it. Between 1948 and 1957, the annual rate of growh in total real production was 3.8 per cent, somewhat higher than the long-run rate.

Real GNP Per Capita. From 1909 to 1957 the annual rate of increase in real GNP per capita was 1.5 per cent. From 1948 to 1957 the rate was 2.0 per cent per year, again somewhat higher.

Industrial production, as measured by the Federal Reserve Board Index, increased from 1919 (when the index begins) to 1957 at an average annual rate of 3.7 per cent. Between 1948 and 1957 the annual rate of increase was 4.4 per cent, a little higher, but within the range of statistical variation that characterizes this series.

Real private output per man hour worked increased from 1889 to 1957 at an average annual rate of 2.0 per cent. From 1948 to 1957 the rate was 3.1 per cent, or about 50 per cent higher.

Real output per unit of labor and capital combined, useful as a measure of overall efficiency, increased from 1889 to 1957 at an average annual rate of 1.7 per cent. From 1948 to 1957 the annual rate of increase was 2.4 per cent, about 40 per cent higher.

Real disposable personal income per capita measures the income available to individuals, after taxes, to use as they please. The annual rate of increase from 1929 (when the data begin) to 1957 was 1.6 per cent, a rate pulled down by depression and pushed up by war booms. From 1948 to 1957 the average annual rate of increase was 1.9 per cent, despite high taxation and rapid population increase.

There are many other indicators of growth: length of the work week, or levels of education, for example. But the six indices that we have looked at suffice to illustrate the nature of the problems in answering the question: What is Economic Growth?

Even this brief look at the record shows the falsity of careless allegations that our economy is slowing down. The recent record, as best we are able to read it at such close range, is very good when judged by historical standards. Indeed, considering the great changes that have taken place and the major adjustments that the economy has made with flexibility and resiliency during the past fifteen years, the record is one which should renew our faith in the vitality of our system. Perhaps we should, can, and will grow faster and better; but that is the "to be continued" part of our growth story.

WHY GROW?—ECONOMIC GROWTH AS A POLICY GOAL

Economic growth has been an important goal of our national policy since the founding of the Republic. It remains an important goal, in no way diminished by our remarkable progress. Indeed, economic growth has recently become a political rallying cry, accompanied sometimes by demands that the government revert to the mercantilist policies by which economic growth was sought in the 17th and 18th centuries.

The issue of economic growth has entered the arena of contemporary politics through a course which has characterized many issues in the past quarter of a century. That is that after we have gotten over the hill by private endeavors, and are on our way at a brisk pace, urgent demands arise that the government expedite and direct us.

Characteristically, individuals, private institutions, or general social forces break the paths and provide the initial momentum. Once the vision of an important goal gains currency, and once we are on our way toward attaining it, suddenly we become impatient for a magic carpet to put us there instantly. Our impatience is exploited by those promoting various political schemes. Some of these schemes have become as wilted and shabby as the proverbial saloon sandwich, as they are pushed decade after decade as means to reach whatever goals have most recently come over the horizon or are most rapidly being attained through private forces.

Much of the current emphasis on economic growth is of this character. All sorts of plans are put forth under the banner of growth, with little or no analysis of the way they might promote growth—except growth in Federal spending. The same spending plans, on the other hand, are often described as reasons for wanting growth. We could afford the spending, the argument runs, if we only had growth; and the implication is that those who paint these glowing pictures of what growth could do to expand Federal spending somehow have the key to growth.

The fact that too many of the considerations raised in discussions of growth cannot be taken seriously should not blind us to the fact that there are a number of important considerations that merit close examination.

The Soviet Threat is one of these. The Soviet threat is real and has many points of thrust. It would be perilous to underestimate the danger. But how is it related to our own economic growth? Some people fear that the Russians will "catch up" to us someday and so fulfill the Khrushchev boast about burying us. Others fear that rapid Soviet growth will increase Russian military potential so greatly as to jeopardize the free world's defenses. Still others fear possible adverse "demonstration effects" of rapid Soviet development—that underdeveloped and uncommitted nations will turn to communism as a way of achieving national strength, politically and economically. All these fears merit sober consideration—more consideration than can be given to them here.

First, it should be pointed out that we have a commanding lead over Russia in terms of both total and per capita output. Even if Russian growth rates continue higher than ours, the absolute gap between us will continue to *increase* for some time to come.

Second, we don't know how large the gap really is—except that it is large. As was mentioned earlier, international comparisons, even if we had good data, are a difficult and unrewarding business. We don't know whether Russian GNP is one-half of ours or one-quarter of ours.

Third, international comparisons of rates of growth can be even more misleading than comparisons of levels of output. The Russians, starting from a lower economic base and in a period of postwar reconstruction, should be expected to have a fairly high percentage rate of expansion. Moreover, they are able to take over the accumulated technology already developed and exploited elsewhere. Furthermore, they are transferring masses of people out of low productivity employment in agriculture to industry with its more highly valued output per man hour. They still have approximately 50 per cent of their labor force in agriculture; we have only about 8 per cent. Our employment is expanding in services, where improvements in output per man hour are slow and limited. In other words, Russian growth is more rapid because they are still in the area where improvement is easy and the way has been shown, whereas we are more heavily involved in the difficult tasks of expanding productivity in medicine, journalism, education, engineering, and other services.

In short, there is no possibility that the Russian economy will overtake ours, at any time in the visible future—certainly not in this century. We should not begrudge the Russian people whatever rise they may achieve in their material levels of well-being in return for the privation and hardships they have suffered in the name of economic growth.

Even the "demonstration effects" of Russian economic expansion may be vastly overemphasized. While her 6 to 8 per cent annual rate of growth in total production in recent years may seem impressive, other countries not under communist domination have and are doing better. The economic progress of West Germany, Japan, and Mexico, for example, is far more striking. As a matter of fact, Russia itself grew faster under the Czars during the decade before the First World War.

Unmet Social Needs is a slogan we hear these days as a call for accelerated growth. According to this argument, if we grow faster we will be better able to provide a greater variety of public services and to eliminate what we now regard as poverty.

One of the more pretentious versions of the "needs" argument is that we have shameful public squalor in the midst of vulgar private opulence. This argument has a strong authoritarian smell, an odor of desire to enforce the advocates' tastes on others through governmental machinery. The argument about "public squalor" would be laughed out of court if confronted with the facts of the past decade on construction of schools, improvements in teachers' salaries, super-highways built, increases in the support of research, expansion in aid to the needy, diseases conquered, urban redevelopment, hospitals built, or indeed almost anything else. Growth in public services has been enormous in the past decade. The unmet-social-needers resort to pointing out plaintively that we don't yet have everything that they think we should want, and to lamenting that private opulence dulls interest in social revolution.

The public squalor argument is, in fact, simply this decade's battlecry of socialism, which—intellectually bankrupt after more than a century of seeing one after another of its arguments for socializing the *means* of production demolished—now seeks to socialize the *results* of production.

Aiding the Economic Development of Other Nations is another reason often advanced for trying to accelerate our own rate of growth. This is a laudable and continuing goal of public policy. But it does not follow that increasing our own rate of growth and raising our own level of living will have much influence on the rate of economic progress elsewhere.

The problems of world economic development are formidable. The pressure of population on arable land, the extremes of ignorance in many underdeveloped countries, the diversity of languages, cultures, and political institutions—these and many other economic and social factors are far more important than the direct and indirect aid that we can give. This is not to underestimate the significant contribution that our foreign aid, investment, and technology can make to world development. But what we can achieve depends primarily upon how we allocate our resources to various ends, and on the kinds of international and domestic policies we pursue, rather than on variations in our own rate of growth. Our import and export policies, for example, are vastly more important to underdeveloped countries than whether our GNP grows at 2 per cent or 5 per cent per year.

The Real Growth Imperatives arise from the fact that a strong economy is a growing economy. An economy with a high per capita income such as ours generates a large volume of private saving which must flow into capital accumulation if the economy is to sustain itself. In other words, the continued vitality of the system requires growth.

But beyond such technical matters, we desire growth to promote our private ends and national purposes. It is that simple; we want growth because it enlarges the opportunities of our children, because it expands our capacities to pursue goals of our own choosing, because it increases the range of choices open to us, because it is a rewarding outlet for our creative energies and imagination, because achievement invigorates and stimulates. In short, through economic growth we lead richer and fuller lives.

Moreover, we desire growth for the preservation of our way of life. By continued growth we demonstrate to ourselves, and perhaps to the world, that our system of free enterprise and representative government is indeed strong and able to fulfill rising aspirations and to enhance the dignity of free men. We need to grow to demonstrate that our system is not headed for inevitable collapse, but will survive even in a world of oppression and hostility.

HOW TO GROW

For a variety of reasons there is general agreement that economic growth is an important goal of economic policy. But there is disagreement over the relative importance of growth as compared with other goals and even more disagreement over the means by which growth should be pursued.

Growth is only one of several major goals of economic policy. Economic freedom, stability of employment, stability of the general price level, economic efficiency, and economic security all are important. Properly conceived and pursued, economic growth is compatible with all these other goals; but it becomes incompatible when pursued too ardently or by inappropriate means. Policies to promote growth or any other goal must reflect a compromise among competing goals.

Growth entails certain costs, and attempts to achieve greatly accelerated statistical growth rates may be costly in terms of human hardship. New machines may reduce prematurely not only the value of old machines but also the value of human skills acquired through long training and experience. New products may reduce the incomes of those producing old products. New industries in new locations may uproot homes and communities near old industries. Unless the costs of economic growth are equitably distributed, it is only reasonable to expect strong resistance to growth and its accompanying changes.

To get high rates of growth through more rapid capital accumulation means that people must save more, either voluntarily or by compulsion. In the Soviet Union people are forced to sacrifice current consumption and liberty to meet targets of capital formation imposed by the authorities. As much as Americans want economic growth, compulsions and depressed levels of consumption are costs which they would not willingly pay except in dire emergency.

A great variety of recipes for growth are in current vogue. Most of them are hackneyed antiques, spruced up a bit with new phrases and served under new names. In the main, these recipes represent two fundamentally different approaches: mercantilism and economic liberalism.

In many ways the debate about economic growth today is similar to the great debate two centuries ago over how best to promote the wealth of nations. The mercantilist approach of the 17th and 18th centuries was an engineering approach. The government by detailed design and elaborate regulation of economic life attempted to impose a coordinated plan of growth on society. Sumptuary laws to prevent frippery and waste, public monopolies to channel investment wisely, detailed regulation of labor and trade—all these were part of the scheme of things. Mercantilism gave way to economic liberalism—a biological approach to growth with the government cultivating growth, not imposing it.

The great success of the biological approach, especially in Great Britain and the United States, is a matter of historical record. It remains to be seen whether our basically liberal approach will give way to a rising tide of mercantilist reaction.

Today one school of thought, the modern mercantilists, says that the government should create growth by massive increases in the quantity and diversity of government services and activity— in short, that government should force growth on the economy. This approach also involves forcing people to save more either through taxes or through inflation, in order to divert resources into collective use.

The opposite school of thought, the supporters of an open society, holds that the kinds and levels of public services should be determined on the basis of what we really want government to produce, that each governmental activity should be justified either on cost-benefit principles or on sound grounds of social responsibility, and that government can best promote growth by policies which release and give effect to the creative energies of private citizens.

While the factors that determine percentage rates of growth over a span of years are not fully understood, the success of past growth efforts and accumulated economic knowledge do tell us a good deal about the conditions of economic progress and how the government can best cultivate growth.

The underlying forces that promote national economic growth are basically the same as those that account for the economic progress of individuals. An individual's desire for a higher and more secure standard of living for himself and for his family is the basic stimulus. To this end he studies, plans, works, saves, and invests. He searches out new ways of doing things, and develops new techniques and processes. Hence, one of the most effective means of stimulating economic growth—and at the same time one of our fundamental objectives in seeking economic growth—is to provide expanding opportunities for every individual to realize his own potentialities to the utmost and to open wider vistas for his children; to encourage initiative, independence, and integrity; to preserve and enlarge the moral worth of the individual; and to approach more closely to our ideals of personal freedom, justice and fair play, broad and equal opportunity, the rule of law, and mutual respect and charity.

Growth requires a flexible and adaptable economic system with freedom to experiment. New industries must spring up, and others must decline. New methods must be accepted and old ones discarded. Labor and capital must shift easily and cooperatively in response to economic rewards and penalties. The combination of an abundant flow of new ideas, a willingness to take risks, and the speedy adoption of successful new methods is a condition for a high rate of growth.

The translation of new ideas into practical processes is speeded by a high rate of saving, through which new equipment can be financed and put into use. Saving also contributes to growth even where new methods are not involved, since it makes possible a larger stock of plant and equipment, housing, and other physical capital, which add to our potential supply of goods and services. In this way, the prudence and responsible foresight of people in providing for future needs makes an essential contribution to our growth.

All of this requires an economic environment that can be brought about and maintained only by positive and progressive governmental actions. The government has a two-fold function in promoting growth. First, it must provide a legal and institutional climate conducive to private economic progress. Second, the government must provide various public services and facilities which, while valuable to the nation as a whole, do not offer sufficient rewards to induce private producers to provide them for sale, or do not offer sufficient direct benefits to induce private individuals to buy them.

We are in the midst of a great national debate over economic growth. But until we understand what growth is, why it is an important policy goal, and how it can be achieved within a framework of economic and political freedom, the debate will range over many false and confused issues.

True growth in economic welfare involves both material and nonmaterial benefits, widely diffused. True growth must conform to the values and aspirations of a free people. The "right" or optimum rate of growth is that rate which conforms to the voluntary choices of the people, rather than a rate obtained by coercion, compulsion, or excessive social costs. The rate of growth can be increased by improving the efficiency of the economic system and by pursuing wise public policies to create a favorable environment for growth.

The future chapters of our story of economic growth are still to be written. We can be confident that these chapters will be happy ones if we have the wit and wisdom to preserve and strengthen the forces of progress that have produced in America an abundant economy, a great nation, and a free people.

Public Responsibility for Growth and Stability

PAUL A. SAMUELSON

Paul A. Samuelson is Professor of Economics at the Massachusetts Institute of Technology. A widely known theorist, he frequently testifies at Congressional hearings on government economic policy. The present essay, originally entitled "The New Look in Tax and Fiscal Policy," appeared in Federal Tax Policy for Growth and Stability, *a compendium of contributions by panelists before a subcommittee of the Joint Economic Committee in 1956.*

THERE IS much talk about taxes. When I flick on the dial of my radio in the morning, I hear a Congressman quoted on how our high level of taxes is ruining the Nation. Scratch the barber who cuts my hair and you find a philosopher ready to prescribe for the Nation's monetary ills.

This is as it should be. We expect sweeping statements in a democracy. Yet such sweeping statements have almost no validity from a scientific point of view. Campaign oratory aside, the more assuredly a man asserts the direction along which salvation is alone to be found, the more patently he advertises himself as an incompetent or a charlatan.

The plain truth is this, and it is known to anyone who has looked into the matter: The science of economics does not provide simple answers to complex social problems. It does not validate the view of the man who thinks the world is going to hell, nor the view of his fellow idiot that ours is the best of all possible tax systems. Quite the contrary, economists would indeed be useless if any sensible man could quickly infer for himself simple answers to the big policy questions of fiscal policy. No need then to feed economists while they make learned studies of the obvious. It is precisely because public policy in the tax and expenditure area is so complex that we find it absolutely indispensable to invest thousands of man-years of scholarly time in scholarly economic research in these areas.

COMPETING GOALS

Turning now to the goals of any tax system, we can ask: What tax structure will give us the most rapid rate of growth? What tax system will give us the highest current standard of living? What tax structure will make our system most immune to the ups and downs in employment and prices that make American families insecure? What tax structure will realize most closely the community's sense of fairness and equity? What tax structure will maximize the efficiency with which we produce what our citizens most want?

Upon careful thought it will be obvious that there cannot exist a tax system which will simultaneously maximize these five quite different goals of social life.

It is easy to see that high current living standards and rapid growth of our ability to produce are conflicting ends: you have only to look at a collectivized society like the Soviet Union, which decides to sacrifice consumption levels of the current generation in favor of a crash program of industrialization; you have only to reflect that historically in the slums of Manchester working families might have lived longer in the 19th century if England and the other nations had during the industrial revolution slowed down their rates of material progress; you have only to consider the problem of conserving scarce exhaustible natural resources to realize that every society must all the time be giving up higher future resource potentials in favor of keeping current generation consumption, as high as it is.

You can imagine a society that decides to devote its income in excess of the bare physiological existence level 100 per cent to capital formation. You can imagine it—but there never has been such a society. Nor would any of us want to live in such a one. It should be obvious, therefore, that no sane person would ever seek a tax program which literally maximized our rate of economic growth. It is just as obvious that no sane person would want to maximize present living levels if this meant eating up all our capital on a consumption bender that would leave us an impoverished nation.

There is no need to go through all the other pairs of the five listed goals to show their partial incompatibility. If we are willing to frame a tax system that strongly favors thrifty men of wealth, we may thereby be able to add to our rate of current growth; if we encourage a gentle rate of inflation, we may be able to increase the profits in the hands of the quick-reacting businessman, perhaps thereby stepping up our rate of growth. So it goes, and one could easily work through the other permutations and combinations.

But not all of our five goals are necessarily competing. Some when you realize them, help you to realize the others. If we succeed in doing away with the great depressions that have dogged the economic record, we may thereby add to our rate of growth. If we shape a graduated tax system that enables lower income groups to maintain minimum standards of life, we may ease the task of stabilizing business activity. If we replace distorting taxes by less distorting alternatives, the fruits of the resulting more efficient production can add to our current consumption and to our rate of progress in capital formation.

I shall not prolong the discussion of the degree to which the diverse goals of tax policy are competing or complementary. For we can formulate proper policies without having to measure these important, but complicated, relationships.

IMPLEMENTING COMMUNITY PREFERENCES

Upon being told by the economist that it is absurd for Congress to aim at the most rapid rate of growth possible and that it is equally absurd for Congress to aim at the highest possible current level of consumption, the policymaker may be tempted to say: "I understand that. Won't you therefore as an economist advise us as to just what is the best possible compromise between these extremes?"

A good question but, unfortunately, not one that the expert economist can pretend to give a unique answer to. If he is honest, he must reply: "The American people must look into their own hearts and decide on what they consider to be the best compromise rate of growth."

Just because I have advanced degrees in economics and have written numerous esoteric works in the field, I am not thereby empowered to let my personal feelings, as to how much the present generation ought to sacrifice in favor of generations to come, become a prescription for society. It would be as presumptuous for me to offer such specific advice as to let my family's notions about dental care determine how much the typical American family ought to spend on toothpaste. But it is legitimate for me as an economist to say this: *Whatever rate of capital formation the American people want to have, the American system can, by proper choice of fiscal and monetary programs, contrive to do.* This can be shown by an example.

Suppose the vast majority of the American people look into the future or across the Iron Curtain at the rate of progress of others. Suppose they decide that we ought to have a more rapid rate of capital formation and technological development than we have been having recently. Then the economist knows this can be brought into being (a) by means of an expansionary monetary policy that makes investment funds cheaper and easier to get. Admittedly, such an expanded investment program will tend, if it impinges on an employment situation that is already full and on a price level that is already stationary, to create inflationary price pressures and over-full employment—unless something is done about it. What would have to be done about this inflationary pressure? Clearly (b) a tight fiscal policy would be needed to offset the expansionary monetary policy: By raising taxes relative to expenditure, we would reduce the share of consumption out of our full employment income, releasing in this way the real resources needed for investment.

From these remarks it will be clear that economic science is not only neutral as to the question of the desired rate of capital accumulation—it is also neutral as to the ability of the economy to realize any decided-on rate of capital formation.

I repeat: With proper fiscal and monetary policies, our economy can have full employment and whatever rate of capital formation and growth it wants.

I want to cap the daring doctrine that an economy can have the rate of capital formation it wants with a doctrine that may seem even more shocking. Naturally, I cannot here develop all of the underlying reasoning, nor give all the needed qualifications. But I do in advance want to stress the earnestness with which I put it forward, and to underline that it does spring from careful use of the best modern analyses of economics that scholars here and abroad have over the years been able to attain.[1] The doctrine goes as follows:

1. [Samuelson has elsewhere described that analysis as a *neoclassical synthesis* of modern income determination theory and the truths of classical capital theory. *Editor.*]

A community can have full employment, can at the same time have the rate of capital formation it wants, and can accomplish all this compatibly with the degree of income redistribution taxation it ethically desires.

This is not the place to give a detailed proof of the correctness of this general proposition. It will suffice to illustrate it with two extreme examples.

In the first, suppose that we desire a much higher rate of capital formation but stipulate that it is to be achieved by a tax structure that favors low-income families rather than high-income. How can this be accomplished? It requires us to have an active expansionary policy (open-market operations, lowering of reserve requirements, lowered rediscount rates, governmental credit agencies of the FHA and RFC type if desired) which will stimulate investment spending. However, with our taxes bearing relatively lightly on the ready-spending poor, consumption will tend to be high at the same time that investment is high. To obviate the resulting inflationary pressure, an increase in the overall tax take with an overly balanced budget [*i.e.*, budgetary surplus] would be needed.

Alternatively, suppose the community wants a higher level of current consumption and has no wish to make significant redistributions away from the relatively well-to-do and toward the lower income groups. Then a tighter money policy that holds down investment would have to be combined with a fiscal policy of light taxation relative to expenditure. But note that in this case, as in the one just above, any qualitative mix of the tax structure can be offset in its effects by appropriate changes in the overall budget level and in the accompanying monetary policy.

A SOBERING PUBLIC RESPONSIBILITY

Modern societies necessarily are pursuing monetary and fiscal policies. These policies interact with private thrift to shape the pattern of high employment consumption and investment. Hence it is these public policies that determine to an important degree how fast society builds up its capital. This power over the community's rate of capital formation should constitute a sobering responsibility for the voters in any modern democracy.

Governmental "Neutralism" and "Activism" in Growth Decisions

EDMUND S. PHELPS

Edmund S. Phelps is Professor of Economics at the University of Pennslyvania. This essay reports some of his recent writings on the foundations of economic growth policy, especially his book Fiscal Neutrality Toward Economic Growth *published in 1965.*

ONE OF THE folkloric propositions about the predominantly capitalistic economy is that its consumers are sovereign over its rate of growth; at least they are sovereign over the volume of private investment, notably the rate of tangible private capital accumulation, on which the growth rate heavily depends. The subscribers to this proposition include many political conservatives who are pleased to think that consumers acting individually in the free marketplace, not the government, choose the investment rate.[1] The subscribers include many socialists who believe that capitalism is inferior to socialism precisely because capitalist governments cannot control the aggregate investment rate. And they include some liberals whose arguments for new public policies to boost the growth rate implicitly assume that the market or the government cannot already err on the side of excessive investment.

The fundamental error of this proposition, viewed from the standpoint of contemporary fiscal and monetary theory, arises from its neglect of the role played by government taxation. If consumers happen to be sovereign when the central government

---

1. Some conservatives would qualify the proposition. They would concede that the marketplace is an imperfect instrument by which consumers can realize the growth—more precisely, the time paths of family consumption—that they really want. No system after all can solve perfectly the awesomely complex problems of intertemporal choice in this uncertain world. But they hold that the free choice which the capitalist system gives to consumers comes tolerably close to giving households the time-profile of consumption goods that they wish among all feasible profiles. I shall return soon to questions of the efficiency of the markets in making intertemporal allocations for they lie at the heart of the controversy over growth policy.

runs a 10 billion dollar deficit, say, they surely cannot also be sovereign if tax rates should place the government budget in deficit by 20 billion dollars. If a sufficiently tighter money policy is coupled with an easier tax policy, aggregate employment will be left unchanged; but we shall have a greater share of aggregate production devoted to consumption goods and a smaller share left for capital formation.

To save the proposition of consumer sovereignty, its supporters must fall back on the contention that, fortuitously or not, the "mix" of taxes and monetary policy over the business cycle has happened to be about right to make consumers in fact sovereign. It must be contended that the treasury of the central government, together with the other taxing authorities, has in fact been "neutral" toward consumer spending and saving. What does this mean? In what sense—by what standard—can we say that the treasury is or is not "neutral"?

CLASSICAL "NEUTRALITY" TWICE SPURNED

The effect of tax policy on the rate of private investment, accepted now by neo-Keynesian economists, was orthodox doctrine in classical economics. David Ricardo and others recognized that an already existing government debt, internally owned, does not subtract from existing productive resources.[2] After denying that taxation to service an already existing public debt is a real burden —on the ground that the interest on the debt is a transfer from one citizen to another—Ricardo added: "From what I have said it must not be inferred that I consider the system of borrownig as the best calculated to defray the . . . expenses of the state. It is a system which tends to make us less thrifty—to blind us to our real situation."[3] The suggestion here is that had the government expenditure been financed instead by taxes, consumers would have felt appropriately poorer in terms of their command over resources for *private* use and would have reduced their (private)

2. It should be added that governmental indebtedness to the private sector will have some effect upon the uses of existing resources, particularly upon consumption and hence upon the volume of resources left available for capital formation, unless taxes are increased enough to offset this effect.

3. David Ricardo, *Principles of Political Economy and Taxation* (E. P. Dutton, 1911), p. 162.

consumption accordingly; the reduction of consumption would have released resources for the government's use and thus reduced or eliminated any diversion of resources from the investment sector.[4]

Ricardo's objection to deficit finance makes the earliest statement of what I call fiscal *neutralism,* a doctrine that government taxes ought to be at a level which conveys to consumers the value or "opportunity costs" of the resources being diverted from private to public use. He presumed that the neutral level of taxation is that which puts the government budget in "balance," neither in surplus nor deficit.

The notion that there is some special virtue in a balanced budget from the point of view of investment and growth was first spurned by the early post-Keynesians who wished to employ tax-rate variations to keep the economy operating at the desired level of employment. The "budget" was placed exclusively in the service of economic stability and any yearning for budget balance was put down as prescientific. If the private components of aggregate demand were buoyant, taxes must be set high, high enough perchance to put the government budget in surplus; if private demand were depressed, taxes would have to be low and the budget might thereby be placed in deficit. Monetary policy was given little part to play.

Monetary policy came back to intellectual life in the 1950s, not so much as an anticyclical weapon but as a long-run force. Neo-Keynesians like Paul Samuelson wrote of the choice between having, on the one hand, easy money to promote high investment and growth with tax policy to restrain consumption demand and, on the other, tight money to restrain growth with low taxes to promote consumption.[5] Taxes were once again assessed for their

4. In a "lifetime saving" model of consumer behavior, only a fraction of the extra tax bill would be financed by a reduction of consumption in the early months, the remainder of the reduction occurring later on.

5. See P. A. Samuelson, "Public Responsibility for Growth and Stability," in this volume, pp. 70–74.

In the wake of Russia's Sputnik in 1957 a number of economists desiring faster growth urged a new "mix" between monetary and fiscal policy in favor of resolutely easier money and a postponement or cessation of tax-rate cuts. The inhibiting effect of the balance-of-payments problem on the monetary authorities and the large growth of "potential" or capacity

effects on growth, as in classical doctrine. Taxes might still be called upon to a limited extent for stabilization purposes, especially if monetary policy was slow to have effect or was harmful in quick and large doses. But monetary instruments would be employed to make the tax level expected to be appropriate in the future consonant with long-run government fiscal objectives. A more serious qualification arises if changes in interest rates and rates of return on capital have an important permanent effect on the balance of payments, given aggregate demand. Then the possibility of exchange-rate adjustments must be assumed to keep international reserves at desired levels.

Several writers drew the conclusion that if fiscal and monetary tools give rise to political control over investment, then the volume of private investment will be determined by a political process. Some writers evidently envisioned that the governing political party (and perhaps the rival party) would formulate an investment policy or a growth policy for popular approval. Samuelson wrote: "This [governmental] power over the community's rate of capital formation should constitute a sobering responsibility for the voters in any modern democracy."

There was no intent here to deny any individual the free choice to consume whatever portion of his disposable after-tax income he likes. Households need not be equally thrifty, nor some thriftier than others. The instruments of the politically determined growth policy were to be just the everyday tools of fiscal and monetary policy. Nor was there any intent by and large to engineer a rate of investment at variance with popular desires. Consumers might yet be sovereign over growth. But through a political process. The market would have little or no role. Indeed, changes in market behavior as such might not have even a marginal effect upon the politically determined growth rate. In the absence of political expressions for greater investment and growth, an overall increase in the thriftiness of consumers would presumably be offset by a reduction of tax rates lest consumption decline.

The marketplace was apparently not seen as even potentially useful in promoting consumer sovereignty over investment. It was

---

output that mounted over the years, however, ultimately won economists and legislators over to another tax cut (legislated in 1964) as the one means available to bring the economy back towards high employment.

not conceived that a suitable fiscal environment might bestow sovereignty on the consumer in his market role. It was tacitly assumed that there exists no fiscal principle, no rule of taxation, the application of which would cause private markets to find the sovereign rate of investment through the dollar votes of consumers and savers. In particular the rule of taxing so as to balance the budget was not presumed to induce private markets to choose the "right" rate of investment. The concept of neutrality was again rejected, or else neglected.

A MODERN CONCEPT OF FISCAL NEUTRALITY

Contrast this novel position on the role of politics in determining resource allocations to economic growth with the position of most Western economists on resource allocations to individual consumer goods. These economists recognize that when there are externalities and decreasing-cost phenomena the government will usually need to intervene with public expenditures to achieve a more "efficient" mix of consumption goods. Without (perfect) intervention the allocation of resources will not generally be "Pareto optimal": that is, it will be possible by some reallocation of resources to make everyone better off. Consider, however, the residue of private consumption goods for which there are perfectly competitive markets and which give off no externalities. It is agreed that the government does not, in order to achieve a Pareto-optimal mix of consumption goods, require a "consumption policy" to determine the mix of outputs of these goods. There is no need to submit alternative consumption mixes to a popular vote. From the fact that the various levels of governments, through their excise taxes and subsidies, can *control* the mix of these goods it does not follow that the government must in any natural sense of the term *decide* the consumption mix. Although society can alter the relative production of pots and pans by political means, few suggest that we must therefore have a pot-or-pan policy. The government can exercise its power in a "neutral" way, hoping that the market will allocate resources among these consumption goods at least as well as can be done by a political process.

With respect to economic growth, how might a neutral policy be defined? I shall say that tax policy is neutral if it produces the same allocation of resources—between aggregate consumption and investment especially, but also among different consumption goods and among individuals—as would occur if there were no government treasury at all (hence no government debt and no government taxes of the ordinary kind) but only a government agency to conscript resources for use in the production of public goods supplied by the government and an agency to redistribute wealth so as to achieve the desired distribution of lifetime income. The conscription or draft of resources here is taken to be efficient: the government is imagined to conscript that set of resources, among all sets sufficient to produce the programmed public goods, which entails the least reduction of the output of private goods valued at their relative prices. And it is imagined that future conscriptions on each person are known insofar as they interest any living person. It does not matter that such a conscription system would be impractical compared to the potentialities of a system of taxation using money or credit. The purpose is only to use conscription as a standard for judging whether tax policy causes the economy to duplicate the way an economy would grow under this idealized system of conscription. Note finally that a neutral tax policy causes the economy to imitate the resource allocations of an economy with the public sector the present economy actually has, not to imitate some otherwise similar economy without any public sector at all.

The virtue of the hypothetical conscription system, though not necessarily an adequate virtue, is that it would not, to use Ricardo's term, "blind" the members of the economy to their true command over private consumption goods now and in the future, as might an arbitrary level of taxes. Each household would know the real costs to itself, in terms of the consumption it expects to be able to make, of the planned program of government-supplied goods. (That the government must form expectations of its future provisions of public goods is not only a prerequisite of a neutral tax policy but, presumably, a prerequisite of any rational use of fiscal instruments.)

Though a neutral tax policy does not distort people's vision of their lifetime consumption possibilities, it should quickly be admitted that people's eyesight in this respect may be astigmatic to begin with. If people see themselves as poorer than they really are, for example, a non-neutral policy that makes them feel a little richer might be better. The shortcomings of fiscal neutrality will shortly be discussed. But let us first examine the workings of fiscal neutrality to understand its strengths. Consider an increase in the government debt without any accompanying change in other economic conditions. We know that such a change in "paper wealth" does not increase the community's true power to consume goods now and in the future, given its present assortment of capital goods. A neutral tax policy will therefore respond with additional taxes to make people feel poorer by just the amount that the increase of the public debt makes them feel richer. The "neutralizing" tax addition will normally exceed the interest on the added national debt, for if taxes were raised just enough to service the additional debt, finite-lived taxpayers, who can sell the debt and thus consume the principal, would still feel that they were richer on balance. A balanced budget therefore is not generally neutral. Or consider a planned increase in future free government services. The Rockefeller Brothers Fund in 1958 saw in the expected enlargement of government expenditures within ten years a reason for larger current private investment. A neutral tax policy would give this result. It would raise taxes by an amount such that people's expectations of their present and future private consumption possibilities would fall by the amount of the increase in future government withdrawals of resources (suitably discounted back to the present according to their distance); present private consumption expenditures would thus fall and resources would be freed for private capital formation.

THE TROUBLE WITH FISCAL NEUTRALITY

Operating in the fiscal environment of a neutral tax policy, the private market will produce a Pareto-optimal growth path of "private" consumption goods if a competitive equilibrium is attained; if there is complete information about future as well as current prices (including wage rates and interest rates) and also perfect information about current and future supplies of public goods; if producers have complete information about the future as well as the current technology; if there are no externalities in production; if consumers know their tastes and their preferences are unchanging over time; if there are no externalities in consumption other than the public goods whose production we take as given.

These are stringent "ifs" and of course they are not satisfied precisely by any economy. In what follows the most frequently cited and perhaps most important ways in which market economies fail to satisfy these conditions will be discussed.

Many of the points listed here as objections to a policy of fiscal neutrality were originally voiced as objections to the growth rate produced by a *laissez faire* economy. Many of these arguments suggest that investment and growth would be too little under *laissez faire*. Since modern economies are not *laissez faire*, and especially since they contain fiscal and monetary instruments that influence the growth rate, these particular arguments do not necessarily show that present-day capitalist economies grow too little. What they may suggest is that growth would be too little under a neutral fiscal policy. But not all the objections to fiscal neutrality have this same upshot.

Pigovian "Myopia" · One of the oldest objections to the *laissez-faire* market solution to growth problems—and by extension to the market solution under a neutral tax policy—is the "myopia" argument of Alfred Pigou. He wrote that "our telescopic faculty is defective," that we "see future pleasures on a diminished scale" and accordingly consume in the present to an extent we later regret. Thus "people distribute their resources between the present, the near future and the remote future on the basis of a wholly irrational preference." Pigou wanted government policies that would steer the economy along a growth path dictated by consumer preferences which were rid of these irrational elements. But the very meaning of consumer sovereignty and "optimality" comes into question.

Absence of Comprehensive Futures Markets · One of the facts of economic life is that our economy lacks futures markets that would bring together buyer and seller of future goods at known prices. The reasons for this lie partly in the awkwardness of allowing for technological and demographic uncertainty. In any case, the absence of these markets compounds the uncertainty about future prices, wage rates and interest rates. No one knows how much other people are going to save in the future, and hence what future interest rates and wage rates will be. Thus people may misjudge their lifetime purchasing powers even under neutral taxation. It would be interesting to know whether today's middle-aged overestimated or underestimated their real earning possibilities today when they were making work and saving decisions ten and twenty years ago.

Social vs. Individual Risk · Another way that capitalism fails to produce the right rate of growth, under a neutral fiscal environment, arises from the tendency of firms and wealthowners on the whole to shy away from risky investments. Robert Solow, James Tobin, and others have argued that to the extent that the risks of various investments are statistically independent, society would ideally "pool" these risks in the manner of an insurance company, making investments pretty much on the basis of their "actuarial" returns, on the mathematical expectations of their returns, without much worry that any individual investment would go sour. But even the largest firms are not large enough to spread the risks of investments on the scale, say, of the supersonic transport. This is one reason why there is frequently a discrepancy between the rates of interest that savers and lenders typically earn and the rates of return that firms require their investments to promise. As a result there is likely to be the wrong amount of saving as well as too little risky high-yield investment relative to safe low-yield investment. Some departure from fiscal neutrality is required to improve the situation. Rather than simply tax above the neutral level, however, which could be the wrong medicine, it would be best that the government arrange to subsidize risky investment or to engage in risk-sharing with firms.[6] Such fiscal actions would cause interest rates to rise, bringing them nearer to actuarial returns, and this rise might increase total saving; at least private saving would (on this account alone) be better attuned to the prospective average returns on the economy's aggregate investment.

6. To some extent, the corporate income tax causes the government to share in the profits and losses from investments and thus reduces risk as well as expected returns.

Monopoly · Another reason that many firms do not accept all investments which have an expected social rate of return in excess of the rate of interest available to savers is that these firms have monopoly power. Where there is a natural monopoly or there are artificial restrictions on entry, other firms are prevented from competing away the resulting monopoly profit. The latter shows up as an excess of the value of market value of the firm over the replacement cost of the firm's assets. (Other factors, like the costs of expansion and the costs of increasing customers can impose this excess valuation though they do not have the same significance.) One effect of this monopoly is likely to be an increase in the quantity of capital allocated to the more competitive sectors of the economy. The inflated asset valuation and the reduction in the rate of interest available to savers is also likely to reduce total saving and investment.

Externalities from Investment · It is often argued nevertheless that without monopoly we would have less growth and ultimately less capital formation on the ground that we depend upon patent protection and other restrictions upon entry in order to encourage technological research. To this Kenneth Arrow, Richard Nelson, and other economists reply that the system of monopoly produces less than the ideal amount of research, especially an inadequate amount of pure research. This is because the benefits of research are potentially "external" to the firm undertaking it. Since information of any kind is technically a "public good" whether offered by the government or not—it can be shared by all with only a negligible transmission cost—there would ideally be no price charged to producers for the use of and access to research performed by another producer. There seems to be a dilemma for economic policy here: no price should be charged for the use of research yet denial of the right to charge a price, to demand royalty payments for its use or to retain monopoly rights in its use, would virtually destroy any incentive for firms to do research. Many economists see a way out of this dilemma through extensive government finance or subsidization of research with little or no patent protection allowed. But clearly the government cannot be expected to make perfect decisions in so complex an area as technological research. So it is probably wise to leave

some room for private initiative. Whatever the best practical solution to these problems, the shortcomings of our technological institutions do not seem to signal clearly that the neutral level of
overall taxes is definitely too low or too high.[7]

Externalities from Consumption · Just as production, like the
production of knowledge, can produce an external effect (neighborhood effect) or at least a potential one if no obstacle to it is
placed in the way, so consumption can produce externalities.
Amartya Sen and Stephen Marglin have offered the example of
the "isolation paradox." Suppose that everyone living today feels
a kind of generalized altruism toward his contemporaries as well
as people in the next generation. Suppose further that the increased amount of consumption by each person in the next
generation which is necessary to compensate the representative
individual living today for a one-unit reduction in the consumption of each of his contemporaries is less than the increase of the
amount of per capita consumption the next generation can have
if each member of the present generation gives up one unit of
consumption. If the number of people is large enough, there will
then be a net gain for all if every individual is made to give up
some consumption. This is because the favorableness of the terms
at which society can exchange present consumption for future
consumption by investing capital exceeds the favor the representative man has for his contemporaries relative to the next generation—and it does so by more than enough to compensate each
individual for the reduction of his own consumption. Note that
despite this gain, the individual is not implied to be willing to
consume less *on his own.* He will be happy consuming less only if
his contemporaries must match him. If these externalities are important, a neutral fiscal policy will produce the wrong quantity
of consumption. Some departure from neutral taxation is required
to induce people collectively to consume less when there is a gain
from so doing (as just described) or to consume more when there
is a loss from a collective increase of consumption. But the market
behavior of savers cannot tell us by how much to depart or even
in what direction to depart from the neutral level of taxation.

7. Note that other kinds of investment, like education or even tangible
capital formation, may give off externalities.

Overlapping Generations · Fresh troubles assail the policy of fiscal neutrality when generations overlap, when the old coexist for a time with the young. Samuelson, Peter Diamond and others have studied the possibility of a market malfunction if the procession of generations is going to be infinitely long. In some no-government models of such an economy it can be shown that, while each household acts rationally, the economy may very well oversave in a certain sense, driving the capital stock beyond what is fruitful if it is to be maintained at that level forever. In a stationary economy with no population growth and no technological progress, this phenomenon would be signalled by a continuously negative rate of return on capital. This possibility exists in these models because there is no way that people can save for their retirement years except by accumulating tangible capital. The same oversaving can occur in an economy with a government and neutral taxation. A departure from fiscal neutrality would be called for if this phenomenon arose in order to eliminate the oversaving.

Another difficulty arises when generations overlap from the fact that the true private consumption possibilities of those living today, particularly those who will survive to coexist the succeeding generations, depend not only on the technology and upon future government uses of resources but also upon the way the succeeding government distributes the tax burden among the various generations then living. (The size of any negative taxes paid to the aged is a case in point.) This consideration alters somewhat and makes conjectural the neutral level of taxation. It is the taxes future governments will impose on the present generations, not the level of overall future government expenditures they will make, that will determine (along with current government outlays) the neutral level of taxes. The overlap of generations may also create an opportunity for those living today to improve upon a neutral tax policy. By reducing its present tax level, the present generation may be able to foist some of the cost of its current government programs onto future generations to the extent that future governments do not penalize surviving members of the present generation for so doing. Whether those with an interest in their heirs' well-being would only deceive themselves in thinking themselves to be better off and whether they might anticipate the larger tax burden on their heirs and accordingly bequeathe more are intricate issues in the theory of saving behavior that cannot be pursued here.

Exact Neutrality Unrealizable · The last objection to fiscal neutrality is that precise neutrality is not realizable in practice. Some economists believe that neutrality is a will-of-the-wisp. It is not only the overall budgetary position, the overall level of taxes, that influences consumption, after all, but also the specifics. A precisely neutral tax policy requires exclusive reliance on "lump-sum" taxes, taxes which the taxpayer believes to be independent of the amount of leisure he takes, the amount of saving he does and the amount of investment he undertakes. Such taxes, of course are not feasible, not for any length of time. Thus governments must decide upon a mix of income taxes, profits taxes, wage taxes, excise taxes and so on; each of these has substitution effects upon the incentive to work and to save. Yet the quantitative importance of these substitution effects is not yet established and if they were quantified one could adjust the overall tax level so as approximately to nullify these substitution effects.

THE TRIALS OF ACTIVISM

What should we conclude from this long (though much condensed) critique of fiscal neutrality and of the marketplace it intends to make sovereign over growth? Note that any *non*-neutral policy towards the overall level of taxation would be as afflicted by many of the faults of capitalism as would a neutral policy. The questions of monopoly and technological progress would bedevil any architect of a politically determined growth policy. But some of the objections—especially uniformed judgments about future prices, externalities in consumption and the possibility of gain at the expense of future generations (who will probably be better off than we anyway)—strike at the heart of the case for using markets to realize consumers' wishes regarding growth.

The good neutralist will answer that the estimates of the future by the uncoordinated market, while imperfect, are not worse than would be the imperfectly informed estimates made by the government; that the failure of the market to cope with external effects is not less than the ability of governments to encompass the side-effects of its actions. Some neutralists will contend that the errors from following a neutral policy would be as small as those from any other policy and that it is hard to tell whether fiscal neutrality would produce too little growth or too much. Other neutralists will argue that calculation of the neutral tax level will indicate the right general magnitude of growth and that back-of-the-envelope estimates of the resulting errors may provide a basis for deviating a little in some direction from the neutral tax level.

Others will conclude in favor of activism towards growth decisions. Finding the objections to fiscal neutrality overwhelming, they will want to rethink economic growth from scratch. The presumption of these activists is that the marketplace under a neutral policy would err so badly that a carefully constructed growth program is likely to be superior.

It should be understood that the activists' road is the hard one, not the easy one. The problems which activists see as unsolved by fiscal neutrality the activists must set for themselves to solve. The imperfectly informed voter is as unlikely to meet these problems as is the decision-maker in the marketplace.

In place of the estimates by consumers of what future the market will bring, calculations must be made of the consequence for future consumption possibilities of alternative government tax programs for growth. Production functions and technological-progress functions must be estimated; future technologies and demographic patterns must be studied. Thorniest of all these calculations is the problem of estimating how future governments will respond to the resources made available to them. If the present government departs radically from the tradition of balanced budgets, will future governments also? If future governments are assumed by each government to behave as it would in their shoes, this problem takes on a conjectural game-theoretic aspect, and it can lack a solution. How convenient by contrast to imagine that the consumer is expert in these matters!

Digging into the preferences of the people is the other half of the task. The difficulty is compounded when people are deemed to care about the external effects of growth upon their contemporaries and upon future people. When we widen reasonably further their areas of concern, the mind boggles. A decision, say, to reduce significantly the rate of economic growth could affect human happiness more than consumption. It might bring a mood of tedium and futility. Rapid growth may perform deeper functions than the economist ordinarily supposes. It is said that many a household saves and invests in private securities in order to feel a participant in the development of the economy. Surrogate saving and investing in government bonds used to finance a portion of public expenditure instead of taxes might not give the same sense of satisfaction. On the other hand, the diversion of resources and of national attention away from investment might pave the way for new social and humanistic pursuits.

The groundwork for "optimal economic growth" is just beginning to be laid. Economics is not yet able to describe the welfare consequences of our growth choices with any confidence. Pending the further development of this research, intuitions and perceptions about the rightness of our present fiscal norms and investment rate will continue to be offered. The complexity of optimal economic growth should warn us against acting upon any of them uncritically. But neither should we fear to drift from the arbitrary fiscal policies of the present.

PART TWO The Means of Growth

Fixed Investment and Economic Growth

Robert M. Solow is Professor of Economics at the Massachusetts Institute of Technology. This essay appeared in 1968 in a volume edited by Walter W. Heller, Perspectives on Economic Growth.

IN ECONOMICS, as in more exact sciences, it sometimes happens that progress comes from exploiting the implications of rather simple insights or observations. The original observation itself may be nothing new; what counts is the realization that it is the key to something else. Thus, much of the modern analysis of economic growth begins from the simple truism emphasized by Sir Roy Harrod and by Evsey Domar: Investment in plant and equipment differs from other possible uses of output in an important way. Investment adds both to current demand for output and to future capacity to produce output. Consumption and military expenditures, on the other hand, may be important sources of demand for current output, but they do not add to capacity.

From a short-run point of view it hardly matters whether an increment to this year's national product takes the form of consumption or investment. It matters to the particular firms that make the sales and the particular workers and places affected. But it matters much less to the economy as a whole. From a longer-run point of view, however, it matters quite a lot. There is an optimistic way and a pessimistic way to state the difference. If the extra expenditures are investment, next year the economy will be able to produce more; it will have grown. That is the optimistic side. But if the economy is having trouble generating enough demand to employ its people and resources fully, then next year it will have an even harder problem if it invests this year, because still more demand will be needed to achieve full employment than if the investment had not taken place. That is the pessimistic view. Which view is more appropriate depends on circumstances. An economy which has been growing smoothly at full employment can "choose" confidently between slightly faster and slightly slower growth. An economy beset by unemployment and slack must be more cautious about the hurdles it sets for itself.

This approach dovetails perfectly with what has come to be called "the new economics" (though to professional economists it is thoroughly middle-aged). The analytical foundation of the Kennedy-Johnson economic policy was the proposition that the appropriate indicator for policy needs is the relationship between the potential output of the economy and the current state of demand, the Gap. When the Gap is large, when demand and production fall short of potential, there is room—and need—for expansionary policy, even if production is already rising. When the Gap is narrow or nonexistent, rapid expansion of demand will waste itself in inflation, because production can advance no more rapidly than potential output rises. If the democratic process suggests that more rapid growth is desirable, then the appropriate goal for policy is to shift some resources from current consumption to investment, to build capacity for the future, as discussed by James Tobin. The tension between demand and capacity, crucial for short-term policy decisions, is also the thing to watch when it comes to long-run economic growth.

Changes in national product can be decomposed into changes in potential output and changes in unemployment and capacity utilization. From year to year, changes in unemployment and the rate of capacity utilization can be the dominant source of changes in national product. But over long periods of time, barring major economic collapse, the change in potential must dominate. If a twenty-year period begins with a Gap of 10 percent and ends with none at all, then Gap-closing contributes something under 0.5 percent a year to the rate of growth of production. For the United States, the long-period growth of potential output has been something between 3 and 4 percent a year. So it is clear that when we turn attention to growth over several decades, the recorded growth of the economy *is*, to a good approximation, the growth of potential output.

INVESTMENT AND POTENTIAL OUTPUT

The effect of investment on potential output can be separated into three components. Without a heavy burden of extra assumptions, it is a terribly difficult matter to measure the three component effects of investment, but nevertheless it pays to keep them separate for clarity of thought. The first effect is usually called "capital-widening" by economists. When employment is growing, the stock of plant and equipment must grow at the same rate simply to provide each of the new workers with the same amount of capital on the average as those already at work. A simplified numerical example—with numbers of about the right size—will help to explain this. Suppose that 70 million people are employed this year, and employment will grow by about 1.5 percent to 71 million next year. If each worker, on the average, is equipped with $20,000 worth of plant and machinery, $20 billion of net investment is required to outfit the new workers up to the standard of the old. If production per man is about $10,000, the national product amounts to $700 billion; the "capital-widening" investment is a bit under 3 percent of the national product.

In the course of time, however, the amount of capital per worker goes up. Even if invention did not generate new processes of production using new kinds of equipment, it would be possible (and might be profitable) to provide more of already known types of capital for each worker. There are always a few more ways to increase productivity per worker: mechanize materials-handling, for example, or replace hand-mixed concrete by machine-mixed. This process is often called "capital-deepening." Suppose—in the numerical example already mentioned—capital per worker were rising ("being deepened") by about 2 percent a year, from $20,000 to $20,400, for instance. Then the net investment required to bring all 71 million workers up to the new standard would be $400 × 71,000,000 or about $28.5 billion, another 4 percent of the national product.

A certain amount of capital-deepening does go on all the time. But invention rarely stands still. The hypothetical process of providing *more* capital per worker is inextricably mixed up with the theoretically different process of providing *better* capital for each worker. This aspect of investment has no such conventional name as the others. I once called it "capital-quickening," for the following reason. Plant and equipment has a fairly long life. It takes a while to wear out; and even if more efficient types of plant and equipment are invented every year, it takes a while before an older type becomes truly obsolete. This means that the stock of capital goods in an economy represents many "layers" of technology—old, not-so-old, and relatively new. The more investment occurs this year, the newer or younger, on the average, will be the stock of capital goods. In fact, the more investment occurs this year, the more old capital will be forced into idleness or out of existence by the competition of newer, more efficient capacity. Since new capital is generally more productive than old, a higher rate of investment has an additional productivity-increasing effect. This "quickening" effect can, in principle, be measured, even though one can not hope to isolate a particular dollar sum of new plant and equipment and identify it as the quickening part of total investment.

These three effects are worth distinguishing because they explain something about the effects of investment and about the motives for investment. Widening increases capacity without increasing productivity per worker. Deepening and quickening increase capacity by increasing productivity, but they do it differently. When more capital is provided per worker, there is likely to be pressure on profits, because the more profitable uses of capital are likely to be tried first. This is an application of the famous "law of diminishing returns." But when better capital is provided for some workers, there need be no weakening of profitability. Invention is the historical answer to the law of diminishing returns.

In principle, any expenditure or use of resources is an investment if it will yield a return in the future. Evidently, then, plant and equipment spending is investment spending, but so are some other types of expenditure. In particular, research and development expenditures are investment, and so is at least some—

perhaps most—spending on education. In this essay, investment means "plant and equipment spending." The one-word description is used, not with imperialistic intent, simply to avoid circumlocution. Casual observation as well as some more systematic evidence suggest that productivity can increase solely as a result of intangible investment. Nevertheless, it is fair to say that any commitment to economic growth involves, sooner or later, a commitment to investment in plant and equipment. Investment in that narrow sense may not be a sufficient condition for rapid growth, but it is almost certainly a necessary condition.

International Comparisons · Some evidence for this assertion comes from international comparisons. There is no doubt at all that, generally speaking, fast-growing countries are high-investment countries. Table 1 gives a sample of the evidence. Table 2 covers fewer countries for a more recent period. The first column gives the rate of growth of productivity, *i.e.*, of output per man-hour, not of output itself. The part of output growth that just reflects the growth of population and employment is excluded as not specially interesting. The second column shows for each country the proportion of Gross National Product devoted to gross investment (including inventories but excluding housing) on the average between 1950 and 1960. The third column is a crude experiment. Since the growth of employment has been eliminated from the first column by concentrating on productivity, it is natural to exclude from investment the part that constitutes capital-widening. Unfortunately, the third column is sheer guess; indeed, it is not even that, but a rule of thumb applied indiscriminately to all countries.

Table 1 shows that the very fast-growing economies—West Germany, Norway, and Japan, for instance—did a lot of investment, more than most others. The very slow-growing economies —especially the United States and the United Kingdom—did much less investment than anyone else. But Table 1 also shows that no simple generalization will quite describe the facts, because once the extreme cases are set aside, the connection between growth of productivity and investment is loose. France has invested rather less, Norway and Canada rather more than their growth rates might lead one to expect. The tremendous

TABLE 1.

	(1) Rate of Growth of Output per Man-hour, Annual Average 1950–60	(2) Proportion of GNP Invested, Annual Average 1950–60	(3) "Nonwidening" Investment as Proportion of GNP
Belgium	2.5	12.1	11.5
Denmark	2.9	15.3	14.5
France	3.9	15.3	14.3
Germany	6.0	19.0	15.8
Italy	4.1	16.1	12.5
Netherlands	3.7	20.0	17.8
Norway	3.9	23.0	24.0
Sweden	3.5	16.3	16.7
United Kingdom	2.0	12.1	10.9
Canada	2.5	20.1	17.5
United States	2.4	14.6	12.8

Source: Angus Maddison. *Economic Growth in the West,* The Twentieth Century Fund, New York, 1964; (W. W. Norton & Company, Inc., paperbound edition 1966).

increase in German productivity from 1950 to 1960 undoubtedly contained a nonrepeatable element of recovery from war. Table 2 gives a fairer picture. Indeed, more detailed research has indicated that fast-growing countries grow fast as much because their investment is more productive as because they invest more in the first place. Some of this is easily understood: Cold countries like Norway and large, sparsely populated countries like Canada use up a lot of capital simply overcoming weather and distance. But it is not all so obvious. Some students of the problem have emphasized that the causal arrow points both ways: High investment may contribute to growth, but growth—especially un-

TABLE 2.

	Rate of Growth of Output per Man, Annual Average 1955–64	Proportion of GNP Invested, Annual Average, 1955–64	"Nonwidening" Investment as Proportion of GNP
France	4.7	15.7	15.1
Germany	4.4	20.1	17.5
Italy	5.7	16.9	16.8
Japan	8.8	30.2	27.2
United Kingdom	2.6	13.7	12.7
United States	1.9	13.9	11.5

Source: Angus Maddison in *Lloyds Bank Review,* January 1966.

interrupted growth—both motivates investment and permits more productive, less defensive, investment.

Evidence from American History · It is not necessary to go outside the United States to find evidence of this kind. Different periods of our own history can be used as the raw material for similar comparisons. The advantage of this procedure is that it avoids the vague implication that one country is pretty much like another except in those respects explicitly mentioned in Tables 1 and 2. We know that is not so. Table 2 must not be read as saying that if the British would only invest as large a fraction of their national income as the Japanese, they could grow as rapidly. The truth is that there is probably nothing the British economy could do that would make it grow as fast as the Japanese; the two countries differ in natural resources, social structure, attitudes, industrial composition, the scope for imitation and the willingness to imitate, and all sorts of things. When we deal with different slices of American history, many of these unmeasured and unmeasurable factors are constant or changing only slowly. The disadvantage of this historical procedure is that we need to compare fairly long periods—so that changes in potential dominate changes in output—and good statistics do not go back very far.

The periods from 1929–47 and from 1947–65 are comparable and fairly long. The end points were years of fairly high employment, so rates of growth are not much distorted by Gap-opening and Gap-closing. Between 1929 and 1947, the stock of plant and equipment (in constant prices) increased only about as fast as the number of people employed. Capital was widened, but not deepened. Moreover, the 1947 stock of capital was certainly older on the average than the 1929 stock; there was no gain in productivity from that source. There is no mystery about this; the period spans the deep depression of the 1930's, when very little investment occurred because very few opportunities for profit presented themselves, and the Second World War, when civilian investment was severely restricted. But we are interested in effects, not causes. Between 1929 and 1947, output per worker in American industry rose at the relatively slow rate of 1.5 percent a year. We can attribute this productivity gain mainly to technological progress, to the improved education and training of workers, and perhaps to other, minor, sources. That productivity rose at all between 1929 and 1947 shows that productivity can rise without much investment. That productivity rose so slowly suggests that without much investment there can not be very rapid progress.

Between 1947 and 1965, the stock of capital goods increased much more rapidly than employment. High investment increased the stock of plant and equipment per worker by something near 3 percent a year. During the same interval, production per worker also rose by nearly 3 percent a year. It would be too simple-minded to compare the prewar and postwar histories and conclude that capital-deepening at a rate of 3 percent a year generates a growth in productivity of about 1.5 percent a year (the 3 percent observed in 1947–65 less the 1.5 percent observed without deepening in 1929–47). One would have to pay more attention to changes in the hours of work, in the "quality" of the labor force, and in the industrial composition of the national product. One would have to attribute some gain in productivity to the fact that the 1965 stock of capital was a few years younger, on average, than the 1947 stock. Still, when all is said and done, it is hard to dodge the implication that the recovery of plant and equipment spending after the doldrums of depression and the rationing of wartime had quite a lot to do with the accelerated growth of productivity.

The same sort of correlation between investment and productivity gain is revealed by the comparison of shorter intervals of time. But the meaning of the correlation is much less clear. The productivity movements may have more to do with fluctuations in capacity utilization than with anything else. And the correlation may simply reflect the fact that rapid growth in output eliminates excess capacity and stimulates investment. That cannot be the mechanism underlying the longer-period comparisons.

The "Natural" Rate of Growth · Here I must deal with a fine point. Modern economic theory suggests that in the very long run the rate of economic growth is approximately the rate of growth of the labor force plus something that might be broadly identified as the rate of increase of economic efficiency. This last catchall is meant to include the rate of technological progress, the increase in output resulting from changes in industrial composition, movements from low-productivity to high-productivity activity, gains from the elimination of discrimination in employment, and many other things. The most important is technological progress. Another important component, stemming from the improvement in quality of the labor force, through more and better education and better health, can be included either as part of the growth of the labor force or as part of the increase of economic efficiency, so long as it is included somewhere. Barring the appearance of a growing Gap, the rate of economic growth will not in the very long run fall short of this "natural" rate of growth. Neither can it for very long be greater.

This implies that for the very long run the rate of growth does not depend on the rate of investment. It implies, roughly speaking, that the only way to create a permanent increase in the rate of growth is somehow to speed up the rate of technological progress. The reasoning behind this conclusion is complicated, but it goes something like this. If an economy that has been growing at its "natural" rate tries to grow faster by investing, say, 15 percent of its output instead of 10 percent, it will at first succeed in doing so. It will supply each worker with more capital and so enable each worker to produce more. The higher output means a higher rate of growth. On the average, too, each worker will have newer capital, and this will add to productivity and growth. But then the law of diminishing returns sets in. Each successive addition to capital per man is able to generate only successively smaller increases in productivity. And as the increments to output get smaller, so do the increments to capital, because investment remains a steady percentage of output. There is a permanent gain in production; that is very important to remember. An economy investing 15 percent of its annual income will forever after have a higher annual income than if it had continued to invest 10 percent. But eventually the gain tapers off. Suppose it tapers off at 20 percent; that is, eventually the economy will have a 20 percent higher output when it invests 15 percent than it would if it had continued to save 10 percent. At the end of twenty years, the economy will have added something under 1 percent a year to its growth rate; but at the end of fifty years, its growth rate will be only 0.4 percent higher than it would have been; and after a century, only 0.2 percent higher. These are not necessarily realistic numbers, but they illustrate the point. The very long-run growth rate may be determined by more fundamental forces than the rate of investment in plant and equipment. But the very long run may be very long. There may be quite respectable increases in the rate of growth achievable over spans of a decade or two. For an economy at 4 percent a year, the addition of a half of a percentage point to the growth rate is no mean achievement.

It appears, then, that meaningful increases in economic growth can result either from higher investment or faster invention. Moreover, there are many subtle interconnections between the two. Some inventions are no use without investment; investment often stimulates invention. If necessity is the mother of invention, investment may well serve as midwife.

This excursion into theory provides us with an understanding of the looseness of the relation between investment and growth revealed in Table 1. Some part—it is no casual matter to say how much—of international differences in growth rates reflects differences in "natural" rates of growth: in the rate of innovation or imitation, in the rate at which the efficiency of use of existing resources under existing technology is being improved, in the rate at which the education and training of the labor force is being upgraded. Some part, of course, does reflect differences in the rate of investment. If the analysis I have mentioned is right, this part is in a very long-run sense transitory. But in the medium run it is quite real; and the investment rate differs from the other determinants of growth by being more easily and quickly changeable through the influence of public policy. It is also more directly a mere instrument. Society does or may have an intrinsic interest in education for its own sake, in innovation for its own sake, in the movement of people for their own sake out of low-productivity agriculture into high-productivity industry, but investment in plant and equipment has no reason for being other than the generation of new capacity. If investment were not necessary for economic growth, it would surely be better to produce consumer goods instead.

Future Investment Requirements · The next question follows naturally. Suppose the United States were to grow for the next ten years at its natural rate: About how much plant and equipment investment would be required? And how much extra investment would be needed as part of a policy to speed the rate of growth a little?

Only the most uncertain sort of answer can be given. We do not even know for sure what the natural rate of growth is: The Council of Economic Advisers estimates 3.75 percent a year, with the possibility that some speed-up has taken place, while the National Industrial Conference Board, in a recent study, settles on a figure near 4.25 percent a year for the decade to 1975. Even if we take a round number like 4 percent as a compromise, there remain uncertainties. Something depends on how much of the 4-percent represents increase in employment, and how much represents increased productivity. Employment growth must be accompanied by capital-widening; productivity growth comes in part, but only in part, from capital-deepening. Another uncertainty has to do with the character of technological progress. Some students of the problem believe that there has been, in the past decade or more, a reduction in capital requirements per unit of national product. If this saving of capital is projected into the future, the investment requirements for any given rate of growth are reduced. Others prefer not to project a decline in capital requirements, either because they do not believe it has occurred or because they believe it to be temporary. They do not foresee any independent reduction in investment requirements from that source.

With all due caution, it is probably fair to say that most estimates of the fixed investment necessary to support 4 percent growth for a decade would cluster around 10 percent of GNP, some a little higher, others a little lower. Is that a lot of investment or a little? The easiest way to answer is to say that since the end of the Second World War the American economy has spent roughly 9 percent of its GNP on plant and equipment. The figure has dipped to 8.5 percent in bad years, and has risen to 10 percent or better only in 1947 and 1948, again in 1956 and 1957, and again in 1965–67 and, according to most forecasts, in 1968. The investment requirements of 4-percent growth are likely to be met by our economy in good years, and missed by 1 percent of GNP—which is 10 percent of the required investment—in slack years.

Now suppose it were desired to raise the growth rate to 4.25 percent: By how much would investment requirements rise? The difference between 4- and 4.25-percent growth sounds almost trivial, but it is not; it amounts to 2.5 percent of GNP in the tenth year alone, or between $15 and $20 billion at current levels. Now there are many ways of adding a little to the growth rate: working longer hours, inducing more women or old people into employment, speeding up the rate of migration from agriculture, to name a few. To do it all by increasing the rate of investment means fighting harder against diminishing returns, and that may be expensive. It would not be easy to get agreement on the magnitudes involved; much of the necessary research has not yet been done. But I suppose that to add 0.25 percent to the "natural" growth rate and sustain it for a decade would require fixed investment to rise above 12 percent of GNP; some might say well above 12 percent of GNP. That is very high by historical standards in this country. It would undoubtedly require special policies to stimulate investment. And not simply to induce business to more of the kind of investment it had been doing. To "deepen capital," to work against diminishing returns, means to encounter less profitable opportunities for investment. Policy must overcome this drag.

INVESTMENT AS DEMAND

From consideration of the capacity-creating effect of investment, logic has returned us to consideration of investment as a component of aggregate demand.

Directly or indirectly, all incomes are earned in production. The national income and the national product are opposite sides of the same coin. Moreover, earners of income spend to buy back the product they have collectively produced. It is possible for changes in inventories to absorb short-run fluctuations in spending; but over any substantial period of time, total expenditures and total production must move together. If spending falls off, production will drop too. But then incomes will fall and spending will drop still further, and then . . . these are the "multiplier effects" that every schoolboy knows, now.

At full employment—however that is defined—the economy can produce a certain volume of output; in so doing it generates the corresponding total of incomes. Full employment will be maintainable only if the recipients of income are collectively willing to buy back the full-employment output. It seems, then, that they are required to spend all that they earn. Many people and many corporations, however, spend less than they earn; they save. Somewhere in the economic system, then, there must be someone or some institution prepared willingly to spend more than it earns. Otherwise the initial level of output and employment will be unmaintainable.

Imagine the economy grouped into three big consolidated sectors: families, businesses, and governments. Families earn wages, rents, dividends, salaries, and buy consumer goods. Businesses retain some part of their profits, accumulate depreciation allowances, and buy plant and equipment. Governments collect taxes from families and businesses and buy all the various things governments do buy. Typically, all families taken together spend considerably less than they earn, saving the difference. Typically, governments spend somewhat more than they take in—they run budget deficits—but except in wartime the difference is small and there are many more surplus years than the mythology suggests. Businesses together spend on investment considerably more than they retain in undistributed profits and depreciation allowances; they run a big deficit. In 1965 the saving of households amounted to $25 billion and the saving (budget surplus) of governments to $2 billion. Against this, the gross saving of businesses was about $82 billion and their gross investment $109 billion. The $27 billion of saving by families and governments was offset by the excess of investment over retained earnings and depreciation allowances of business. (In these figures gross investment includes housebuilding, inventory accumulation, and net foreign investment in addition to plant and equipment spending; and a certain amount of personal saving is really the "business saving" of unincorporated businesses. But the principle is clear.)

Full employment can be maintained only if business and government together have a big enough deficit (or surplus) to offset the saving (or overspending) that families will do from the incomes they earn at full employment. (Personal saving has been positive every year since 1929 except for 1932 and 1933; at full employment it would certainly be positive.) If we freeze the consolidated budget deficit of all governments at zero or any convenient positive or negative number, this means that investment spending must be big enough to absorb the gross saving of business and the net saving of families. If it is not big enough to do so, markets are not strong enough to buy up the full-employment output of the economy; production, employment, and income will shrink to squeeze out the excess saving. If investment is bigger than it need be, aggregate expenditure will exceed the value of production at the going prices; prices and production will both rise, but the nearer the economy is to capacity operation, the more the excess demand will waste itself in inflation.

ECONOMIC POLICY

Economic policy in this context—there are many other goals of economic policy—has two objectives. Above all, the fiscal—tax and budget—and monetary policy of the Federal Government should aim to balance the economy at full employment. This can be accomplished by influencing the spending decisions of private families and businesses, and therefore their net saving. It can also be accomplished by operating on tax rates and government spending, and therefore on the net saving of governments. In fact, both devices will always be used. The immediate purpose is to guarantee that total expenditure from full-employment income is just enough to buy full-employment output, or that total investment should just offset total saving at full employment; these are two ways of saying the same thing.

This objective of economic policy can be achieved, in principle, by many combined fiscal-monetary strategies. The full-employment objective bears primarily on the total of expenditures, not on the way the total is divided among the three major sectors of consumption, investment, and government purchases. Of course, the allocation of total production cannot be haphazard; it must conform roughly to the pre-existing distribution of industrial capacity, which can itself be changed only slowly. There is much evidence, for example, that the sharp capital-goods boom of 1956-57 strained the capacity of the equipment-producing industries with inflationary consequences for the whole economy. Despite this limitation, it remains true that there can be full employment with a broad range of "mixes" of personal consumption, business investment, and government spending. The second major objective of fiscal and monetary policy is to bring about a mix that corresponds generally to society's preferences.

It has been the burden of this essay that if a society wishes to have rapid growth it will have to divert a part of its output from current consumption to investment. This means that if aggregate demand is deficient, policy should aim to fill the gap with a strong dose of investment. If demand is excessively strong, policy should aim at cutting back noninvestment expenditures more sharply than plant and equipment outlays. If aggregate demand is just right, it may be necessary to build up investment at the expense of other uses of output and, at the same time, provide the corresponding saving either by creating incentive to save in the private economy or by generating a government budget surplus.

If society wishes temporarily to push its growth-rate above the "natural" rate, an additional problem arises. The investment to support growth will run into diminishing profitability; extra investment now reduces the incentive to invest next year or the year after. Without luck and care, the consequence may be not only a relapse of the growth rate—which may not be so important, after all—but a shortage of total demand and the emergence of temporary slack and unemployment.

The policy tools for operating on the composition of output are pretty clear. There are many ways of reducing or increasing taxes: Investment credits and corporate tax concessions sweeten the return on investment, and increases are likely to put pressure on plant and equipment plans. Easy credit conditions and low interest rates are likely to favor investment, because financing becomes easier and because anything that reduces the return on alternative assets is likely to make capital goods look better. Restrictive monetary policy, in reverse, is likely to contract demand mainly by decreasing the attractiveness of long-lived investments.

All this is fairly clear in principle. In fact there are two unsettled problems. The first is that different people place different values on growth as an objective of policy. It is not easy to see how any delicate consensus can be struck.

The second difficulty is a matter of "economic engineering." We have very little experience with managing the rate of investment through tax and monetary means. In 1961, fixed investment was 9.0 percent of GNP; no more could be expected in a slack economy with plenty of idle capacity. Considerations like those discussed here led the Kennedy Administration to propose the 7 percent investment credit as part of the Revenue Act of 1962; indeed, as first proposed the credit would have been a more precise instrument for stimulating marginal investment. Other, similarly intended actions were undertaken on both the fiscal and monetary fronts.

The result was that fixed investment rose to 9.2 percent of GNP in 1962 and 1963! So small an increase might have been expected simply as a result of the gradual reduction in unemployment and excess capacity, even in the absence of any deliberate intent to stimulate investment. Doubts accumulated as to whether any such policy could succeed without intolerable government interference in the private economy. But in 1964 the investment ratio rose to 9.6 percent, and in 1965 to 10.3 percent, reminiscent of the investment boom of the mid-fifties.

Does this reflect simply the luck of the game, the revival of confidence, the expectation of continued prosperity and/or inflation? Or does it mean that policies aimed at stimulating investment work with a fairly long lag, especially when they have to overcome an aversion to risk fostered by long years of economic slack? It will take a few more years of observation before anyone can know.

Investment in Human Capital

THEODORE W. SCHULTZ

Theodore W. Schultz is Professor of Economics at the University of Chicago. This essay is taken from his Presidential address before the American Economic Association in December, 1960.

ALTHOUGH IT IS obvious that people acquire useful skills and knowledge, it is not obvious that these skills and knowledge are a form of capital, that this capital is in substantial part a product of deliberate investment, that it has grown in Western societies at a much faster rate than conventional (nonhuman) capital, and that its growth may well be the most distinctive feature of the economic system. It has been widely observed that increases in national output have been large compared with the increases of land, man-hours, and physical reproducible capital. Investment in human capital is probably the major explanation for this difference.

Much of what we call consumption constitutes investment in human capital. Direct expenditures on education, health, and internal migration to take advantage of better job opportunities are clear examples. Earnings foregone by mature students attending school and by workers acquiring on-the-job training are equally clear examples. Yet nowhere do these enter into our national accounts. The use of leisure time to improve skills and knowledge is widespread and it too is unrecorded. In these and similar ways the *quality* of human effort can be greatly improved and its productivity enhanced. I shall contend that such investment in human capital accounts for most of the impressive rise in the real earnings per worker.

SHYING AWAY FROM INVESTMENT IN MAN

Economists have long known that people are an important part of the wealth of nations. Measured by what labor contributes to output, the productive capacity of human beings is now vastly larger than all other forms of wealth taken together. What economists have not stressed is the simple truth that people invest in themselves and that these investments are very large. Although economists are seldom timid in entering on abstract analysis and are often proud of being impractical, they have not been bold in coming to grips with this form of investment. Whenever they come even close, they proceed gingerly as if they were stepping into deep water. No doubt there are reasons for being wary. Deep-seated moral and philosophical issues are ever present. Free men are first and foremost the end to be served by economic endeavor; they are not property or marketable assets. And not least, it has been all too convenient in marginal productivity analysis to treat labor as if it were a unique bundle of innate abilities that are wholly free of capital.

The mere thought of investment in human beings is offensive to some among us. Our values and beliefs inhibit us from looking upon human beings as capital goods, except in slavery, and this we abhor. We are not unaffected by the long struggle to rid society of indentured service and to evolve political and legal institutions to keep men free from bondage. These are achievements that we prize highly. Hence, to treat human beings as wealth that can be augmented by investment runs counter to deeply held values. It seems to reduce man once again to a mere material component, to something akin to property. And for man to look upon himself as a capital good, even if it did not impair his freedom, may seem to debase him. No less a person than J. S. Mill at one time insisted that the people of a country should not be looked upon as wealth because wealth existed only for the sake of people.[1] But surely Mill was wrong; there is nothing in the concept of human wealth contrary to his idea that it exists only for the advantage of people. By investing in themselves, people can enlarge the range of choice available to them. It is one way free men can enhance their welfare.

The failure to treat human resources explicitly as a form of capital, as a produced means of production, as the product of investment, has fostered the retention of the classical notion of labor as a capacity to do manual work requiring little knowledge and skill, a capacity with which, according to this notion, laborers

1. J. S. Nicholson, "The Living Capital of the United Kingdom," *Econ. Jour.* Mar. 1891, *1*, 95; see J. S. Mill. *Principles of Political Economy*, ed. W. J. Ashley, London, 1909, p. 8.

are endowed about equally. This notion of labor was wrong in the classical period and it is patently wrong now. Counting individuals who can and want to work and treating such a count as a measure of the quantity of an economic factor is no more meaningful than it would be to count the number of all manner of machines to determine their economic importance either as a stock of capital or as a flow of productive services.

Laborers have become capitalists not from a diffusion of the ownership of corporation stocks, as folklore would have it, but from the acquisition of knowledge and skill that have economic value.[2] This knowledge and skill are in great part the product of investment and, combined with other human investment, predominantly account for the productive superiority of the technically advanced countries. To omit them in studying economic growth is like trying to explain Soviet ideology without Marx.

ECONOMIC GROWTH FROM HUMAN CAPITAL

Many paradoxes and puzzles about our dynamic, growing economy can be resolved once human investment is taken into account. Let me begin by sketching some that are minor though not trivial.

When farm people take nonfarm jobs they earn substantially less than industrial workers of the same race, age, and sex. Similarly nonwhite urban males earn much less than white males even after allowance is made for the effects of differences in unemployment, age, city size and region. Because these differentials in earnings correspond closely to corresponding differentials in education, they strongly suggest that the one is a consequence of the other. Negroes who operate farms, whether as tenants or as owners, earn much less than whites on comparable farms.[3] Fortunately, crops and livestock are not vulnerable to the blight of discrimination. The large differences in earnings seem rather to reflect mainly the differences in health and education. Workers in the South on the average earn appreciably less than in the North or West and they also have on the average less education. Most migratory farm workers earn very little indeed by comparison with other workers. Many of them have virtually no school-

2. H. G. Johnson, "The Political Economy of Opulence," *Can. Jour. Econ. and Pol. Sci.*, Nov. 1960, *26*, 552–64.

3. Based on unpublished preliminary results obtained by Joseph Willett in his Ph.D. research at the University of Chicago.

ing, are in poor health, are unskilled, and have little ability to do useful work. To urge that the differences in the amount of human investment may explain these differences in earnings seems elementary.

Of more recent vintage are observations showing younger workers at a competitive advantage; for example, young men entering the labor force are said to have an advantage over unemployed older workers in obtaining satisfactory jobs. Most of these young people possess twelve years of school, most of the older workers six years or less. The observed advantage of these younger workers may therefore result not from inflexibilities in social security or in retirement programs, or from sociological preference of employers, but from real differences in productivity connected with one form of human investment, i.e., education. And yet another example, the curve relating income to age tends to be steeper for skilled than for unskilled persons. Investment in on-the-job training seems a likely explanation, as I shall note later.

Let me now pass on to three major perplexing questions closely connected with the riddle of economic growth. First, consider the long-period behavior of the capital-income ratio. Estimates now available show that less reproducible capital tends to be employed relative to income as economic growth proceeds. Are we to infer that the ratio of capital to income has no relevance in explaining either poverty or opulence? Or that a rise of this ratio is not a prerequisite to economic growth? These questions raise fundamental issues bearing on motives and preferences for holding wealth as well as on the motives for particular investments and the stock of capital thereby accumulated. For my purpose all that needs to be said is that these estimates of capital-income ratios refer to only a part of all capital. They exclude in particular, and most unfortunately, any human capital. Yet human capital has surely been increasing at a rate substantially greater than reproducible (nonhuman) capital. We cannot, therefore, infer from these estimates that the stock of *all* capital has been decreasing relative to income. On the contrary, if we accept the not implausible assumption that the motives and preferences of people, the technical opportunities open to them, and the uncertainty associated with economic growth during particular periods were leading people to maintain roughly a constant ratio between *all* capital and income, the decline in the estimated capital-income ratio [4] is simply a signal that human capital has been increasing relatively not only to conventional capital but also to income.

The bumper crop of estimates that show national income increasing faster than national resources raises a second and not unrelated puzzle. The income of the United States has been increasing at a much higher rate than the combined amount of land, man-hours worked and the stock of reproducible capital used to produce the income. Moreover, the discrepancy between the two rates has become larger from one business cycle to the next during recent decades. To call this discrepancy a measure of "resource productivity" [technological progress] gives a name to our ignorance but does not dispel it. If we accept these estimates, the connections between national resources and national income have become loose and tenuous over time. Unless this discrepancy can be resolved, received theory of production applied to inputs and outputs as currently measured is a toy and not a tool for studying economic growth.

Two sets of forces probably account for the discrepancy, if we neglect entirely the index number and aggregation problems that bedevil all estimates of such global aggregates as total output and total input. One is returns to scale; the second, the large improvements in the quality of inputs that have occurred but have been omitted from the input estimates. Our economy has undoubtedly been experiencing increasing returns to scale at some points offset by decreasing returns at others. If we can succeed in identifying and measuring the net gains, they may turn out to have been substantial. The improvements in the quality of inputs that have not been adequately allowed for are no doubt partly in material (nonhuman) capital. My own conception, however, is that both this defect and the omission of economies of scale are minor sources of discrepancy between the rates of growth of inputs and outputs compared to the improvements in human capacity that have been omitted.

A small step takes us from these two puzzles raised by existing estimates to a third which brings us to the heart of the matter, namely the essentially unexplained large increase in real

4. I leave aside here the difficulties inherent in identifying and measuring both the nonhuman capital and the income entering into estimates of this ratio. There are index number and aggregation problems aplenty, and not all improvements in the quality of this capital have been accounted for, as I shall note later.

earnings of workers. Can this be a windfall? It seems far more reasonable that it represents rather a return to the investment that has been made in human beings. The observed growth in productivity per unit of labor is simply a consequence of holding the unit of labor constant over time although in fact this unit of labor has been increasing as a result of a steadily growing amount of human capital per worker. As I read our record, the human capital component has become very large as a consequence of human investment.

SCOPE AND SUBSTANCE OF THESE INVESTMENTS

What are human investments? Can they be distinguished from consumption? Is it at all feasible to identify and measure them? What do they contribute to income? Granted that they seem amorphous compared to brick and mortar, and hard to get at compared to the investment accounts of corporations, they assuredly are not a fragment; they are rather like the contents of Pandora's box, full of difficulties and hope.

Human resources obviously have both quantitative and qualitative dimensions. The number of people, the proportion who enter upon useful work, and hours worked are essentially quantitative characteristics. To make my task tolerably manageable, I shall neglect these and consider only such quality components as skill, knowledge, and similar attributes that affect particular human capabilities to do productive work. In so far as expenditures to enhance such capabilities also increase the value productivity of human effort (labor), they will yield a positive rate of return.[5]

How can we estimate the magnitude of human investment? The practice followed in connection with physical capital goods is to estimate the magnitude of capital formation by expenditures made to produce the capital goods. This practice would suffice also for the formation of human capital. However, for human capital there is an additional problem that is less pressing for physical capital goods: how to distinguish between expenditures for consumption and for investment. This distinction bristles with both conceptual and practical difficulties. We can think of three

5. Even so, our *observed* return can be either negative, zero or positive because our observations are drawn from a world where there is uncertainty and imperfect knowledge and where there are windfall gains and losses and mistakes aplenty.

classes of expenditures: expenditures that satisfy consumer preferences and in no way enhance the capabilities under discussion —these represent pure consumption; expenditures that enhance capabilities and do not satisfy any preferences underlying consumption—these represent pure investment; and expenditures that have both effects. Most relevant activities clearly are in the third class, partly consumption and partly investment, which is why the task of identifying each component is so formidable and why the measurement of capital formation by expenditures is less useful for human investment than for investment in physical goods. In principle there is an alternative method for estimating human investment, namely by its yield rather than by its cost. While any capability produced by human investment becomes a part of the human agent and hence cannot be sold; it is nevertheless "in touch with the market place" by affecting the wages and salaries the human agent can earn. The resulting increase in earnings is the yield on the investment.[6]

Despite the difficulty of exact measurement at this stage of our understanding of human investment, many insights can be gained by examining some of the more important activities that improve human capabilities. I shall concentrate on five major categories: (1) health facilities and services, broadly conceived to include all expenditures that affect the life expectancy, strength and stamina, and the vigor and vitality of a people; (2) on-the-job training, including old-style apprenticeship organized by firms; (3) formally organized education at the elementary, secondary, and higher levels; (4) study programs for adults that are not organized by firms, including extension programs notably in agriculture; (5) migration of individuals and families to adjust to changing job opportunities. Except for education, not much is known about these activities that is germane here. I shall refrain from commenting on study programs for adults, although in agriculture the extension services of the several states play an important role in transmitting new knowledge and in developing skills of farmers. Nor shall I elaborate further on internal migration related to economic growth.

Health activities have both quantity and quality implications. Such speculation as economists have engaged in about the ef-

6. In principle, the value of the investment can be determined by discounting the additional future earnings it yields just as the value of a physical capital good can be determined by discounting its income stream.

fects of improvements in health,[7] has been predominantly in connection with population growth, which is to say with quantity. But surely health measures also enhance the quality of human resources. So also may additional food and better shelter, especially in underdeveloped countries.

The change in the role of food as people become richer sheds light on one of the conceptual problems already referred to. I have pointed out that extra food in some poor countries has the attribute of a "producer good." This attribute of food, however, diminishes as the consumption of food rises, and there comes a point at which any further increase in food becomes pure consumption.[8] Clothing, housing and perhaps medical services may be similar.

Surprisingly little is known about on-the-job training in modern industry. About all that can be said is that the expansion of education has not eliminated it. It seems likely, however, that some of the training formerly undertaken by firms has been discontinued and other training programs have been instituted to adjust both to the rise in the education of workers and to changes in the demands for new skills.[9] The amount invested annually in such training can only be a guess. H. F. Clark places it near to equal to the amount spent on formal education.[10] Even if it were only one-half as large, it would represent currently an annual gross

7. Health economics is in its infancy; there are two medical journals with "economics" in their titles, two bureaus for economic research in private associations (one in the American Medical and the other in the American Dental Association), and not a few studies and papers by outside scholars.

8. For instance, the income elasticity of the demand for food continues to be positive even after the point is reached where additional food no longer has the attribute of a "producer good."

9. To study on-the-job training Gary Becker [in a preliminary draft of a study undertaken in 1960 for the National Bureau of Economic Research] advances the theorem that in competitive markets employees pay all the costs of their training and none of these costs are ultimately borne by the firm. Becker points out several implications. The notion that expenditures on training by a firm generate external economies for other firms is not consistent with this theorem. The theorem also indicates one force favoring the transfer from on-the-job training to attending school. Since on-the-job training reduces the net earnings of workers at the beginning and raises them later on, this theorem also provides an explanation for the "steeper slope of the curve relating income to age," for skilled than unskilled workers, referred to earlier. Becker has also noted still another implication arising out of the fact that the income and capital investment aspects of on-the-job training are tied together, which gives rise to "permanent" and "transitory" income effects that may have substantial explanatory value.

10. Based on comments made by Harold F. Clark at the Merrill Center for Economics, summer 1959; also, see [4].

investment of about $15 billion. Elsewhere, too, it is thought to be important. For example, some observers have been impressed by the amount of such training under way in plants in the Soviet Union.[11]

Happily we reach firmer ground in regard to education. Investment in education has risen at a rapid rate and by itself may well account for a substantial part of the otherwise unexplained rise in earnings. I shall do no more than summarize some preliminary results about the total costs of education including income foregone by students, the apparent relation of these costs to consumer income and to alternative investments, the rise of the stock of education in the labor force, returns to education, and the contribution that the increase in the stock of education may have made to earnings and to national income.

It is not difficult to estimate the conventional costs of education consisting of the costs of the services of teachers, librarians, administrators, of maintaining and operating the educational plant, and interest on the capital embodied in the educational plant. It is far more difficult to estimate another component of total cost, the income foregone by students. Yet this component should be included and it is far from negligible. In the United States, for example, well over half of the costs of higher education consists of income foregone by students. As early as 1900, this income foregone accounted for about one-fourth of the total costs of elementary, secondary and higher education. By 1956, it represented over two-fifths of all costs. The rising significance of foregone income has been a major factor in the marked upward trend in the total real costs of education which, measured in current prices, increased from $400 million in 1900 to $28.7 billion in 1956. The percentage rise in educational outlays was about three and a half times as large as in consumer income, which would imply a high income elasticity of the demand for education, if education were regarded as pure consumption.[12] Educational outlays also rose about three and a half times as rapidly as did the gross formation of physical capital in dollars. If we were to treat education as pure investment this result would sug-

11. Based on observations made by a team of U. S. economists of which I was a member, see *Saturday Review*, Jan. 21, 1961.

12. Had other things stayed constant this suggests an income elasticity of 3.5. Among the things that did change, the prices of educational services rose relative to other consumer prices, perhaps offset in part by improvements in the quality of educational services.

gest that the returns to education were relatively more attractive than those to nonhuman capital.[13]

THE STOCK OF EDUCATION AND ITS RETURN

Much schooling is acquired by persons who are not treated as income earners in most economic analysis, particularly, of course, women. To analyze the effect of growth in schooling on earnings, it is therefore necessary to distinguish between the stock of education in the population and the amount in the labor force. Years of school completed are far from satisfactory as a measure because of the marked increases that have taken place in the number of days of school attendance of enrolled students and because much more of the education of workers consists of high school and higher education than formerly. My preliminary estimates suggest that the stock of education in the labor force rose about eight and a half times between 1900 and 1956, whereas the stock of reproducible capital rose four and a half times, both in 1956 prices. These estimates are, of course, subject to many qualifications. Nevertheless, both the magnitude and the rate of increase of this form of human capital have been such that they could be an important key to the riddle of economic growth.

The exciting work under way is on the return to education. In spite of the flood of high school and college graduates, the return has not become trivial. Even the lower limits of the estimates show that the return to such education has been in the neighborhood of the return to nonhuman capital. This is what most of these estimates show when they treat as costs all of the public and private expenditures on education and also the income foregone while attending school, and when they treat all of these costs as investment, allocating none to consumption.[14] But surely

13. This of course assumes among other things that the relationship between gross and net have not changed or have changed in the same proportion. Estimates are from my essay, "Education and Economic Growth" [in Social Forces Influencing American Education, H. G. Richey, ed., Chicago, 1961].

14. Several comments are called for here. (1) The return to high school education appears to have declined substantially between the late 'thirties and early 'fifties and since then has leveled off, perhaps even risen somewhat, indicating a rate of return toward the end of the 'fifties about as high as that to higher education. (2) The return to college education seems to have risen somewhat since the late 'thirties in spite of the rapid influx of college-

a part of these costs are consumption in the sense that education creates a form of consumer capital which has the attribute of improving the taste and the quality of consumption of students throughout the rest of their lives. If one were to allocate a substantial fraction of the total costs of this education to consumption, say one-half, this would, of course, double the observed rate of return to what would then become the investment component in education that enhances the productivity of man.

Fortunately, the problem of allocating the costs of education in the labor force between consumption and investment does not arise to plague us when we turn to the contribution that education makes to earnings and to national income because a change in allocation only alters the rate of return, not the total return. I noted at the outset that the unexplained increases in U. S. national income have been especially large in recent decades. On one set of assumptions, the unexplained part amounts to nearly three-fifths of the total increase between 1929 and 1956.[15] How

trained individuals into the labor force. (3) Becker's estimates based on the difference in income between high school and college graduates based on urban males adjusted for ability, race, unemployment and mortality show a return of 9 per cent to total college costs including both earnings foregone and conventional college costs, public and private and with none of these costs allocated to consumption. [See his study, "Underinvestment in College Education?" which follows.] (4) The returns to this education in the case of nonwhite urban males, of rural males, and of females in the labor force may have been somewhat lower (see Becker). (5) My own estimates, admittedly less complete than those of Becker and thus subject to additional qualifications, based mainly on lifetime income estimates of Herman P. Miller ["Annual and Lifetime Income in Relation to Education: 1939–1959," *Am. Econ. Review,* Dec. 1960, 50, 962–86], lead to a return of about 11 per cent to both high school and college education as of 1958. See [Schultz, *op. cit.*]

Whether the consumption component in education will ultimately dominate, in the sense that the investment component in education will diminish as these expenditures increase and a point will be reached where additional expenditures for education will be pure consumption (a zero return on however small a part one might treat as an investment), is an interesting speculation. This may come to pass, as it has in the case of food and shelter, but that eventuality appears very remote presently in view of the prevailing investment value of education and the new demands for knowledge and skill inherent in the nature of our technical and economic progress.

15. Real income doubled, rising from $150 to $302 billion in 1956 prices. Eighty-nine billions of the increase in real income is taken to be unexplained, or about 59 per cent of the total increase. The stock of education in the labor force rose by $355 billion of which $69 billion is here allocated to the growth in the labor force to keep the per-worker stock of education constant, and $286 billion represents the increase in the level of this stock. See [Schultz, *op. cit.*] for an elaboration of the method and the relevant estimates.

much of this unexplained increase in income represents a return to education in the labor force? A lower limit suggests that about three-tenths of it, and an upper limit does not rule out that more than one-half of it came from this source.[16] These estimates also imply that between 36 and 70 per cent of the hitherto unexplained rise in the earnings of labor is explained by returns to the additional education of workers.

A CONCLUDING NOTE ON POLICY

One proceeds at his own peril in discussing social implications and policy. The conventional hedge is to camouflage one's values and to wear the mantle of academic innocence. Let me proceed unprotected!

1. Our tax laws everywhere discriminate against human capital. Although the stock of such capital has become large and even though it is obvious that human capital, like other forms of reproducible capital, depreciates, becomes obsolete, and entails maintenance, our tax laws are all but blind on these matters.

2. Human capital deteriorates when it is idle because unemployment impairs the skills that workers have acquired. Losses in earnings can be cushioned by appropriate payments but these do not keep idleness from taking its toll from human capital.

3. There are many hindrances to the free choice of professions. Racial discrimination and religious discrimination are still widespread. Professional associations and governmental bodies also hinder entry; for example, into medicine. Such purposeful interference keeps the investment in this form of human capital substantially below its optimum.[17]

4. It is indeed elementary to stress the greater imperfections of the capital market in providing funds for investment in human beings than for investment in physical goods. Much could be done to reduce these imperfections by reforms in tax and banking laws and by changes in banking practices. Long-term private and public loans to students are warranted.

5. Internal migration, notably the movement of farm people into industry, made necessary by the dynamics of our economic progress, requires substantial investments. In general, families in

16. In per cent, the lower estimate came out to 29 per cent and the upper estimate to 56 per cent.

17. Milton Friedman and Simon Kuznets, *Income from Independent Professional Practice*, National Bureau of Economic Research. New York, 1945.

which the husbands and wives are already in the late thirties cannot afford to make these investments because the remaining payoff period for them is too short. Yet society would gain if more of them would pull stakes and move because, in addition to the increase in productivity currently, the children of these families would be better located for employment when they were ready to enter the labor market. The case for making some of these investments on public account is by no means weak. Our farm programs have failed miserably these many years in not coming to grips with the costs and returns from off-farm migration.

6. The low earnings of particular people have long been a matter of public concern. Policy all too frequently concentrates only on the effects, ignoring the causes. No small part of the low earnings of many Negroes, Puerto Ricans, Mexican nationals, indigenous migratory farm workers, poor farm people and some of our older workers, reflects the failure to have invested in their health and education. Past mistakes are, of course, bygones, but for the sake of the next generation we can ill afford to continue making the same mistakes over again.

7. Is there a substantial underinvestment in human beings other than in these depressed groups? This is an important question for economists. The evidence at hand is fragmentary. Nor will the answer be easily won. There undoubtedly have been overinvestments in some skills, for example, too many locomotive firemen and engineers, too many people trained to be farmers, and too many agricultural economists! Our schools are not free of loafers and some students lack the necessary talents. Nevertheless, underinvestment in knowledge and skill, relative to the amounts invested in nonhuman capital, would appear to be the rule and not the exception for a number of reasons. The strong and increasing demands for this knowledge and skill in laborers are of fairly recent origin and it takes time to respond to them. In responding to these demands, we are heavily dependent upon cultural and political processes, and these are slow and the lags are long compared to the behavior of markets serving the formation of nonhuman capital. Where the capital market does serve human investments, it is subject to more imperfections than in financing physical capital. I have already stressed the fact that our tax laws discriminate in favor of nonhuman capital. Then, too, many individuals face serious uncertainty in assessing their innate talents when it comes to investing in themselves, especially

through higher education. Nor is it easy either for public decisions or private behavior to untangle and properly assess the consumption and the investment components. The fact that the return to high school and to higher education has been about as large as the return to conventional forms of capital when all of the costs of such education including income foregone by students are allocated to the investment component, creates a strong presumption that there has been underinvestment since, surely, much education is cultural and in that sense it is consumption. It is no wonder, in view of these circumstances, that there should be substantial underinvestment in human beings, even though we take pride, and properly so, in the support that we have given to education and to other activities that contribute to such investments.

8. Should the returns from public investment in human capital accrue to the individuals in whom it is made? [18] The policy issues implicit in this question run deep and they are full of perplexities pertaining both to resource allocation and to welfare. Physical capital that is formed by public investment is not transferred as a rule to particular individuals as a gift. It would greatly simplify the allocative process if public investment in human capital were placed on the same footing. What then is the logical basis for treating public investment in human capital differently? Presumably it turns on ideas about welfare. A strong welfare goal of our community is to reduce the unequal distribution of personal income among individuals and families. Our community has relied heavily on progressive income and inheritance taxation. Given public revenue from these sources, it may well be that public investment in human capital, notably that entering into general education, is an effective and efficient set of expenditures for attaining this goal. Let me stress, however, that the state of knowledge about these issues is woefully meager.

9. My last policy comment is on assistance to underdeveloped countries to help them achieve economic growth. Here, even more than in domestic affairs, investment in human beings is likely to be underrated and neglected. It is inherent in the intellectual climate in which leaders and spokesmen of many of these coun-

18. I am indebted to Milton Friedman for bringing this issue to the fore in his comments on an early draft of this paper. See preface of [Friedman and Kuznets, *op. cit.*] and also Jacob Mincer's pioneering paper ["Investment in Human Capital and Personal Income Distribution," *Jour. Pol. Econ.*, Aug. 1958, *66*, 281–302].

tries find themselves. Our export of growth doctrines has contributed. These typically assign the stellar role to the formation of nonhuman capital, and take as an obvious fact the superabundance of human resources. Steel mills are the real symbol of industrialization. After all, the early industrialization of England did not depend on investments in the labor force. New funds and agencies are being authorized to transfer capital for physical goods to these countries. The World Banks and our Export-Import Bank have already had much experience. Then, too, measures have been taken to pave the way for the investment of more private (nonhuman) capital abroad. This one-sided effort is under way in spite of the fact that the knowledge and skills required to take on and use efficiently the superior techniques of production, the most valuable resource that we could make available to them, is in very short supply in these underdeveloped countries. Some growth of course can be had from the increase in more conventional capital even though the labor that is available is lacking both in skill and knowledge. But the rate of growth will be seriously limited. It simply is not possible to have the fruits of a modern agriculture and the abundance of modern industry without making large investments in human beings.

Truly, the most distinctive feature of our economic system is the growth in human capital. Without it there would be only hard, manual work and poverty except for those who have income from property. There is an early morning scene in Faulkner's *Intruder in the Dust,* of a poor, solitary cultivator at work in a field. Let me paraphrase that line, "The man without skills and knowledge leaning terrifically against nothing."

Underinvestment in College Education? [1]

GARY S. BECKER

Gary S. Becker is Professor of Economics at Columbia University. This essay is taken from a paper he contributed to the annual proceedings of the American Economic Association, published in May, 1960.

IN THE LAST few years the United States has become increasingly conscious of its educational program and policies. Not only have Congress, state legislatures, and local bodies paid greater attention to this issue, but large numbers of books, articles, talks, and academic studies have also been devoted to it. This concern has been stimulated by developments in the cold war which apparently have increased the power of the Soviet Union relative to the United States. These developments are primarily the rapid economic growth of the Soviet Union in the postwar period and their obvious success in missiles and space technology.

The near panic in the United States engendered by the more spectacular Soviet accomplishments has in turn spawned a re-examination of American policies and procedures relating to economic growth and military technology. Re-examinations begot by panic almost always overestimate and overstress weaknesses and underestimate points of strength. It is perhaps not surprising, therefore, that most recent studies of American education have found it seriously deficient at all levels and in most aspects, be it the effort required, the subjects pursued, or the amount given. It is widely believed that not enough is spent on education, especially at the college and postgraduate levels, that too few of the ablest high school graduates continue their studies, that school curricula at all levels are insufficiently challenging, and that more students should be majoring in the natural sciences and engineering.

For some time now I have been conducting a study for the

1. I am indebted to A. F. Burns, S. Fabricant, Z. Griliches, J. Mincer, and T. W. Schultz for very helpful comments. Needless to say, I alone am responsible for any conclusions reached.

National Bureau of Economic Research of investment in and returns to education in the United States, especially at the college level. This study is not directly concerned with educational policy but some of the results may have relevance to the issues currently being discussed. They seem to be especially relevant in determining whether too little is spent on college education and whether the quality of our college students could be improved. This paper discusses these questions in light of the contribution of college graduates to economic growth and military technology.

The concept of economic growth used here follows that used in calculations of national income and in comparisons of the economic performance of the Soviets and the United States, and excludes, among other things, nonmonetary income. In restricting this discussion to economic growth and military technology we thus exclude the effect of education on nonmonetary returns as well as on democratic government, equality of opportunity, culture, etc. The effects on growth and technology have been greatly emphasized recently; so it is especially important to discuss them. This limitation does mean, however, that we are not attempting a complete analysis or evaluation of the effects of college expenditures. A detailed derivation of the results used here will be found in the larger study to be published by the National Bureau.

THE RATE OF RETURN ON EDUCATION

The economic effects of education can be divided into the effect on the incomes of persons receiving education and the effect on the incomes of others. This distinction largely corresponds to the distinction between private and social (i.e., external) or direct and indirect effects. Data from the last two Censuses and from other surveys giving the incomes of persons with different amounts of education make it possible to form a judgment about the direct economic effects. The Census data giving the incomes of male college and high school graduates were used to estimate the direct return to college after being adjusted for other differences between high school and college graduates, such as in ability, race, unemployment, and mortality.

The average return from college so computed is related to the average cost of college, the latter including foregone earnings or opportunity costs as well as direct college costs. Returns are related to costs by an internal rate of return—the rate of discount which equates the present value of returns and costs. In other words, it is the rate of return earned by the average college graduate on his college education. If this rate of return was significantly higher than the rate earned on tangible capital, there would be evidence of underinvestment in college education.

The rate of return relevant to a person deciding whether to go to college is a private rate, computed for private returns net of income taxes and for private costs. This was about 12½ per cent in 1940 and 10 per cent in 1950 for urban white males. The difference between these rates resulted almost entirely from the growth in the personal income tax during the forties. The rate of return in 1940, and to a lesser extent in 1950, seems large and is probably larger than the average rate earned on tangible capital. (Some evidence on this is presented shortly.)

But this is not the relevant rate in determining if there is underinvestment in education. First of all, the rate of return should be computed on total college costs, not only on those paid by students. Since in 1940 and 1950 students paid only about two-thirds of these costs, there is a considerable difference between the rates earned on private and on total costs. Second, while returns collected by the state in the form of personal income tax payments are in principle an external return, it is convenient to adjust for them now, especially since this eliminates most of the difference between the rates of return in 1940 and 1950. If then the before-tax return to college is related to the total cost of college, a rate of return of about 9 per cent is found for both 1940 and 1950. The adjustment for taxes raised the return in 1950 to about the same level as in 1940, but the adjustment for private and public subsidies to colleges reduced both rates about three percentage points. The rate of return no longer seems especially high in either year and it is an open question whether it is higher than the return on tangible capital.

Even 9 per cent is probably too high an estimate of the return to all college graduates since it refers only to urban male whites. The rate of return to nonwhites seems to be about two percentage points lower than this.[2] I made no estimates of the return to women and rural graduates and know of none made by others, but since women participate in the labor force less than men, the

2. Presumably, the difference between the return to whites and non-whites partly results from discrimination against nonwhites.

direct money return to them is probably much less than to men.[3] The average return to rural graduates is probably also less than that to urban graduates. Thus the average return to all graduates would be lower than the 9 per cent return to urban white males. That this difference might be substantial is evident, not only from the presumed large difference in returns to urban white males and others, but also from the fact that the former are only about 45 per cent of all graduates.

The average return on college expenditures could be compared to the returns on almost an endless variety of tangible capital goods, ranging from consumers' durables to government capital. It is easiest—and perhaps for our purposes most relevant—to compare it to the average return on capital owned by business enterprises. George Stigler has been preparing estimates of the return to assets owned by manufacturing corporations. Preliminary results indicate that the rate of return on these assets, after payment of the corporate income tax, averaged about 7 per cent, both from 1938 to 1947 and from 1948 to 1954. This does not seem, however, to be the relevant rate to compare with the less than 9 per cent earned on college capital which was computed *before* the deduction of income taxes. The latter should be compared with the return before payment of the corporate income tax. During this period, the before-tax return of manufacturing corporations averaged more than 12 per cent of their total assets. The data for nonmanufacturing corporations are less readily available and I do not have an estimate of the return to them. But since corporate income tax rates were so high during this period, it is extremely unlikely that all corporations averaged less than 10 per cent or greater than 13 per cent before taxes. Although even less is known about unincorporated enterprises, it is unlikely that their rate of return averaged much less than 5 per cent or greater than 8 per cent.

The average rate of return to business capital as a whole depends on the rates of return to the corporate and unincorporated sectors and on the relative importance of each sector. It would appear that corporate capital is about 60 per cent of all business

3. A woman receives indirect returns from college if it enables her to marry a man with a higher income than she would have married if she did not go to college. These returns may be substantial and should be considered when a woman decides whether to go to college. It is not obvious that the total return to women graduates is much less than that to men; such a comparison would require data on the family incomes of the average male and female college graduates rather than on their personal incomes.

capital. If this measures the relative importance of the corporate sector and if 10 and 5 per cent measure the average returns to corporate and unincorporated capital, then the average return to all business capital would be 8 per cent.

The substantial difference between these estimates and those published by others results not from difference in the basic data but in the operations performed. Most studies use private college costs rather than total costs, make no adjustment for the differential ability of college graduates, deal only with urban white or all urban males, and use a long-term interest rate to measure the rate of return elsewhere. They estimate the return to college education at about 15 per cent, and elsewhere at about 5 per cent, clearly suggesting underinvestment in college education. Using total costs reduces the rate of return on college to about 11 per cent; adjusting for differential ability reduces it further to about 9 per cent, and including nonwhites, females, and rural persons reduces it still further. On the other hand, the before-tax rate of return to business is much higher than the long-term interest rate because of risk and liquidity premiums and the heavy corporate income tax. The average rates of return to business and to college education—adjusted for these factors—do not seem very far apart.

The evidence on direct returns is limited and these estimates of direct returns subject to considerable error, but it would appear that direct returns alone cannot justify a large increase in expenditures on college education relative to expenditures on business capital. To justify large increases it is necessary to show either that improved evidence would widen the difference between the estimated returns to college and business capital or that indirect (i.e., external) returns are much larger for college than for business capital. The direct return to college was estimated from the incomes of persons differing in age and education; ideally one would like to have the lifetime incomes of persons known to differ only in education. Improvements in panel techniques and in our knowledge of the abilities of different persons may someday produce evidence close to the ideal. It remains to be seen, however, whether our conclusion about the relative returns to college and business capital is greatly changed.

External or indirect effects are very embarrassing to the economist, since his theories say little about them, he has few techniques for measuring them, and he usually does not even think that he knows much about them. In particular, little is known about the external effects from college education, although it is easy to give some examples. Thus college graduates did the pioneering work in molecular physics, and it may eventually benefit (or hurt) everyone. Einstein, Fermi, and the other pioneers received only a small fraction of the total increase (or decrease) in income resulting from their work. But it is much easier to give these examples than to assess their quantitative importance or, what is even more difficult, to compare them with external effects from business capital. Some maintain, quite persuasively, that college education had little to do with American economic growth throughout most of its history; others, equally persuasive, point to the importance of science in recent years and argue that future growth is closely related to scientific achievement; still others cite the laboratory and general increasing returns as examples of the sweeping external economies from investments in tangible capital.

Since direct returns alone do not seem to indicate under-investment in education, those arguing this have to rely heavily on external returns. These may well be very important, but in light of our ignorance it is not surprising that no one has yet demonstrated that they are (or are not) sufficiently important to push the total return from college education much above the return elsewhere. It is this ignorance about external returns which prevents any firm judgment about the adequacy of expenditures on college education.

The Education of Scientists · Even those maintaining that external economic and military effects are important would not maintain that they are equally important in all college specialties. But there would probably be little agreement on which specialties were likely to produce these effects, and with our present knowledge it would be impossible to prove that any specialty— no matter how removed it seems from economic and military questions—was unlikely to do so. Recent discussions of the role of college education in the cold war have, however, tended to emphasize scientific specialties to the exclusion of most others, and it is possible to determine whether important external economic and military returns [4] from science alone would imply large-

4. If all persons working on military technology were employed by the government and if salaries measured expected (or actual) military contribution, there would be no external military effects since the full marginal pro-

scale underinvestment in college education.

Science majors include persons majoring in natural science, mathematics, engineering, and applied biology, and in recent years they received about one-quarter of all bachelor's and first professional degrees.[5] This is probably a large overestimate of the number likely to produce external economies. Only science majors with advanced graduate training are likely to, but less than 5 per cent of all science graduates go on for their doctorates. Scientists are more likely to produce these economies if they engage in research and development but just about 25 per cent of all scientists are so engaged. Thus it would seem that well under half of all science majors or under 13 per cent of all college graduates have a reasonable chance of producing important external economies.

It was seen that the average direct return to college graduates is about the same as the average direct return to business capital. If the direct return to scientists was no lower than the direct return to other graduates [6] and if the external military and economic effects from scientists were important, the total return to scientists would be greater than the returns to business capital. There would be underinvestment in scientists, and government assistance to the scientific field would be required to attain a more optimal allocation of capital. The number of scientists would be increased partly at the expense of business investment, partly at the expense of current consumption, and perhaps partly at the expense of other professions.

The important point to note, however, is that even a large underinvestment in scientists implies only a small underinvest-

---

ductivity would be directly measured by salaries. This argument clearly holds for all government employees regardless of their specialty.

5. Business had about 14 per cent, education about 20 per cent, and humanities and social sciences about 25 per cent of all first degrees.

6. Few systematic studies have been made of the return to different college specialties. According to the 1950 Census the average income of engineers was about $5,100, much lower than the $6,600 average income of college graduates. This seems to indicate that the direct money return to engineering graduates is less than that to other graduates. But about 40 per cent of the Census engineers are not college graduates, and they may receive less income than graduate engineers simply because they have less training. Moreover, even if they have the same total amount of training—received on the job rather than in college—they would tend to report lower incomes because their incomes would be net of training costs, while the reported incomes of graduate engineers (and other college graduates) would be gross of training costs.

ment in college education as a whole. For example, the number of scientists with prospects of producing external effects could be increased by as much as 50 per cent—a very sizable increase—and yet less than a 7 per cent increase in the total number of college graduates would be required. The 7 per cent figure is arrived at by assuming that none of the increase in scientists is at the expense of other college specialties and that a full 13 per cent of all graduates fall into the relevant "scientist" category. Even 7 per cent must, therefore, be considered a liberal upper estimate. So the current demand for a large increase in scientists (or, more generally, expenditures on scientific training) to stimulate development could be met with a very modest increase in total expenditures on college education. This does not mean that underinvestment in scientists is unimportant, but only that it could be corrected with a relatively small expenditure.

Let me conclude by briefly summarizing the discussion. Several aspects of college education in the United States were examined in terms of their contribution to economic and military progress. The limited available evidence did not reveal any significant discrepancy between the direct returns to college education and business capital, and thus direct returns alone do not seem to justify increased college expenditures. This puts the burden on external or indirect returns since they would have to be important to justify increased expenditures. Unfortunately, very little is known about them; so a firm judgment about the extent of underinvestment in college education is not possible.

Many recent discussions have emphasized the external contributions of scientists to economic and military progress and have called for large increases in scientific personnel. Such an increase could be accomplished with a small increase in total college expenditures. A large increase in expenditures would be warranted only if external returns were produced by a much larger fraction of all college graduates.

Research and Economic Growth:
The Role of Public Policy

BENTON F. MASSELL AND RICHARD R. NELSON

Benton F. Massell and Richard R. Nelson are economists at the RAND Corporation. RAND engages in research related to matters of national security. This article first appeared in the Winter 1962 California Management Review.

SINCE HAMILTON's first report on manufactures, this country has not let decisions affecting economic growth be made exclusively by private individuals and groups. Our tariff history, the patent laws, the homestead act, the land grants to railroads, the establishment of numerous government agencies to help private industry prosper and grow, the public development of land and water resources in many areas, public support of education and research —all these testify to the large role that public agencies have played in our growth.

But those who argue that economic growth is a useful means to several desired ends should be well aware of the fact that there are other and alternative means. For example, rapid economic growth is essential to the maintenance of full employment only to the extent that we let investment take much of the burden of providing aggregate demand. We could aim for a higher level of consumption and of government services, in which case investment would be a less important source of demand, and the amount of economic growth needed to call forth that investment would be significantly smaller. The authors, though strong advocates of economic growth both as an end in itself and as a means to other ends, are concerned lest alternative and complementary policies to these other ends may tend to get lost in the din of growthmanship.

In our economy the government sector spends about one-fifth of Gross National Product, taxes take an equal share, the operations of the Treasury and the Federal Reserve Board comprise a significant fraction of our total transactions in paper assets, and government debt is a major portion of total debt outstanding. The everyday fiscal and monetary operations of the government thus have a significant impact on investment and, consequently, on economic growth.

Over half of our Research and Development is government financed, and though the objective of the bulk of this program is improved defense, it obviously affects the rate of economic progress. In these areas, and in many others, government policies do affect our economic growth rate, and in an important way. The real question, though, is, should the government consciously pursue a set of policies *expressly designed* to step up the growth rate? And, if so, what sorts of measures are called for?

We think that one promising avenue to explore is an expanded government participation in our research effort. In recent years, economists have begun to realize that technological progress is a key to rapid economic growth. As scientific research is an important element in the creation of technological change, policies aimed at stimulating various areas of science may be useful instruments of a national growth policy.

Economic Progress and Technical Change · Atomic energy, modern drugs, plastics, electronic computers, synthetic fibers— these products, which have resulted directly from twentieth-century science, should make us aware of the great role that invention has played in our economic progress. Scientific research enters the picture by creating the knowledge which permits us to develop these new and improved products and processes.

Perhaps, therefore, we can gain a better understanding of the importance of research by attempting to gauge the contribution of technical change to our economic progress. The resulting measure will be crude. Much technical progress is independent of research, and, moreover, sometimes research contributes to economic progress by routes other than that of creating technical change. Nevertheless, measuring the relative importance of technical change will provide us with a better notion of the significance of research.

Let us use increase in per worker productivity as an index of economic progress. In order to isolate the contribution of technological change, we must separate this factor from other factors which contribute to increased productivity: (1) Greater use of capital equipment per worker, or what the economist terms "capital deepening," (2) more efficient allocation of resources in firms, and among firms and industries, and (3) increase in the level of education and skill of both labor and management.

A recent study by one of the authors suggests that between 30 percent and 40 percent of the past increase in output per worker was accounted for by capital deepening and improved resource allocation. Consequently, at least 60 percent must be explained by technical change and improved working force quality. Similar studies by other economists and statisticians have tended to support these conclusions. Thus, education and technical change emerge as potent economic forces.

Of course these statistical results must be qualified by the existence of interactions among the four sets of factors. For example, changes in technology frequently need to be incorporated in new capital goods before becoming effective. Thus it would be wrong to use the importance of technical change as an argument for abandoning investment activity.

Nevertheless, the results of these statistical procedures are illustrative of the major role which technical change has played. Moreover, these results are supported by other, more direct, evidence of the importance of research. Technical change starts with invention, and there is convincing evidence that science is playing an increasingly instrumental role in inventive activity.

Patent statistics, research and development expenditure data, and counts of "important inventions" have all recently been used in attempts to measure the rate of invention and the level of inventive activity in various industries and sectors of the economy. The data reveal a secular shift in inventive activity away from industries based on craft and simple mechanical engineering, and toward industries based on modern chemistry and physics—in other words, toward those industries where science is important. The data also suggest a growing importance of the industrial research and development laboratory—the modern institution harnessing science to technical progress.

As one would expect, there is a significant correlation between the amount of research and development work a firm does and the number of significant inventions accredited to it. And the firms which do a lot of inventing tend to grow faster, and be more profitable.

Additional indirect evidence of the contribution of research is provided by studies of the returns earned by investment in research and development. The studies which have been done are of success stories, but the figures they suggest are remarkably high, even granting this source of bias. For example, the research which led to hybrid corn has yielded returns of several hundred percent a year. And calculations made by some of the larger industrial laboratories also suggest rates of return to research well above profits earned from investment in plant and equipment.

One study, attempting to measure directly the impact of research on productivity, and on the technological change component of productivity increase, showed that the firms of an industry which do the most research and development tend to have the most rapid rate of technological change; and the industries where productivity is growing the fastest have typically been the research-intensive industries.

RESEARCH AS INVESTMENT IN KNOWLEDGE

How does research contribute to technical change? In one sense, by increasing and enriching our stock of knowledge. There are many difficulties connected with defining the stock of knowledge. Certainly it involves much more than formal scientific knowledge, and research is by no means the sole activity by which knowledge is increased. Indeed, writers who use as their examples the inventions of the 18th and 19th centuries have tended to argue that formal scientific knowledge is unimportant to inventors—what is important is general technological know-how.

However, writers who have used as their examples the more recent advances in chemical and electronic technology have argued that, though formal science may not have been particularly important in the more distant past, it has played a more major role in recent inventive activity.

The stock of knowledge may play a permissive role or a triggering role. In its permissive role the stock of knowledge and changes in it acts primarily through its effect on the costs of solving already perceived practical problems. Knowledge serves primarily as a reference book determining the skill with which people concerned with solving practical problems are able to surmount the difficulties. Where knowledge plays this permissive role, the evidence is that demand, or social need, is the primary factor determining what problems people try to solve, and the stock of knowledge determines how, and with what success, they go about solving them.

In some industries, the stock of knowledge has played a more active role, and advances in scientific knowledge have served to trigger inventive activity. That is, advances in knowledge have generated searches for problems the knowledge could be applied to. This seems to be the case with a number of advances in chemical technology and in electronics.

It is useful to treat both fundamental scientific research and the more applied forms of inventive activity as part of a spectrum of activities aimed at increasing our stock of technical knowledge. At one end of the spectrum is fundamental research, at the other end practical engineering and inventing. Moving from the pure science end of the spectrum to the engineering end, the goals become more clearly defined in terms of specific practical problems; the predictability of the results tends to increase; the chances that the results will be directly of use increases; and the chances of patenting improve.

There are some important implications of this. Though knowledge is always a difficult commodity to buy and sell on a market, the chances that a company will be able to capture on the market a good share of the benefits created by the research and development it undertakes are much greater toward the engineering end of the spectrum than toward the basic science end of the spectrum. For this reason, profit incentives work a good deal better in applied research and development than in fundamental research. It is important to keep this point in mind—it is of major importance in designing effective public policy.

Government's Role in Research · The actions of the federal government already impinge on scientific research in a vast number of areas, in many different ways, and for a wide diversity of reasons. In some cases, the responsibilities of the federal government are almost accidental. The Smithsonian Institute is under the jurisdiction of our government because long ago a wealthy

Englishman admired American democracy. In many cases, the
original problems which led the government into an area of
science have long disappeared. But perhaps the main reasons why
the government has become involved in science are the following:

First, we have the concern with certain areas of science derived from problems of managing efficiently those sectors of
our political economy where we have established public, as con-
trasted with private, decision-making organizations. Examples
of this type of interest are defense, research to improve public
health, weather forecasting, and geographical surveys. These all
have in common the fact that the goods and services involved
are public goods.

Second, fundamental scientific knowledge itself can be considered a public good, for the total benefits which accrue from a
fundamental scientific advance exceed those which can be traded
on the free market. In recent years, the Federal government has
acted to sponsor research in certain key areas, such as peacetime
atomic energy and space technology, on the grounds that the
advances which might result would be sufficiently widespread in
their impact to be treated as public goods.

A third, and more restricted, reason for federal involvement has
been the existence of a number of industries and sectors in
which, though nonresearch decisions are largely made by private
organizations, it is felt that public interest in advancing technology surpasses the interests or capabilities of the private organizations involved. Agriculture, civil aviation, and the work
of the National Bureau of Standards are examples of this interest.

We are suggesting a fourth reason for federal encouragement
of science and technology—to stimulate economic growth.

PUBLIC POLICY TOWARD RESEARCH

One of the main tasks of policy formation is to decide which
areas of science can be financed and managed by nongovernmen-
tal organizations in such a way as to lead to socially satisfactory
results, and which areas need the financial support, and perhaps
the direction of governmental agencies. In the United States, we
have developed a satisfactory division of labor between public

and private agencies, between agencies whose goals are the general welfare and organizations whose goals are those of the controlling individuals. We have thus achieved decentralization and flexibility with only a relatively small degree of discord and coordination failure.

This division of labor has worked so well principally because of a correlated set of institutions which have tended to make private incentives reflect the social interest. It is important to keep this division of labor within our scientific institutions, and this means two things. First, where the public interest is reasonably well reflected in private profit opportunities, we should continue to rely on private groups to do the job. Second, in those areas where private incentives and the public interest are not in accord, we should take steps either to bring them into accord or to get the job done through public agencies.

In addition to selecting areas where governmental action is desirable, the formulation of effective policy depends upon the choice of appropriate policy instruments. The instruments of public policy toward science are many and varied. Consider, for example, the following: government establishment and administration of research laboratories; special public agencies which contract for private research; the provision of relatively untied research funds; and various laws and institutions which can influence and aid private institutions in undertaking research. Government policy is synonymous neither with government decision making nor with government funding.

How Good Is Industrial Research? · Direct subsidization of private industrial research should be the least important aspect of our over-all policies to accelerate growth by stimulating science. There is some room for useful change in our tax, patent, and industrial organization laws. And the whole area of patent rights on government financed research needs rethinking. Indeed, perhaps we should reconsider the entire patent system.

But it seems likely that in the type of work done by industrial laboratories there is a smaller gap between public benefit and private incentives than in any other area of research and development. And, given that our over-all scientific resources are limited (as is government ability to formulate and manage policy effectively), the industrial research laboratory does not appear to need immediate government attention. Though direct public support of industrial research does not seem a wise move, there may be significant gains from public policies designed to strengthen the link between scientific knowledge and research and development.

The preponderance of the work done in industrial research laboratories is not scientific research as it has been defined in this paper, and as it is traditionally defined. Most of it is problem solving, and development and design work, involving little or no effort to achieve a greater understanding of underlying physical principles. Although industrial research and development draws heavily on science, it does not contribute much to science.

There are good reasons why this is so; why the research groups at the Bell Telephone Laboratories, General Electric, and a few other companies are the exceptions, not the rule. The results of fundamental research are quite unpredictable. At the outset of a fundamental research effort it is very difficult to predict with any real precision just what practical problems will be illuminated as a result of the research. Only companies operating on a very broad technological base and producing a wide range of products can have any real confidence that the applied areas which are illuminated are areas of immediate interest to them.

Further, the way that advances in fundamental knowledge yield practical advances is usually extremely diffuse. Cases like the transistor and nylon, where the results of laboratory research led directly to the invention of new products, are rare. Indeed, many of the companies that maintain fundamental research groups do not consider the principal role of these groups to be the creation of knowledge the companies can use. Rather, these groups are seen as the windows through which the company views the general world of science.

It is the primary job of these groups to keep the company, and in particular the applied research and development people, aware of scientific knowledge, new and old, which can be used profitably in the development of new products and processes. For very rarely do specific advances in science yield specific advances in technology. More generally, a particular technical advance clothes a number of applied scientific principles, some new, most of them old.

Thus if we separate scientific research from invention and development, we cannot expect profit-oriented companies to play a major role in our research effort. Some companies in some industries will find scientific research profitable. But in only a few of the giant companies, with a great range of diversified products, is real research a paying proposition, if the direct benefits of in-house research are considered alone.

The main contribution of the groups in industry doing fundamental research is the excellent contact with the general world of science which they provide. However, fundamental research groups are expensive to maintain. Many companies are not sufficiently large to make it profitable for them to keep a staff of good scientists whose main function is to keep the company abreast of developments.

In a number of industries, no company is of sufficient size, or diversity of product line and technology, for a fundamental research group to be profitable. This suggests that it may be promising to do more experimentation with industry-wide research organizations. And the support and encouragement of these organizations may be a legitimate function of government.

In those industries where production techniques and market structure tend to lead to firms of small size, and in those industries which are characterized by the dominance of mature firms with no research tradition, there may be significant payoffs from sponsoring cooperative research institutions which stress relatively fundamental work on the sciences that underlie the industries' technology. The main function of these institutions should be the closer linking of the industry with science.

Government Aid for Basic Research · While cooperative research laboratories may have a positive contribution to make, policies aimed at stimulating fundamental science, improving the efficiency of the over-all scientific effort, and, over the long run, increasing our supply of trained scientists and engineers should be the core of our policy. For it is in just these areas that private financing is most inadequate to serve the public's needs. Fundamental research has all of the characteristics of an activity where public benefits exceed private profit opportunities.

Because public support of fundamental research need not imply direct governmental controls of any major sort, policies in this area have the advantage of not extending the area of direct governmental decision making in our society. Further, since the recipients of government support would be, by and large, non-profit organizations, the economic and political pressures—and the consequent conflict of interest—are relatively small. Nor are there major problems of public control and private incentives which tend to arise when government-supported research in a profit-oriented laboratory results in something of significant commercial worth.

However, an effective public policy must be formulated in awareness of the way that fundamental research contributes to economic progress. As we have seen, the results are unpredictable and, if planning is used in a tight sense, unplannable. Obtaining results from basic research is not like getting candy from a slot machine.

The organization of fundamental science reflects this fact. Within basic science the allocation of effort is determined in part by the interests of individual scientists, in part by the professional judgment of an elite who have considerable control over resources and rewards, and in part by incentives and funds provided by organizations interested in research in certain areas.

The first two factors tend to cause research resources to be shifted toward areas which seem ripe for new discoveries, where ripeness is usually signaled by interesting goings-on. The third factor tends to draw scientific resources toward areas where certain practical payoffs are perceived.

There are two broad questions of social policy raised here. One is the extent to which considerations other than those of scientific interest should influence the allocation of research resources. The evidence is reasonably clear that really major advances in knowledge are more likely to come when scientists are able to follow their own interests, than when scientists are constrained to work in fields where certain immediate payoffs are expected.

On the other hand, it is important that research be done in areas where success is likely to be socially, politically, or economically important. An enlarged Federal role in the support of basic research, if it is to be effective, clearly must strike a balance between these two considerations.

A successful basic research program is heavily dependent upon the quality of our educational system; support of scientific and technical education may well be the most effective long-run policy for stimulating economic progress. People with scientific training are needed not only to do research and development work. They are needed in many other functions. Indeed, less than one-third of our engineers and scientists are engaged in research and development.

Technically trained people are needed in production management, in sales, in administrative positions of all sorts, and in top management. One of the more important roles of the scientist in management, not actively doing research and development, is as a sympathetic and critical appraiser of the new ideas which come out of the labs. The non-research-and-development scientist and engineer is a vital link between invention and innovation.

Encouraging Major Breakthroughs · Another extremely promising area of Federal policy lies in helping the development of major new technological breakthroughs. Atomic energy and space have set the precedent here. The decision to establish a quasi-governmental agency to sponsor and play a major role in developing the peacetime atomic energy industry represented a significant, if not unprecedented, break with tradition. (A similar decision had been made in the 1920s with respect to aviation when the NACA was established.)

One significant reason for this decision was that the risks and costs of the major research effort considered necessary for a satisfactory rate of progress seemed larger than those which private companies would be willing to undertake by themselves. Research relating to the introduction of major new technologies, by its very nature, offers a small probability of a tremendous gain and a large probability of no gain at all. Some sort of risk-sharing and profit-sharing scheme is consequently called for. The result of such a scheme may well be to tilt the risk-gain scale in such a way as to create incentives for research in areas which were previously regarded as unprofitable.

The establishment of the National Aeronautics and Space Administration to direct our research on peacetime uses of space technology reflects these considerations. It appears likely that modern science will open up new technological fields with similar characteristics in the future; and if public agencies aren't established to explore these fields, we may fail to devote sufficient scientific resources to them.

At the present stage of our knowledge, it is nonsense to talk about such things as an "optimum" research effort in anything but a highly theoretical manner. Perhaps some day our knowledge of the way that research contributes to economic growth will be sufficiently sound to enable quite precise predictions of the impact of various policies to be made. But at the present the best strategy is to be flexible and experimental.

We are convinced that policy toward science should recognize the division of labor between governmental and private units, and focus on those areas of science where the evidence is clearest that private incentives do not reflect adequately the public interest.

These areas include almost all of fundamental research, the whole field of scientific education, major and costly research efforts that are likely to open up new areas of technology, and perhaps industry research of the sort which will enable firms which cannot afford to support research to gain closer links with the world of science. Because the public interest is better reflected by profit opportunities in the applied fields, where there is a well established industrial research structure, the gains from increased public support in this area seem much less than in the areas marked out above.

The gains from public attention to these issues are potentially vast. Hopefully, by mobilizing our scientific resources, we can accelerate the rate of growth in economic activity sufficiently to meet the Soviet challenge.

Can There Be Too Much Research?

FRITZ MACHLUP

Fritz Machlup is Professor of Economics at Princeton University. This article first appeared in Science. *It is part of a series of papers emerging from the author's study of the economics of knowledge.*

THIS ARTICLE deals with an important question arising from the recent growth of research and development and the loud cheers that have accompanied this growth. Several kinds of research will be touched upon, but my chief subject will be industrial research and development. This four-word phrase will be referred to often, and the use of "IRAD" as a code word for it will save space.

PHENOMENAL GROWTH OF IRAD

It has been estimated that the expenditures for IRAD in 1930 were less than $120 million; in 1953 they were $3700 million, and in 1956 they were $6500 million. One might make two reservations concerning the legitimacy of measuring the growth of IRAD by dollar outlays: that the data for the earlier years are not reliable and that the value of the dollar has diminished over the period. Yet neither of these considerations can throw any doubt on the order of magnitude of the figures in question.

The figures for recent years include large amounts of public funds spent by industry under government contracts; in 1956 no less than 49 percent came from the Federal Government. In addition there were direct expenditures of the Government for research and development performed by its own agencies ($1400 million) and expenditures for research, basic and applied, in universities and other nonprofit institutions. Some expenditures for *basic* scientific research are included in the figures for IRAD, but this is only a small portion—about 5 percent in 1953—of the activities of industrial organizations. Hence, when we speak of IRAD we mean primarily *applied* research and development, designed to produce new or improved technology—some of it in the form of inventions, patentable or unpatentable; some of it concerned with the application or adaptation of inventions and the acquisition of know-how; but all of it useful in industrial production involving new products, new devices, new processes.

Much of the phenomenal growth of IRAD has been connected with the war and defense effort of the nation, either directly, as in the execution of "crash programs" for the development of weapons and other defense materiel, or indirectly through the transfer of the "research-mindedness" of defense production to industry in general. Some of the increase in IRAD expenditures has probably been connected with the tax laws, especially the combination of high corporate income tax rates (and still higher excess-profits tax rates after the war) with the deductibility of IRAD payrolls from taxable income. In any case, industrial research has become very popular, not only among industrialists but also with the consuming public, as one can infer from the public-relations emphasis upon industrial research. In the main, the new research-mindedness of industry has probably proved profitable as well as productive, and everybody is satisfied that the increase in industrial research has been a splendid thing all around.

THE MORE THE BETTER?

If this past increase has been such a desirable development, should we be content with the level attained or should we press for more? Should we devote an ever-increasing portion of our resources (chiefly human resources) to industrial research, or is there perhaps some limit beyond which we should not go? It is easy to see that an economy might fail to allocate enough of its resources to IRAD. But can there ever be too much? Is not more research and development always better than less?

For most noneconomists the answer looks simple: More IRAD will produce more invention of better products and of better production techniques; this, in turn, will raise our standard of living; hence, we should always encourage industrial research, by allotting more government funds, by further liberalizing the tax laws, by strengthening the patent system, by employing whatever methods seem appropriate. "Let us have more IRAD, the more the better."

This view fails to recognize the existence of an economic problem—that is, a problem of choosing among alternatives. Economics comes in where more of one thing means less of another. To be sure, it would be nice to have more of a good thing, but if this implies that there will be less of something else, one should compare and choose. It is the economist's task to analyze what alternatives society will have to forego when it does what seems so desirable to many or to all. The social cost of what *is* done is the value of what *might* be done instead. In technical terms, the social cost of any action is equal to the value of the most valuable alternative opportunity that has to be foregone.

Many highly sophisticated economists will likewise incline to the view that there should be more inventive activity, not because it would be without social cost, but because the social cost is apt to be much smaller than the social benefit from the increased activity. They are convinced that society stands to gain from a shift of resources toward "inventing." By and large, economists in the free world are willing to rely on the price mechanism to guide or steer resources into the most wanted uses. But they recognize that there are certain situations or areas in which market prices and business profits will not adequately reflect the social benefits derived from particular goods or services. The private benefits that can be derived from inventive work are, as a rule, less than the potential social benefits. To express it in the economists' lingo: Since the "external benefits" of inventions —"external" because they accrue to individuals other than their producers and users—are substantial, the "social marginal product" of inventive activity is greater than the "private marginal product"; this implies that without government intervention not enough resources are allocated to the business of inventing, and that the total social product—the flow of real output—could be increased by shifting additional resources to IRAD.

WHENCE THE MANPOWER?

From what sectors of the economy can one withdraw the productive resources that are to be transferred to IRAD? Let us list all conceivable "sectors" that might be raided for manpower and then ask how likely each of them is to give up the human resources wanted for increased IRAD. (There are also IRAD expenditures for resources other than human, but the problems of finding buildings, apparatus, and materials needed for IRAD are not so serious.) "Inventive personnel" may be recruited by getting qualified persons away from (i) involuntary leisure, (ii) voluntary leisure, (iii) the production of security from invasion and revolution (including the production of military goods), (iv) the production of consumers' goods, (v) the production of capital goods, (vi) basic research, or (vii) education.

A shift of qualified persons from "involuntary leisure" to inventive activities would surely be the best of all possibilities, since the diminution of involuntary idleness would be a boon rather than a sacrifice. It would mean that there have been unemployed talents waiting to be used—talented individuals anxious to give up the leisure that had been imposed on them. This possibility, however, must be written off as an illusion if we are engaged in serious economic analysis. "Depression economics," based on the assumption that there are pools of unemployed resources ready to be put to work, has its uses, but only for what has been called an "upside-down economy." Economic theory and economic policy for the "right-side-up economy" would be badly vitiated by the assumption that there are ever-ready pools of productive resources that can be drawn upon at any time, to any extent, for any use.

A shift from "voluntary leisure" would be the next best possibility. It would mean that some qualified people are ready, with some inducements, to devote more time to inventive activity, not at the expense of any other productive activity but at the expense of some of their leisure time. These people may be professionals or amateurs. The former are the scientists and eng ·neers already in IRAD and possibly willing to work overtime. This pool of potential resources may be of great importance for the implementation of "crash programs" of research and development in a national emergency. But long-run programs, not directed toward specific goals (like winning a war or an international race for accomplishment of a particular technical feat) but designed for "progress in general," cannot successfully be based on the continuous and continual supply of overtime labor. The other source of volunteer labor—amateur researchers and tinkerers, busy with other jobs during their regular hours but glad to use their free evenings and weekends for inventive activity—can probably be drawn upon regularly. (Mobilization of these "individual inventors" was perhaps one of the achievements of the patent system in times past.) But this is a very limited source of supply, perhaps already fully utilized; in addition, the role of the "evening-and-Sunday inventors" has become quite insignificant in our age of organized research and development. Thus, the possible sacrifice of leisure cannot be counted on to provide the labor for additional inventive activity.

One must assume that society has allocated to national defense the resources that its experts consider indispensable. If the threat of invasion or revolution increases, resources will have to be withdrawn from other uses; if that threat is reduced, resources can be transferred and larger allocations can be made elsewhere. But one cannot reasonably assume that civilian industry, when it wants to increase its IRAD staff, will be able to raid the defense establishment or defense production for large numbers of engineers, even if one could find there the men qualified to do inventive work.

ALTERNATIVE OR COMPLEMENTARY GROWTH?

Having disposed of—as illusory—the first three hypothetical pools of manpower for additions to the IRAD staff, we may find it expedient to stop a moment for reorientation. The sectors left for consideration are the production of consumers' goods, the production of capital goods, basic research, and education. Let us now combine basic research, education, and applied research and development (including IRAD) into one sector, called "production of knowledge," and examine its relation to the other two. Is it really correct to regard these three sectors of production as alternatives? Since they actually have grown together, should they not rather be considered as complementary? Has not every increase in the production of capital goods helped, rather than hindered, the growth in the production of consumers' goods? Has not every increase in the production of knowledge accelerated, rather than retarded, the growth in the production of both capital goods and consumers' goods? Evidently, here is a conflict in economic interpretation that must be resolved before we can proceed.

Historically, production has increased simultaneously in all three areas; looking back over long periods, one does not find any absolute reduction in the production of consumers' goods when more resources were allocated to the production of capital equipment and of knowledge. Simultaneous increases in all areas have been possible because of the increase in the total labor force and because of the advance of productivity. As more manpower became available, absolutely larger numbers could be allocated to all lines of endeavor; an increased allocation to one sector did not presuppose an absolute curtailment of others. But in percentage terms the allocation was still a matter of alternatives. And it is in these terms, and in terms of output per head, that the problem of resource allocation in an economy with rising population must be analyzed. Clearly, a relative increase in the allocation of resources to any one line of endeavor implies relative curtailments of others.

Even with a constant labor force it is possible for production in all areas to increase if productivity—output per worker—increases. And productivity will almost certainly increase as more capital equipment and more technical knowledge are accumulated. Hence, with the advance of productivity it becomes possible to reduce the allocation of resources to the production of consumers' goods, and to increase the allocation to other areas, without causing any decline in final output. Indeed, this gradual reallocation of resources from consumers' goods production to the accumulation of capital and of knowledge will cause the output of consumers' goods, in the long run, to increase even faster.

This does not contradict the truth about the fundamental "alternativeness" of production of consumers' goods, capital equipment, and knowledge. At any moment of time, the three "departments of production" compete for the available resources, and increases in the allocations to the production of capital and knowledge at a rate faster than the rate of growth of manpower and of productivity will reduce the per capita output of consumers' goods in the near future.

COMPETITION FOR SCARCE RESOURCES

The notion that an increase in the production of capital goods or in the production of knowledge should, if only temporarily, hold back the production of consumers' goods is so contrary to widespread preconceptions that we must not expect it to be easily accepted. Some slightly more thorough elaboration, or even a repetitive reformulation, may therefore be appropriate, or at least forgivable.

An increase in the stock of knowledge may lead to a rise in productivity and thus to increases in the output of consumers' goods and capital goods. Similarly, an increase in the stock of capital goods may raise productivity and thus permit increases in production. This may suggest that the most rapid accumulation of capital goods and knowledge will permit the fastest increase in consumption. But, alas, such accumulation presupposes the availability of resources. If resources are being fully used, increased appropriations for investment in capital and knowledge must imply reduced appropriations to the production of consumers' goods. There is, therefore, a dilemma: The way to increase consumption is first to reduce it. Only by reducing the production of consumers' goods can society transfer resources to the production of capital goods and useful knowledge, and only subsequently can the increased stocks of capital and knowledge raise productivity enough to enable the diminished resources that are allotted to consumers' goods production to bring their output back to the former level and above it.

Increased research and development in order to increase the stock of knowledge is a splendid thing for society; so is increased production of productive equipment, and both are so highly valued because they eventually allow increased consumption. Yet, these three—more knowledge, more equipment, and more consumption—are alternatives in the sense that, even though all three can increase when productivity increases, a greater increase of one must mean, for the time being, smaller increases of the others. At any one moment, an increase in the production of knowledge means less equipment or less consumption than might otherwise be available, or less of both. A choice by society to increase research and teaching implies a choice, though usually unconscious, to have in the next years less productive equipment or less consumption, or less of both, than they might have had. Should a relative cutback of consumption prove impracticable, the choice is between "knowledge" and "equipment."

The Choice Between Research and Education · If resources are shifted from education to IRAD, the accumulation of new technical knowledge may be accelerated at the expense of the dissemination of established general knowledge. It is possible for industry, by providing more attractive job opportunities (for IRAD as well as for other kinds of qualified work), to drain schools of the teachers needed for the instruction of the new generation. The time may come when a lack of adequately trained graduates of the schools creates a bottleneck, obstructing not only further progress in the arts but also the maintenance of the general productivity of the people.

As in the formation and reproduction of capital, the problem is one of timing. Pushing IRAD *now*, in order to increase the production of new technical knowledge, may be at the expense of the reproduction of established knowledge and may result in an eventual decrease of general productivity with a forced reduction of IRAD *later,* perhaps even with a net loss in the production of technical knowledge in the long run.

BASIC AND APPLIED RESEARCH

It has been customary to divide knowledge, teaching, and research into two main categories, one of which is characterized as general, fundamental, liberal, basic; the other, as applied, practical, vocational, technical. The distinction is a useful one, even if blurred in many instances. The difference between basic and applied research happens to be significant for our present inquiry: whether there can be too much research.

We have stated that IRAD competes for the kind of human resources that are required for educating the young. Schoolteaching and applied research are largely alternative occupations. The instances in which a man in IRAD work also teaches an evening class, or in which a teacher also serves as an industrial consultant, are merely exceptions which confirm the rule that applied research and teaching are alternatives. This is not the case with basic research, which to some extent is a complementary activity of teachers at advanced levels.

The essential complementarity between teaching (especially postgraduate) and basic research has always been recognized by institutions of higher education. The performance of university professors is judged, as a rule, by their research work, and it is from the great research scholars that advanced students have received their most lasting inspirations. Of course, teaching and research cannot be complementary where heavy teaching loads

make it impossible for college teachers to carry on any sign
research. Perhaps, if the amount of teaching is measured by
hours of classroom work, all research must be considered an
alternative to teaching; only when the amount of teaching is
measured by the results achieved—in terms of the intellectual
capacities developed—will basic research be recognized as complementary to teaching on the highest levels.

The social benefits of basic research are invaluable, and its
social cost is probably not too high. For apparently only a relatively small number of people can qualify as workers in basic research, and, hence, the promotion of basic research will not encroach heavily on other pursuits. If those who do basic research
are engaged in higher education, their usefulness as teachers may
be increased, not diminished. And when the funds for basic research go to institutions of higher education, such outlays stimulate the employment not only of better but also of *more* academic
teachers by enabling universities to meet more successfully the
attractive salaries industry offers to qualified scholars in administrative posts and IRAD positions. In other words, increased
public outlays for basic research are not likely to encroach on
education. On the contrary, they may aid education by allowing
universities to hold on to scholars who might otherwise be lured
into industry, by allowing scholars to improve their qualifications
as teachers, and by attracting more qualified young people into
careers of scholarship. On these grounds one may say that there
is little danger of there being "too much basic research."

IRAD AND ADEQUATE EDUCATION

However, IRAD and education—the acquisition of new applied knowledge and the dissemination of established basic
knowledge—may be in serious competition with each other, especially if the teaching profession serves as a recruitment pool
for IRAD personnel and if IRAD job opportunities attract promising college graduates away from schoolteaching.

Since the production and reproduction of knowledge nowa-
days is almost completely a government concern, an imbalance
cannot be corrected by free enterprise. Schools are maintained
chiefly by local government with the help of state government;
more than 50 percent of research and development is financed

he central government; and a substantial part of
nced IRAD is indirectly paid for by the government
ows the IRAD payrolls to be deducted from the cor-
taxable incomes. Even the part of IRAD that is not
by the Government is—according to many authorities—
gely dependent on incentives held out by the governmental
system of patent protection for inventions. Thus, whatever imbalance develops within the area of the production and reproduction of knowledge, as well as between the production of knowledge and the production of investment goods and consumers'
goods, is not to be blamed on the competitive economic order
but on the inadequacies of governmental planning.

These are not just academic speculations but very real problems of urgent concern to our democratic process. The high taxes
needed to finance education and research cannot but impinge on
the production of other things, and industry feels the pinch not a
little (as does every taxpayer). On the other hand, the neglect
of education is becoming increasingly notorious and is to a large
extent attributable to the inflationary increases of wages and
salaries in industry, which have made the financial rewards to
teachers and scholars inadequate for the maintenance of the required supply.

RATIONAL RESOURCE ALLOCATION

With the pressure of competing demands on the productive
resources of the nation that exists today, the problem of allocation of resources deserves more thought than it has been given.
According to their special interests, or often out of sheer enthusiasm, different groups try to promote increased outlays for capital investment, increased expenditures for education, increased
disbursements for IRAD, and increased consumer spending, all
at once—not just in times of depression (when it would make
sense) but all the time. Of course, every one of these increases
would be fine to have, but since they compete with one another
we should first make up our collective minds regarding the com-
parative advantages. No matter whether an increase in industrial
research is financed by the Government or by private industry
(under the patent system or with some other stimulus), the decision to increase inventive activities is fully rational only when

it seems likely that productivity can be raised faster and maintained more securely through more new technical knowledge than through more capital equipment, more basic research, or more education. If the total amount of productive resources that can be withheld from the production of consumers' goods is limited (as it must be), how much should be allocated to the production of capital goods, how much to the reproduction of established knowledge, how much to the acquisition of new basic knowledge, and how much to the production of increased technical knowledge? This is a matter for economic judgment, tempered by important political and moral considerations. It would surely be foolish to allot to IRAD *all* the resources that can be spared from the consumption sector; it would be stupid to allot *none* of the available resources to IRAD. Even very far within these extremes there may be too much promotion or too little promotion of IRAD.

It has become fashionable among students of economic growth and development to acclaim technological progress as the number-one factor in the process. This may be perfectly justified, but it does not imply that IRAD should be singled out as the most important of all pursuits. Some of those who stress IRAD in order to reduce the emphasis upon capital investment forget that the increase in the stock of capital goods may have been a necessary condition of all technological development. Others who play up IRAD at the expense of liberal education and of basic research forget the dependence of technological research upon advances in basic knowledge and upon an adequate supply of highly educated people. If one puts education, training, research, and development all into one category and sets it against investment in industrial plant and equipment, then one might possibly find evidence for the contention that—in some countries and over some periods of time—the investment in knowledge has contributed more per dollar to the increase in labor productivity than the investment in physical industrial facilities. The bracketing of research with education is necessary for this statement to be tenable; for, among other things, the researchers and developers must have been previously educated and trained, and the utilization of new technical knowledge often requires degrees of dissemination and comprehension that cannot be attained without broad and general education.

If it should be possible to find statistical criteria for the identification of the specific contributions which "investment in knowledge" and investment in physical facilities have made to the increase in productivity, and thereby to obtain evidence for claiming "major credit" for the former, one would have to guard against the mistakes of regarding these findings as pertinent for other places, other times, and other allocations of resources. Particularly one would have to guard against the fallacy of confusing "total utility" and "average utility" with "incremental (marginal) utility." It is perfectly possible for technological research to deserve first prize in the distribution of merits for economic growth and, nevertheless, not to deserve first claim on additional resources.

Lest these remarks be understood as an attack on IRAD, or as a plea for drastic curtailments of IRAD expenditures, be it noted that such has not been my intention. I have intended to show that there *can* be too much IRAD work, not that there *has* been too much of it. Whether the present rate of IRAD expenditures is too high, too low, or just right, I do not know—though I am impressed with the present plight of education and cannot help looking askance at any so clearly identified rival bidder for potential teachers. In any case, a warning is in order against the position of the IRAD enthusiasts who champion the idea of "the more the better."

Technological Change and Industrial Research

Edwin Mansfield is Professor of Economics at the University of Pennsylvania. His recent book The Economics of Technological Change, *from which this selection is taken, is an important source on technological progress.*

DETERMINANTS OF THE RATE
OF TECHNOLOGICAL CHANGE

What determines the rate of technological change in an industry? Existing theory is still in a relatively primitive state, for it is only recently that economists have begun to give this question the attention it deserves. On a priori grounds, one would expect an industry's rate of technological change to depend to a large extent on the amount of resources devoted by firms, by independent inventors, and by government to the improvement of the industry's technology. The amount of resources devoted by the government depends on how closely the industry is related to the defense, public health, and other social needs for which the government assumes major responsibility; on the extent of the external economies [1] generated by the relevant research and development; and on more purely political factors. The amount of resources devoted by industry and independent inventors depends heavily on the profitability of their use. Econometric studies indicate that the total amount a firm spends on research and development is influenced by the expected profitability of the research and development projects under consideration and that the probability of its accepting a particular research and development project depends on the project's expected returns. Case

1. External economies and diseconomies are benefits and costs which accrue to bodies other than the one sponsoring the economic activity in question—which in this case is the firm or agency financing the research and development.

studies of particular inventions and studies of patent statistics seem to support this view.

If we accept the proposition that the amount invested by private sources in improving an industry's technology is influenced by the anticipated profitability of the investment, it follows that the rate of technological change in a particular area is influenced by the same kinds of factors that determine the output of any good or service.[2] On the one hand, there are demand factors which influence the rewards from particular kinds of technological change. For example, if a prospective change in technology reduces the cost of a particular product, increases in the demand for the product are likely to increase the returns from effecting this technological change. Similarly, a growing shortage and a rising price of the inputs saved by the technological change are likely to increase the returns from effecting it. As an illustration, consider the history of English textile inventions. During the eighteenth century, there was an increase in the demand for yarn, due to decreases in the price of cloth and increased cloth output. This increase in demand, as well as shortages of spinners and increases in their wages, raised the returns to inventions that increased productivity in the spinning processes and directly stimulated the work leading to such major inventions as the water frame, the spinning jenny, and the spinning mule.[3]

On the other hand, there are also supply factors which influence the cost of making particular kinds of technological change. Obviously, whether people try to solve a given problem depends on whether they think it can be solved, and on how costly they think it will be, as well as on the expected payoff if they are successful. The cost of making science-based technological changes depends on the number of scientists and engineers in relevant fields and on advances in basic science; for example,

2. Needless to say, these factors are not the only ones that influence the rate of technological change. As emphasized in subsequent chapters, there is considerable uncertainty in the research and inventive processes, and laboratories, scientists, and inventors are motivated by many factors other than profit. Nonetheless, the factors discussed in this section seem very important.

3. It is easy to see why an increase in product demand raises the expected returns from an investment in improving the industry's technology. It raises the total, absolute returns from a given percentage cost reduction, and tends to increase the total returns from a given product improvement.

advances in physics clearly reduced the cost of effecting changes in technology in the field of atomic energy. In addition, the rate of technological change depends on the amount of effort devoted to making modest improvements that lean heavily on practical experience. Although there is often a tendency to focus attention on the major, spectacular inventions, it is by no means certain that technological change in many industries is due chiefly to these inventions, rather than to a succession of minor improvements; for example, Gilfillan has shown that technological change in ship-building has been largely the result of gradual evolution. In industries where this is a dominant source of technological change and where technological change is only loosely connected with scientific advance, one would expect the rate of technological change to depend on the number of people working in the industry and in a position to make improvements of this sort.[4]

Besides being influenced by the quantity of resources an industry devotes to improving its own technology, an industry's rate of technological change depends on the quantity of resources devoted by other industries to the improvement of the capital goods and other inputs it uses. Technological change in an industry that supplies components, materials, and machinery often prompts technological change among its customers. Consider the case of aluminum. For about thirty years after the development of processes to separate aluminum from the ore, aluminum technology remained dormant because of the lack of low-cost electrical power. Technological change in electric power generation, due to Thomas Edison and others, was an important stimulus to the commercial production of aluminum and to further technological change in the aluminum industry. In addition, there is another kind of interdependence among industries. Considerable "spillover" occurs, techniques invented for one industry turning out to be useful for others as well. For example, continuous casting was introduced successfully in the aluminum industry before it was adapted for use in the steel industry. The

---

4. See S. Gilfillan, *Inventing the Ship*, New York: Follett Publishing Company, 1935; S. Hollander, *The Sources of Increased Efficiency*, Boston: M.I.T. Press, 1965; and K. Arrow, "The Economic Implications of Learning by Doing," *Review of Economic Studies*, June 1962. Of course, there are problems in defining "major" and "minor" inventions and in allocating credit among them.

inventor, Siegfried Junghans, turned his attention to steel after inventing a process for non-ferrous metals, which were easier to cast because of their lower melting points. Similarly, when shell molding was first introduced, its value was thought to be limited to molding non-ferrous items, but recent work indicates that it can be used for ferrous items too.[5]

Other factors which influence an industry's rate of technological change are the industry's market structure, the legal arrangements under which it operates, the attitudes toward technological change of management, workers, and the public, the way in which the firms in the industry organize and manage their research and development, the way in which the scientific and technological activities of relevant government agencies are organized and managed, and the amount and character of the research and development carried out in the universities and in other countries. We describe now the results of several studies that have tried to quantify the effects of some of the factors discussed in this section. . . .

Total Productivity Indexes · The total productivity index relates changes in output to changes in both labor and capital inputs alone. Specifically, this index equals $q/(zl+vk)$, where q is output (as a percent of output in some base period), l is labor input (as a percent of labor input in some base period), k is capital input (as a percent of capital input in some base period), z is labor's share of the value of output in the base period, and v is capital's share of the value of the output in the base period. Substituting values of q, l, and k over a given period into this formula, one can easily compute the value of the index for that period.[6] As a measure of technological change, this index has important advantages over labor productivity, the most important being that it takes account of the changes over time in the amount of capital inputs. However, it has the disadvantage of assuming that the marginal products of the inputs are altered only by technological change and that their ratios remain constant and independent of the ratios of the quantities of the inputs.

5. J. Jewkes, D. Sawers, and R. Stillerman, *The Sources of Invention*, New York: St. Martin's Press, Inc., 1959.
6. This formula comes from E. Domar, "On Total Productivity and All That," *Journal of Political Economy*, December 1962.

This formula, or variants of it, has been used to estimate the rate of increase of total productivity in the United States for the period 1899–1957, with these results: First, total productivity for the private domestic economy increased by about 1.7 percent per year over the whole period. Second, there seems to have been an increase in the rate of productivity growth to about 2.1 percent per year in the period following World War I. Third, the rate of productivity increase seems to have been higher in communications and transportation than in mining, manufacturing, and farming (Table 1). Fourth, within manufacturing it seems to have been highest in rubber, transportation equipment, tobacco, chemicals, printing, glass, fabricated metals, textiles, and petroleum.

What factors seem to influence the rate of growth of total productivity in an industry? Apparently, an industry's rate of

TABLE 1. *Estimates of Annual Rate of Increase of Total Productivity in Various Sectors of the U.S. Private Domestic Economy, 1899–1953*

Sector	Estimate (% per year)	Sector	Estimate (% per year)
Farming	1.1	Manufacturing	2.0
Mining	2.2	Foods	1.7
Metals	2.2	Beverages	1.6
Anthracite coal	0.7	Tobacco	3.5
Bituminous coal	1.6	Textiles	2.4
Oil and gas	3.0	Apparel	1.7
Nonmetals	2.6	Lumber	1.0
Transportation	3.2	Furniture	1.4
Railroads	2.6	Paper	2.3
Local transit	2.5	Printing	2.6
Residual transport	4.0	Chemicals	2.9
Communications and public utilities	3.6	Petroleum	2.4
Telephone	2.0	Rubber	4.1
Telegraph	1.8	Leather	1.2
Electrical utilities	5.5	Glass	2.6
Manufactured gas	4.7	Primary metals	1.9
Natural gas	2.0	Fabricated metals	2.6
Residual sector	1.3	Machinery, nonelectric	1.7
		Machinery, electric	2.2
		Transportation equipment	3.5

Source: J. Kendrick, *Productivity Trends in the United States,* Princeton, 1961.

growth of total productivity is related in a statistically significant way to (1) its ratio of research and development expenditures to sales, (2) its rate of change of output level, and (3) the amplitude of its cyclical fluctuation. Specifically, the rate of growth of total productivity increases (on the average) by 0.5 percent for each tenfold increase in the ratio of research and development expenditures to sales and by 1 percent for every 3 percent increase in the industry's growth rate.[7] These empirical results seem to be consistent with the theories above. However, they are somewhat ambiguous; for example, the observed relationship between the rate of productivity growth and the industry's growth rate could be due partly to an effect of the former on the latter. Correlation does not prove causation.

Other Measures of Technological Change · Economists have tried to devise better measures of the rate of movement of the production function than the total productivity index. These measures rest on somewhat different assumptions about the shape of the production function, the Cobb-Douglas and CES production functions sometimes, but not always, being used. For example, in an important paper published in 1957, Robert Solow provided an estimate of the rate of technological change for the nonfarm economy during 1909–1949.[8] The results suggest that, for the entire period, the average rate of technological change was about 1.5 percent per year. That is, the quantity of output derivable from a fixed amount of inputs increased at about 1.5 percent per year. In addition, Solow found evidence that the average rate of technological change was smaller during 1909–1929 than during 1930–1949. Benton Massell carried out a similar analysis for United States manufacturing, his estimate of the annual rate of technological change during 1919–1955 being about 3 percent.[9] In contrast with Solow, his results show little

7. N. Terleckyj, *Sources of Productivity Advance*, Ph.D. Thesis, Columbia University, 1960.
8. R. Solow, "Technical Change and the Aggregate Production Function," *Review of Economics and Statistics*, 1957. Solow assumed that there were constant returns to scale, that capital and labor were paid their marginal products, and that technological change was neutral.
9. B. Massell, "Capital Formation and Technical Change in U.S. Manufacturing," *Review of Economics and Statistics*, May 1960.

or no evidence of a higher rate of technological change during the thirties and forties than in previous decades.

The studies by Solow and Massell assume implicitly that technological change is disembodied—that is, that all technological change consists of better methods and organization that improve the efficiency of both old capital and new. Examples of such improvements are various advances in industrial engineering (for example, the development of time and motion studies) and operations research (for example, the development of linear programming). Although technological change of this sort has undoubtedly been of importance, many changes in technology must be embodied in new equipment if they are to be utilized. For example, the introduction of the continuous wide strip mill in the steel industry and the diesel locomotive in railroads required new investment in plant and equipment. No one has attempted to measure fully the extent to which technological change in recent years has been capital-embodied, as this kind of technological change is called. But the available evidence clearly indicates that a great deal of capital-embodied technological change has taken place.

If technological change is assumed to be capital-embodied, not disembodied, somewhat different methods must be used to estimate the rate of technological change. What do the results look like? Solow has estimated that the rate of technological change in the private economy during 1919–1953 was 2.5 percent per year.[10] This estimate is higher than his earlier estimate based on the assumption that technological change was disembodied. Turning to individual firms, estimates have been provided for ten large chemical and petroleum firms in the postwar period, one set of estimates assuming that technological change was disembodied, the other assuming that it was capital-embodied.

10. R. Solow, "Investment and Technical Change," *Mathematical Models in the Social Sciences,* ed. by Arrow, Karlin, and Suppes, Stanford, Calif.: Stanford University Press, 1959. It is important to note that the two rates of technological change are not entirely comparable, the capital-embodied rate of technological change generally being the larger. See E. Phelps, "The New View of Investment," *Quarterly Journal of Economics,* November 1962; and R. Solow, "Capital Labor and Income in Manufacturing," *The Behavior of Income Shares,* Princeton, N.J.: Princeton University Press, 1964.

TABLE 2. *Estimates of the Rate of Technological Change,
Disembodied and Capital-Embodied, Ten Chemical and
Petroleum Firms, 1946–1962*

Firm [1]	Disem-bodied	Capital-Embodied
	(% Per Year)	
C1	0.4	0.5
C2	2.4	6.2
C3	2.6	2.0
C4	1.4	3.5
C5	[2]	5.3
P1	0.3	2.1
P2	1.9	5.9
P3	3.2	6.6
P4	1.1	9.5
P5	1.8	8.8

Source: E. Mansfield, *Industrial Research and Technological Innovation,*
Norton, 1968, Chapter IV.
[1] The basic data were obtained from the firms with the understanding
that their names would not be divulged. Thus, C1 stands for the first chemical firm, P1 stands for the first petroleum firm, etc.
[2] Less than zero.

The results are shown in Table 2.[11] At the industry level, estimates
for ten manufacturing industries suggest that the rate of capital-
embodied technological change during 1946–1962 was highest in
motor vehicles and instruments, next highest in food, chemicals,
electrical equipment, paper, and apparel; and lowest in machinery, furniture, and glass (Table 3).[12] Outside manufacturing,
the rate of capital-embodied technological change in the railroad
industry during 1917–1959 has been estimated at 3 percent per
year.

What factors seem to influence the rate of technological change,
as measured by the estimated change in the production function?
My results, based on data regarding ten large chemical and
petroleum firms and ten manufacturing industries in the postwar
period, indicate that, both for firms and for industries, the rate of

11. E. Mansfield, *Industrial Research and Technological Innovation,* New
York: W. W. Norton & Company, Inc., 1968, Chapter IV. Of course, when
we speak about the rate of technological change in a firm, we mean the
rate at which its production function, not the industry's, shifts over time.
12. *Ibid.*

TABLE 3. *Estimates of Rate of Capital-Embodied Technological Change, Ten Two-Digit Manufacturing Industries, 1946–1962*

Industry	Estimate (% per year)
Chemicals	3.7
Machinery	1
Food	4.7
Paper	3.4
Instruments	8.3
Electrical equipment	3.6
Stone, clay, and glass	1.5
Apparel	3.0
Motor vehicles	8.6
Furniture	1.9

Source: E. Mansfield, *Industrial Research and Technological Innovation*, Norton, 1968, Chapter IV.

[1] Less than zero.

technological change is directly related to the rate of growth of cumulated research and development expenditures made by the firm or industry. If technological change is disembodied, the average effect of a 1 percent increase in the rate of growth of cumulated research and development expenditures is a .1 percent increase in the rate of technological change. If technological change is capital-embodied, it is a .7 percent increase in the rate of technological change. Needless to say, these results are tentative, since they are based on a relatively small amount of data and since, as noted before, correlation does not prove causation.

Patents and Technological Change · The number of patents is sometimes used as a crude index of the rate of technological change, or some important component thereof, in a given field at a certain point in time. Used in this way, patent statistics have important disadvantages. For one thing, the average importance and cost of the patents granted at one time and place may differ from those granted at another time and place. For another, the proportion of the total inventions that are patented may vary considerably. Nonetheless, it is of interest to see what the patent statistics suggest, since they are the basis for some major investigations in this area.

According to a series of studies by Jacob Schmookler, there is a high correlation between the patent rate on capital-goods inventions in an industry and the lagged value of the industry's investment or value-added.[13] That is, a high patent rate on capital-goods inventions is associated with a high previous level of investment or value-added. Turning from comparisons over time to comparisons among industries at a given point in time, there seems to be a tendency for the number of patents on capital-goods inventions to be directly related to the level of investment or value-added in an industry. That is, industries with high investment or value-added account for more patents than those with low investment or value-added. Moreover, this relationship persists when the effects of industry size are taken into account.[14]

What are the implications of these findings? In the past, some, though by no means all, economists assumed that the rate of technological change was determined outside the economic system and was independent of economic variables. To the extent that the patent rate is a useful index of the rate of technological change, or some important component thereof, Schmookler's results seem to contradict this assumption. Going a step further, he concludes that the distribution of inventions according to function, that is, according to the industry expected to use them, is largely determined by demand factors of the sort discussed earlier. The supply factors, reflecting, for example, advances in basic science, enter in as determinants of the form—mechanical, chemical, electrical, and so on—in which the inventions occur. Put differently, demand conditions determine which industries

13. An industry's value-added is its dollar sales minus its purchases of intermediate products from other firms or industries. Griliches and Schmookler found that 84 percent of the variation in the patent rate on process inventions could be explained by the industry's value-added three years before. See their "Inventing and Maximizing," *American Economic Review*, September 1963. For results based on investment data, see J. Schmookler, *Invention and Economic Growth*, Cambridge, Mass.: Harvard University Press, 1966.

14. J. Schmookler and O. Brownlee, using data for eighteen manufacturing industries, show that this relationship is quite strong, particularly when the patent data are lagged several years behind the value-added data. The coefficient of correlation, which is higher in more recent years, exceeded .9 in 1947. See their "Determinants of Inventive Activity," *American Economic Review*, May 1962. For results based on investment data, see J. Schmookler, *Invention and Economic Growth, op. cit.*

or consumer activities inventions are made for; supply conditions determine which industries or branches of science and technology inventions are made by. This is an interesting hypothesis, which undoubtedly will be subjected to further tests using other bodies of data.

As an industry grows older, there seems to be a tendency for the rate of patenting to rise first at an increasing rate, then at a decreasing rate, and finally to decline. This pattern has occurred in a wide variety of industries, the ultimate decline in the patent rate being explained in two quite different ways. According to one hypothesis, the technology in any field rather quickly approaches perfection, with the result that fewer important inventions can be made in it and inventors leave the field. According to the other hypothesis, the decrease in the patent rate occurs because of a decrease in the rewards to be gained from technological change in this industry, these rewards being associated with the growth and profitability of the industry. The decline in the patent rate may be due partly to both hypotheses, but the available evidence, though not entirely unambiguous, seems to indicate that the latter hypothesis is more important. . . .

THE NATURE OF INDUSTRIAL RESEARCH AND DEVELOPMENT

Research and development encompasses work of many kinds, and it is important that we identify the various types. First, there is basic research, which is aimed purely at the creation of new knowledge. Its purpose is to permit changes in ways of looking at phenomena and activities, to identify and measure new phenomena, and to create new devices and methods for testing various theories. For example, the biologist who tries to understand how and why certain cells proliferate, without having any particular application in mind, is carrying out basic research. Industrial laboratories carry out some basic research, but it is a very small proportion of their efforts. The principal bastions of basic research in our society are the universities.

Second, there is applied research, which is research expected to have a practical pay-off. Projects of this sort might be directed at ways of making steel resist stresses at particular temperatures, ways of inhibiting the growth of streptococci, or ways of obtaining the energy from atomic fission directly as electricity. The distinction between basic and applied research is fuzzy. Essentially, the distinction is based on the motivation of the researcher, basic research being aimed at new knowledge for its own sake, applied research being aimed at practical and commercial advances. In many cases both motives are present, and it is difficult to classify a particular project in this way. . . .

Third, there is development, which is aimed at the reduction of research findings to practice. Development projects are of many kinds. The more advanced development projects aim at the construction of entirely new types of products and processes; the more routine development projects, which often constitute the bulk of the total, aim only at relatively minor modification of products already brought into being by previous research and development. By the time a project reaches the development stage, much of the uncertainty regarding its technical feasibility has been removed, but there usually is considerable uncertainty regarding the cost of development, time to completion, and utility of the outcome. The development phase of a project is generally more expensive than the research phase. There is a long road from a preliminary sketch, showing schematically how an invention should work, to the blueprints and specifications for the construction of the productive facilities. The tasks that are carried out depend, of course, on the nature and purpose of the development project. In some cases, various types of experiments must be made, and prototypes must be designed and developed. Frequently, pilot plants are built and the experience with the pilot plant is studied before large-scale production is attempted. The construction of adequate materials and the design of new ways to work with these new materials are sometimes of crucial importance. . . .

The distinction between research and development is often rather hazy. The differences between them relate primarily to the orientation of the work, the degree of uncertainty inherent in a given problem, and the length of time work can be expected to proceed without demonstrable pay-off. Research tends to be oriented more toward the search for new knowledge (rather than toward the capacity to produce a particular product), to involve greater uncertainty of outcome, and to require more time for maturity than development. Nonetheless, although research and development are not the same things, in a particular project, a hard-and-fast distinction between research and development may be very difficult to make.

The Process of Invention · "Invention" has been defined in many ways. According to one definition, an invention is a prescription for a new product or process that was not obvious to one skilled in the relevant art at the time the idea was generated. Other definitions add the requirement that the product or process must have prospective utility as well as novelty. This raises difficult questions as to how one is to find out whether a particular new product or process is prospectively useful, but it has the advantage of eliminating tinkering of an economically irrelevant sort. Thus, we include prospective utility as part of the definition.

Inventions can occur in either the research phase or the development phase of organized R and D activity. Generally, according to officials of the National Science Foundation, the central ideas come from research, and inventions in patentable form arise in the course of development. In addition, of course, many inventions occur through the efforts of independent inventors. How do inventions come about? According to one school of thought, they are due to the inspirations of genius, these inspirations not being susceptible to analysis. According to another school of thought, invention proceeds under the stress of necessity. If the great inventive geniuses had never lived, the same inventions would have been made by others without serious delay. When the time is ripe they are inevitable. Neither of these views is taken very seriously at the present time. The first is useless because the emergence of inventions is regarded as inexplicable. The second minimizes the significance of individual effort, ignores chance elements, and is too mechanistic.

Most economists view the situation differently. To them, invention is an activity characterized by great uncertainty, but one which nonetheless shares most of the characteristics of other economic activities. In particular, they hypothesize that the amount of resources devoted to inventing in a particular field is dependent both on the social demand for inventions of this type and on the prospective costs of making the invention, the latter being related to the state of scientific knowledge. This, of course, is a variant of the conventional theories of expected profit or utility maximization. However, there is no intention of characterizing the inventor as an "economic man." It is recognized that, besides having economic motives, inventors invent for fun, fame, and the service of mankind, and perhaps to express the "instinct of workmanship" or the "instinct of contrivance." [15]

It is also recognized that invention is inherently a very difficult process to analyze, map out, organize, and direct. Contrary to popular impression, this process frequently moves from the observation of a phenomenon to exploration of a use for it, not from a clearly defined goal to the discovery of technical means to achieve this goal. Need and technique interact with one another, and it is not always apparent ahead of time from what disciplines or technologies answers will come. For example, a process for drawing brass rod arose from an adaptation of candle-making technology. Moreover, in trying to solve one problem, an answer to quite a different problem may result. Thus, Avicel, the non-nutritive food, was invented by an American Viscose Company chemist in the course of attempting to produce stronger rayon tire cord.

Turning to the psychological aspects of the process, some, like Abbot Usher,[16] postulate the existence of four steps leading to a successful invention. First, a problem of some kind is perceived. Second, the elements or data necessary for solving the problem are assembled through some particular set of events or train of thought, one of the elements being an individual with the required skill in manipulating the other elements. Third, an act of insight occurs, in which the solution of the problem is found. Fourth, there is a period of critical revision in which the solution becomes more fully understood and is worked into a broader context. To illustrate what Usher means by an act of insight, consider James Watt's most fundamental invention in

15. See J. Schmookler, *Invention and Economic Growth, op. cit.;* F. Taussig, *Inventors and Money Makers,* New York: The Macmillian Company, 1915; and T. Veblen, *The Instinct of Workmanship and the State of the Industrial Arts,* New York: The Macmillan Company, 1914; W. W. Norton & Company, Inc., 1966.

16. A. Usher, *A History of Mechanical Inventions,* Cambridge, Mass.: Harvard University Press, 1954.

the field of steam engine technology—the separate condenser. In 1763, a small model of the Newcomen steam engine was brought for repairs to Watt, a twenty-eight-year-old mathematical instrument maker at the University of Glasgow. Watt was perplexed by several aspects of the model's operation. After some experimentation, he recognized a deficiency in the engine's concept. Then while strolling on the green of Glasgow "on a fine Sabbath afternoon" early in 1765, "the idea came into my mind that as steam was an elastic body it would rush into a vacuum, and if a connection were made between the cylinder and an exhausting vessel it would rush into it and might there be condensed without cooling the cylinder . . . I had not walked farther than the golf house, when the whole thing was arranged in my mind." [17]

Finally, a few words should be added regarding the characteristics of successful inventors. A study [18] based on a random sample of about 100 persons granted patents in 1953 indicates that about 50 percent were college graduates and that about 60 percent were technologists—engineers, chemists, metallurgists, and directors of research and development. Another study [19] investigates the age of inventors when they made "very important" inventions. In proportion to the number of inventors alive at various ages, very significant inventions were made at the highest average rate when inventors were not more than thirty to thirty-four years old. Moreover, the mean age of the inventors of 554 great inventions was about thirty-seven years. Thus the most significant inventions seem to be largely the product of relatively young men. . . .

THE RETURNS FROM INDUSTRIAL RESEARCH
AND DEVELOPMENT

Measuring the returns from research and development is as difficult as it is important. For some years, the McGraw-Hill Economics Department gathered data from firms regarding the

17. Quoted in *ibid.*, p. 71.
18. J. Schmookler, "Inventors Past and Present," *Review of Economics and Statistics*, August 1957. Also, see J. Rossman, *The Psychology of the Inventor*, Inventors Publishing Company, 1931.
19. H. Lehman, *Age and Achievement*, Princeton, N.J.: Princeton University Press, 1953.

TABLE 4. *Expected Average Pay-Out Periods from*
R and D Expenditures, 1958–1961

Industry	1958			1961		
	Less than 3 years	3 to 5 years	6 years and over	3 years or less	4 to 5 years	6 years and over
	(% of companies answering)					
Iron and steel	50	50	0	38	50	12
Nonferrous metals	42	42	16	64	18	18
Machinery	49	45	6	51	39	10
Electrical machinery	23	69	8	61	32	7
Autos, trucks, and parts	40	60	0	54	40	6
Transportation equipment (Aircraft, ships, railroad equipment)	24	65	11	43	44	13
Fabricated metals and instruments	24	71	5	77	14	9
Chemicals	15	56	29	33	41	26
Paper and pulp	25	69	6	50	32	18
Rubber	50	17	33	38	38	24
Stone, clay, and glass	44	50	6	38	46	16
Petroleum and coal products	12	63	25	17	33	50
Food and beverages	37	54	9	54	43	3
Textiles	65	29	6	76	24	0
Miscellaneous manufacturing	66	31	3	71	25	4
All manufacturing	39	52	9	55	34	11

Source: McGraw-Hill Inc., *Business Plans for Expenditures on Plant and Equipment,* annual.

expected profitability of their R and D programs. Table 4 shows for each industry, in 1958 and 1961, the distribution of firms classified by their expected pay-out period for research and development. Although the pay-out period is a very crude measure of profitability, it is all that is available on a widespread basis. According to McGraw-Hill economists, the 1958 expected returns on R and D were "significantly better than the typical return, or pay-off, on investment in new plant and equipment, . . . [which helps to] make it clear why many companies with a given amount of capital to reinvest found it profitable to increase the proportion going to research and development." [20] More

20. D. Keezer, D. Greenwald, and R. Ulin, "The Outlook for Expenditures on Research and Development," *American Economic Review,* May 1960. p. 366.

recently, there is evidence that firms in many industries have become somewhat less optimistic concerning the prospective returns from additional research and development.

For a small group of firms and industries, some very tentative and experimental estimates have been made of the marginal rate of return from R and D expenditures, that is, the rate of return from an extra dollar spent on research and development.[21] If the production function is Cobb-Douglas,[22] if total past R and D expenditures as well as labor and capital are inputs, and if R and D expenditures have grown exponentially, one can obtain relatively simple expressions for the marginal rate of return from research and development, whether technological change is capital-embodied or disembodied. If it is capital-embodied, the marginal rate of return is directly related to the elasticity of output with respect to total past R and D expenditures and the rate of investment, but inversely related to the amount spent in the past on R and D and the ratio of capital to output. If it is disembodied, the marginal rate of return is directly related to the elasticity of output with respect to total past R and D expenditures and inversely related to the ratio of total past R and D expenditures to present output.[23]

Using these theoretical results, estimates of the marginal rates of return in 1960 were made for ten major chemical and petroleum firms and lower bounds for the marginal rates of return were estimated for ten manufacturing industries. Judging from the data for individual firms, the rate of return was very high in petroleum; in chemicals, it was high if technological change was capital-embodied but low if it was disembodied. The rate of return was directly related to a firm's size in chemicals, but inversely related to it in petroleum. Turning to the industry data, the rate of return seems to have been relatively high (15 percent or more) in the food, apparel, and furniture industries.

21. E. Mansfield, *op. cit.,* Chapter IV.

22. The production function is Cobb-Douglas if $Q = I_1^{a_1} I_2^{a_2} \ldots I_n^{a_n}$, where Q is the output rate and $I_1 \ldots I_n$ are inputs.

23. The elasticity of output with respect to total past R and D expenditures is the percent increase in output that would result from a 1 percent increase in total past R and D expenditures. For a complete list of the factors that, under the assumed circumstances, influence the marginal rate of return, see E. Mansfield, *op. cit.,* Chapter IV.

These results are merely experimental and should be viewed with considerable caution. They are based on a number of highly simplified assumptions regarding the shape of the production function, and they contain substantial sampling errors. Moreover, they are incomplete estimates of the social rate of return, since they do not take account of the effects of increased R and D expenditures in one industry or firm on productivity in another industry or firm. (The social rates of return may be higher.) Finally, although it is easy to include lags in the effect of R and D expenditures on the production function, as well as a finite elasticity of supply [24] of R and D inputs to the firm, this was not done because of the lack of relevant data.

On the basis of the crude measurements that can be made, does it seem that a firm's output of significant inventions [25] is closely related to the amount it spends on R and D? Is there any evidence that the productivity of a firm's R and D activities increases with the amount spent on R and D? Is there any evidence that productivity is greater in large firms than in small ones? A study [26] has been made of the chemical, petroleum, and steel industries, using data regarding the number of significant inventions carried out by about ten large firms in each industry. Because of the roughness of the data, the results are crude and tentative. Nonetheless, they are of interest. Holding size of firm constant, the number of significant inventions carried out by a firm seems to be highly correlated with the size of its R and D expenditures. Thus, although the output from an individual R and D projects is obviously very uncertain, it seems that there is a close relationship over the long run between the amount a firm spends on R and D and the total number of important inventions it produces.

The evidence from the study also suggests that increases in R and D expenditures in the relevant range (and holding size of firm constant) result in more than proportional increases in inventive output in chemicals. But in petroleum and steel, there is no

24. The elasticity of supply is the percent increase in the amount supplied resulting from a 1 percent increase in the price.

25. Note that an invention may be of great importance to the industry as a whole, but not particularly profitable to the firm responsible for the invention.

26. E. Mansfield, op. cit., Chapter II.

real indication of either economies or diseconomies of scale within the relevant range. Thus, except for chemicals, the results do not indicate any marked advantage of very large-scale research activities over medium-sized and large ones. Finally, when a firm's expenditures on R and D are held constant, increases in size of firm seem to be associated in most industries with decreases in inventive output. Thus, the evidence suggests that the productivity of an R and D effort of given scale is lower in the largest firms than in the medium-sized and large ones.[27]

27. Note once again that these results are based on only a small amount of very rough data and that they pertain to only three industries. For some results based on the drug industry, see W. Comanor, "Research and Technical Change in the Pharmaceutical Industry," *Review of Economics and Statistics,* May 1965.

PART THREE The Long View

Economic Growth: The Last Hundred Years

DEBORAH C. PAIGE WITH
F. T. BLACKABY AND S. FREUND

Deborah C. Paige and her colleagues are staff economists at the National Institute of Economic and Social Research. The National Institute is supported by British firms to conduct economic research into business conditions and public policy in the United Kingdom. This article first appeared in the July 1961 Economic Review *published by the Institute.*

INTRODUCTION

Since the war the economies of some developed countries appear to have been growing exceptionally fast (Table 1). From

TABLE 1. *Recent and Long-Term Growth Rates in National Product per Man-Year*

| | Long-term rate | | Annual per cent increases | |
	Starting year	Rate	1950– 1959	1954– 1959
Japan	1880	2.9	6.1	7.6
Italy	1863	1.2	4.7	3.8
Germany	1853	1.5	4.5	3.6
France	1855	1.5	3.6	3.3
Netherlands	1900	1.1	3.4	2.9
Norway	1865	1.6	3.1	2.5
Sweden	1863	2.1	2.8	3.0
United States	1871	2.0	2.2	2.2
Canada	1872	1.7	2.0	1.8
Denmark	1872	1.6	1.8	2.5
United Kingdom	1857	1.2	1.7	1.6

1950 onwards six countries have shown growth rates of 3 to 6 per cent; four of these have shown rates of over 3 per cent since 1954, by which time the effects of post-war recovery might be expected to have been over. These rates are nearly all more than twice as high as the long-term averages of the countries concerned. Does this imply that they are some kind of spurt rates which will inevitably revert, sooner or later, to more 'normal' rates of growth?

This is one of the questions raised by a study of long-term growth rates; it leads on to others. Is there any sense in the concept of a normal rate of growth—either a general normal rate for all industrial countries or a specific normal rate for individual ones? Do the same countries show rapid rates of growth over long periods? Do all countries show rapid rates at certain stages of development? Are fast rates linked to population increases?

The amount of information available about growth rates in the last 50–100 years has increased considerably during recent years. This article collects the figures together, appraises them, and attempts to show what conclusions can and cannot be drawn from them. The countries studied include all the eight Western European nations for which adequate long-term series could be found, as well as the United States, Canada and Japan. No attempt has been made to include countries of the Eastern bloc; the problems of the measurement and comparability of their figures are a separate subject.

THE FIGURES

In most economic articles, any assessment of the figures can quite properly be relegated to a statistical appendix; but in a discussion of the rates of economic growth over a century the first question that springs to mind is whether the figures are sufficiently reliable and meaningful for any useful conclusions to be drawn. This must be discussed, at least in broad terms, before any comparisons are made.

In this article, the measure of growth used is the rate of increase in real national product per head of the employed labour force. For most countries, official currently-constructed national product series have only been in existence since the second world war, and estimates for the earlier period have been calculated retrospectively. These retrospective estimates depend on fewer series and have a larger margin of error than post-war figures; but the estimates in current prices appear moderately reliable over quite long periods. A much larger margin of error enters in when they are adjusted for price changes—as they must be before growth can be measured in real terms.

Even if full information were available, it would not be possible to construct one definitive series of national product estimates in constant prices; there is an inherent 'index number problem' that cannot be avoided. There is no unique measure of changes in prices: when the price movements of different goods diverge, the index obtained depends upon the year whose pattern of expenditure is used to provide the weights. In short periods, and periods when most prices move together, different weighting patterns produce fairly similar results. But the price indices linking pre- and post-war years, or spanning periods of rapid technological change, are likely to vary considerably according to the base year taken.

Tentative and indirect evidence suggests that a change from a series corrected by detailed price indices using initial year weights to one corrected by price indices using end-year weights might change the growth rate by 50 per cent or more over a period of, say, thirty years, including a major war. Such differences are seldom found in practice because the series used are usually amalgams of differently-weighted component series, which can only be regarded as a rather inaccurate approximation to the mean of the two extremes.

For earlier periods these index number difficulties are outweighed by the problem of finding any price index which is at all appropriate. Usually the choice is between a wholesale price index and a cost-of-living index based on working-class expenditure patterns. Neither of them is really suitable for adjusting national income figures. The wholesale price indices tend to be little more than indices of primary product prices. The cost-of-living indices give a large weight to food and rent, and only a small weight to manufactured goods. Both indices may therefore overstate the price rise for the national product as a whole, since in parts of the nineteenth century the relative prices of manufactured goods fell sharply.

Growth rates also need to be adjusted for population changes, and preferably for employment changes. (Ideally, they should be adjusted for hours of work, which fell considerably in the earlier period; but there is not enough information to make com-

plete estimates of average hours worked.) For many countries
the employment series before 1938 are not satisfactory. Most of
the estimates used in the inter-war period were obtained by calculating participation rates from the census years, applying these
rates to population estimates for the years between the censuses,
and then adjusting these figures by annual estimates of unemployment. For some countries these unemployment figures are
based on trade union returns, and may therefore show too great
a cyclical fluctuation; thus some of the apparent fluctuations in
output per man in Norway and Sweden may not be real.

Before 1913, since labour force estimates for many countries
are unreliable, the increase in national product was divided by
the increase in population of working age. These figures are a
rather poor substitute for labour force figures; but where separate
labour force estimates exist, the average rate of increase in the
population of working age was not very different from that in
the labour force in the period up to 1913.

Assessment · The margin of error in the figures, therefore, is a
wide one; and the further back the figures go, the wider the
margin is. An estimate made for Norway [1] suggests that the maxi-
mum margin of error in the national product figures since 1930 is
± 3 per cent; in the figures for 1900–1930, ± 7–8 per cent; and
around 1865, ± 20 per cent.

There are, however, some reasons for confidence in the figures.
From 1901 onwards, movements in national product can be
compared with movements in industrial production. This provides some independent check. Although they may share a number of common sources, the industrial production series are based
mainly on physical quantities with value weights, and the national product series are value figures deflated by a price index;
the two series are therefore to some extent independent. Further
in most of our countries they are, to a considerable extent, different ways of measuring the same thing; for industrial production accounts directly for a substantial part of the national
product, and a good deal of the remainder tends to move in line
with it—items such as freight transport and distribution. The

1. Jul Bjerke, *Some Aspects of Long-term Economic Growth of Norway
since* 1865, paper presented to the 6th European Conference of the International Association for Research in Income and Wealth, August 1959.

industrial production series do in fact tend to confirm the national product series. The direction and the turning points are nearly always the same, but—as might be expected—the industrial series show both steeper cyclical swings and a more rapid secular growth.

GROWTH AND POPULATION

It is the rise in output per man-year, much more than any increase in population, which has accounted for the increase in the national products of these countries over the last 50–100 years (Table 2). In Sweden, for instance, the population increase explains only a quarter of the rise in output, and in France hardly any of it. Canada, the Netherlands and the United States are exceptions; here the population rise was important and explains about half the increase in total production.

Further, there is not much evidence to support the commonly-held belief that a stable population is an important obstacle to growth. Kuznets found, from a comparison of the figures for nineteen countries, that there was no clear-cut association between rates of population growth and product per head of total population.[2] The present study also shows only a tentative and inconclusive association between rate of growth of output per head and that of population of working age; neither over the whole period nor in either sub-period before or after 1913 is there any significant correlation. It is true that the two immigrant countries, the United States and Canada, show both rapid population rises and also high rates of economic growth. But it is Japan, ranking fourth in growth of working population, and Sweden, ranking tenth, which are at the top of the list of productivity increases. The United Kingdom, France and Italy rank low in the rate of growth both of population of working age and of production per man year; but the Netherlands, which had the most rapid population growth of the non-immigrant countries, also had the slowest growth of total product per man-year.

If we look at the changes in the rates for separate countries between the periods before and after 1913, there is a slight and tentative suggestion that a slowing down in economic growth

2. See S. Kuznets, 'Levels and Variability of Rates of Growth', *Economic Development and Cultural Change*, vol. 5, no. 1, October 1956.

TABLE 2. Rates of Growth of Working-age Population and National Product per Man-Year

| | | Ranking in total period | | | Annual per cent increases | | | | | | |
| | | | | | Total period | | | Up to 1913 | | 1913–1959 | |
	Start-ing year	Product per man-year	Working-age pop-ulation	Total product	Product per man-year	Working-age pop-ulation	Total product	Product per man-year	Working-age pop-ulation	Product per man-year	Working-age pop-ulation
Japan	1880	1	4	1	2.9	1.2	4.0	3.4	0.9	2.6	1.4
Sweden	1863	2	10	4	2.1	0.7	2.8	2.4	0.7	1.7	0.8
United States	1871	3	2	2	2.0	1.7	3.8	2.2	2.3	1.8	1.2
Canada	1872	4	1	3	1.7	1.8	3.5	1.9	2.1	1.5	1.6
Denmark	1872	5	6	5	1.6	1.0	2.6	2.1	1.1	1.2	1.0
Norway	1865	6	7	8	1.6	0.9	2.5	1.3	0.8	1.9	1.0
France	1855	7	11	11	1.5	0.1	1.5	1.5	0.1	1.5	0.1
Germany	1853	8	5	7	1.5	1.1	2.5	1.5	1.1	1.4	1.1
Italy	1863	9	8	10	1.2	0.8	1.8	0.7	0.6	1.7	0.9
United Kingdom	1857	10	9	9	1.2	0.7	2.0	1.6	1.0	0.8	0.5
Netherlands	1900	11	3	6	1.1	1.4	2.5	0.7	1.5	1.3	1.4

Note: From 1913 onwards product per man-year is obtained by dividing the national product not by the working-age population but by the employed population. For this reason, both for the period 1913–1959 and for the whole period, the changes in population and in product per man-year do not exactly make up the change in the total product. But the differences are very small.

goes with a slowing down in the rise in population, and vice versa. But it does not follow that it was the change in population growth which influenced economic growth; it could as well have been the other way round, or the association may have been accidental.

Six countries have slower rates of economic growth after 1913 than they did before it; and of these, three—Canada, the United States and Britain—also show a significant decline in the rate of population growth. But for two of them, the United States and Canada, it may well be that the change in the trend of immigration was partly influenced by the fact that their economies were growing more slowly for other reasons.

France had a virtually stationary population and about the same rate of growth in both periods. Of the three remaining countries, Norway and Italy had higher rates of growth after 1913 than before it; so did Japan, up till 1941. In all three, the population also rose faster after 1913. Norway and Italy do not appear to have started sustained economic growth until nearly the end of the 19th century and Japan started from an extremely low level. It is certainly possible that population increases stimulated growth in these countries; it is also possible that improvement of very low living standards stimulated population increase through a reduction of the death rate.

This analysis does not exclude the possibility that a rapid rise in population may stimulate output per man in certain circumstances; but it certainly does not suggest that this has been a major determining factor in the last hundred years. There is absolutely no indication that it is a necessary condition of economic growth; some of the fastest growing countries have had relatively stable populations.

GROWTH THROUGH CATACLYSMS: 1913–1959

Since 1913 normal economic development has been drastically affected by three cataclysms—the two world wars and the great depression. It has been suggested that some kind of normal growth rate runs through such major disturbances; and that there is 'a general principle observed in the figures for all countries, for all recoveries from wars and other major upheavals. Growth is naturally much more rapid than usual until the country gets back on its trend line, after which the normal rate of growth is resumed.'[3] Of this there is little evidence. Our series do suggest that growth is especially fast during the recovery period following a major interruption, but that, at least during the twentieth century, countries have never fully made up the ground they lost as a result of the cataclysms.

Consequently the average growth rates of the period since 1913 are not of much use.

In studying economic growth in order to speculate about the future it is obviously not very reasonable to expect a repetition of the great depression; nor is it sensible to assume that—if there is another world war—its economic effects would be some sort of statistical average of the effects of the last two. It is not helpful to incorporate into the answers to hypothetical questions about the future the same number and kind of cataclysms as occurred in an arbitrarily-chosen period of the past.

For the different experience of the various countries in the two world wars and the great depression thoroughly distorted their growth rates. Canada and the United States show higher rates of growth in the combined war period than they do in peacetime. Norway, Sweden, Denmark, Italy and the Netherlands all show some net growth in the two world wars, but at rates ranging from less than a quarter to about a half of their peacetime average. The other four countries show either very slow growth rates or actual falls in output for the war periods together (Table 3).

The effect of these wartime variations is such that neither the long-term rates of growth including the wars, nor the peacetime rates excluding them, can be regarded in any sense as normal. For if we regard the rates over the whole period as normal, it must be because we believe that in peacetime countries made up for their losses in wartime. If this were so, countries whose output fell sharply during the wars would show particularly rapid peacetime rates of growth. Alternatively, if we believe that the peacetime average gives normal growth rates, this must mean that we believe that the peacetime rates were not affected by wartime experience.

Our results suggest, tentatively, something between these two hypotheses: that the nations particularly hard hit in the war

3. Colin Clark, *Financial Times*, 8 June 1960.

TABLE 3. *Rates of Growth in National Product per Man-Year, 1913–1959, Peacetime and Wartime Experience*

Annual per cent increases

| | Total period 1913–1959 | Peace-time | | | War-time average | Ranking | | |
		1922–1938	1950–1959	Peace-time average		Total period	Peace average	War average
Japan	2.6	4.4	6.1	5.0	−0.1	1	1	9
Norway	1.9	2.6	3.1	2.8	0.9	2	4	3
United States	1.8	1.1	2.2	1.5	2.2	3	10	1
Italy	1.7	1.7	4.7	2.8	0.5	4	3	7
Sweden	1.7	2.7 (a)	2.8	2.7	0.6	5	5	6
Canada	1.5	0.6	2.0	1.1	1.9	6	11	2
France	1.5	1.8	3.6	2.4	0.3	7	6	8
Germany	1.4	3.3 (b)	4.5	3.8	−0.8	8	2	11
Netherlands	1.3	0.8	3.4	1.7	0.7	9	7	5
Denmark	1.2	1.5	1.8	1.6	0.7	10	8	4
United Kingdom	0.8	1.5	1.7	1.6	−0.2	11	9	10

Note: Both on account of breaks in the figures, and in order to exclude the period of starting up again after the wars, the "wartime" rates have been taken as covering the years 1913 to 1922 and 1938 to 1950. For Sweden the first world war period is taken as 1913 to 1923, and for Germany 1913 to 1925. Owing to the major difficulty of establishing price links between pre-war and post-war periods for countries with major currency upsets, there is a considerably wider margin of error in the wartime average than in the peacetime periods and the rates shown should only be taken as giving the general direction and magnitude of the change. The margin of error in the wartime changes may in some countries be sufficient to affect the 1913–59 average significantly, although its weight in this average is probably not sufficient to change the order of magnitude seriously.

(a) 1923–38. (b) 1925–38.

may have caught up to some extent in peacetime, but not completely. Canada and the United States, the two countries that grew faster in wartime than peacetime, had the slowest peacetime rates of growth. All the nine countries which had a marked loss of growth in wartime grew faster in peacetime than the United States and Canada. But the catching-up was by no means complete: among the nine countries themselves, there is little evidence that those particularly hard hit by the war did particularly well in peacetime.

The analysis of the effects of the great depression suggests similar results (Table 4)—that there was some catching up afterwards, but that it was not complete: consequently the period spanning the depression, from about 1929 to 1937,[4] cannot be regarded as normal either. First, by 1937 or 1938 most countries had by no means regained the trend indicated by their growth rates up to 1929; 1929–1937 rates were relatively low for most countries, and very low indeed for some. The ground lost in the great depression was in general not made up. Further, there is some tendency, though not a strong one, for the countries worst hit by the depression to show relatively low growth rates over the whole inter-war period. The two countries whose output dropped most in the depression—Canada and the United States —rank seventh and ninth respectively in their inter-war growth rates.

But, although recovery from the depression was clearly not complete, there were some very strong recovery effects: it was, on the whole, the countries whose output had fallen most sharply in the recession which showed the most rapid rates of rise after 1932. So there is no question of using the period 1932–1937 as in any way a normal period: it was dominated by the after-effects of the depression.

THE PERIOD BEFORE 1913

Since the period after 1913 is so disturbed, if we are to find

4. As growth was again interrupted in a number of countries by the recession in 1938, the post-depression period has been taken only up to 1937 for all countries except Japan. Two alternative definitions of national income for Japan produce different movements between 1937 and 1938. The movement over the whole period from 1933 until 1938 appears, however, to be moderately well established.

TABLE 4. Growth Rates and the Depression: 1922–1938

Annual per cent increases

| | Total period 1922(a)–1938 | | Before and after 1929(a) | | | | Depression and recovery | | | |
| | | | 1922(a)–1929(b) | | 1929(b)–1937(a) | | Depression: total product, trough as per cent of previous peak | Trough of depression to 1937(a) | | Period of depression |
	Total product	Product per man-year	Total product	Product per man-year	Total product	Product per man-year		Total product	Product per man-year	
Japan	5.2	4.4	6.5	5.9	3.6	2.4	no fall	4.8	3.7	1931–1933
Germany	4.0	3.3	5.7	6.0	2.8	2.1	84	8.8	3.5	1928–1932
Sweden	3.1	2.7	3.9	3.3	2.3	1.9	87	6.3	4.6	1930–1932
Norway	3.2	2.6	3.9	3.1	2.5	2.0	92	4.3	3.4	1930–1931
France	1.4	1.8	5.8	5.8	–2.1	–1.3	82	(d)	(d)	1929–1936
Italy	1.9	1.7	2.3	2.2	1.9	1.6	95	3.0	2.7	1929–1930
Denmark	2.8	1.5	3.6	2.1	2.0	1.1	98	2.8	0.4	1931–1932
United Kingdom	2.3	1.5	2.7	1.6	2.3	1.6	94	4.9	2.2	1929–1932
United States	1.8	1.1	4.8	2.1	0.1	0.4	70	9.7	4.9	1929–1933
Netherlands	1.8	0.8	4.0	2.0	0.2	0.3	88	5.0	3.4	1929–1934
Canada	2.1	0.6	5.1	2.1	–0.3	–0.9	71	8.4	3.9	1929–1933

(a) From 1925 for Germany and from 1923 for Sweden.
(b) Or year of onset of depression if other than 1929.
(c) 1938 for Japan.
(d) No recovery until 1936.

any historical experience which might be relevant for future growth rates we must look at the period before the first world war. Here the problems of comparison are most acute. Not only is the margin of error in the figures much higher, but we are looking at a different kind of world, with many of our countries still in an early stage of industrialisation. Do the rates of economic growth found in these circumstances have any relevance to present conditions? And if so, are they appropriately measured by today's national accounting conventions?

Fortunately we do not need to try to compare the level of production of 1870 with that in 1960, when we would have the problem of comparing worlds with radically different products: hansom cabs and oil-lamps as against taxis and electricity. Rather we are comparing the rate of growth between, say, 1870 and 1880 with that between 1950 and 1960, and the problems of the introduction of new commodities and techniques are much smaller. In every period growth is affected by the rate of innovation, and it is true that the earlier period was for many countries one of particularly rapid technological change; but this has also been true of the nineteen-fifties.

In one respect, however, nineteenth century economic growth does differ substantially from that of later periods. Part of total economic growth is explained by changes in the distribution of the labour force, in particular the shift from low-paid occupations such as agriculture and domestic service to higher-paid occupations in industry. This shift was very important in the nineteenth century and for some countries in the first quarter of the twentieth century; by the end of the second world war it had almost come to an end in most of our countries, except Japan. For most of the countries we do not have enough information to separate out that part of the total productivity increase which can be attributed to labour force shifts. There are, however, some figures for the United States: it has been estimated that, since 1910, about one-eighth to one-quarter of the total long-term increase in productivity was due to such shifts.

Growth rates calculated from these early series may be too high because the share of sectors which are declining, or growing more slowly than the rest, is underestimated. This is likely because there is much more information about the industrial, rapidly-expanding sectors than about the agricultural and handi-craft sectors. The use of modern national accounting conventions can also lead to overestimates of growth in these earlier periods. National accounting figures in general include only market trans-actions. In less developed countries more needs are satisfied within the family. Consequently there is a difficulty when we calculate changes over time in output per head of population of working age. Throughout, family workers are included in the population, but their non-market product may be excluded from national output. Over a period, therefore, when the share of the non-market product in the total was falling, the increase in out-put per head is overestimated.

These are the qualifications to bear in mind in considering the figures in Tables 5 and 6. The averages for the whole period be-fore 1913 must be treated cautiously, because they cover very different periods for different countries—periods ranging from thirty to sixty years. But it is not sensible—as it is for 1913–1959 —to compare common chronological sub-periods for these coun-tries; for whereas from 1913 onwards two world wars and a great depression dominated the economic trend in all the countries considered here, before 1913 each country's economic develop-ment was largely determined by its domestic circumstances. For instance, the United Kingdom and Sweden, which had been the fastest growing countries in the late 'sixties and early 'seventies, were stagnating in the late 'seventies; this was the time when Ger-many and the United States were growing very fast indeed— Germany after the achievement of political unity and the United States after the American Civil War.

Nor is it possible to isolate with any certainty periods in the history of each country at which they could be said to be in the same stage of economic development. By the middle of the nine-teenth century the United Kingdom and France had left their pre-industrial patterns of economic activity far behind. Our series for Germany and Italy are long enough to show a clear change of trend: Germany immediately after attaining political unity and Italy a good deal later. (For these two countries it is probably useful to exclude the earlier, more slowly growing period.) For the other countries there is tentative evidence that some of our series start around the first period of intensive in-

TABLE 5. Rapid Growth Rates of National Product per Man-Year Before 1913(a)

Annual per cent increases

	Long-term average growth rate, to 1913		Fastest 8-year periods of growth		Periods(b) during which growth exceeded			
					2½ per cent a year		3 per cent a year	
	Starting-year	Rate	Period	Rate	Period	No.years	Period	No.years
Japan	1880	3.4	1891-99	4.7	1880-1911	31	1880-1911	31
Sweden	1863	2.4	1880-88	4.5	1866-98	32	1863-75	12
			1866-74	4.6	1900-11	11	1891-98	7
			1890-98	2.9			1903-08	5
			1900-08	2.8				
United States	1871	2.2	1872-80	5.2	1871-1907	36	1871-89	18
			1896-1904	3.1			1896-1905	9
Denmark	1872	2.1	1877-85	2.4	1877-84	7	1878-82	4
			1888-96	2.4	1887-93	6	1887-90	3
					1895-99	4		
Canada	1872	1.9	1875-83	4.1	1874-90	16	1874-86	12
			1895-1903	2.2	1899-1904	5		
United Kingdom	1857	1.6	1867-75	2.7	1859-73	14	1867-73	6
			1881-89	2.5	1881-89	8		
Germany	1853	1.5	1874-82	3.5	1873-93	20	1873-86	13
			1882-90	2.0				
Norway(a)	1865	1.3	1905-13	2.7	1905-13	8	1909-13	4
Italy	1863	0.7	1871-77	2.4(c)	1898-1902	4	—	—
			1897-1905	2.3	1904-07	3		

(a) The long-term rate is calculated up to the year 1913. All other dates refer to the centre of five year averages; for instance, 1911 = 1909-13. For Norway however, the rates are calculated from single years. (b) Of three years or more. (c) As the series only covers selected years, only a six year period is available.

TABLE 6. *Comparisons of Growth Rates of National Product per Man-Year*

	1950–1959	1954–1959	1922[a]–1929[b]	Fastest 8 years before 1913	Pre-1913 average	Post-1913 average
A. Annual per cent increases						
Japan	6.1	7.6	5.9	4.7	3.4	2.6
Italy	4.7	3.8	2.2	2.3	0.7	1.7
Germany	4.5	3.6	6.0	3.5	1.5	1.4
France	3.6	3.3	5.8	. .	1.5	1.5
Netherlands	3.4	2.9	2.0	(c)	(c)	1.3
Norway	3.1	2.5	3.1	2.7	1.3	1.9
Sweden	2.8	3.0	3.3	4.6	2.4	1.7
United States	2.2	2.2	2.1	5.2	2.2	1.8
Canada	2.0	1.8	2.1	4.1	1.9	1.5
Denmark	1.8	2.5	2.1	2.4	2.1	1.2
United Kingdom	1.7	1.6	1.6	2.7	1.6	0.8
B. Ranking						
Japan	1	1	2	2	1	1
Italy	2	2	6	9	10	4
Germany	3	3	1	5	7	8
France	4	4	3	. .	8	7
Netherlands	5	6	10	(c)	(c)	(c)
Norway	6	7	5	6	9	2
Sweden	7	5	4	3	2	5
United States	8	9	7	1	3	3
Canada	9	10	8	4	5	6
Denmark	10	8	9	8	4	9
United Kingdom	11	11	11	7	6	10

(a) From 1925 for Germany, and from 1923 for Sweden.
(b) Or the onset of the depression (Table 4).
(c) Omitted because pre-1913 figures only cover thirteen years.

dustrialisation.[5] Some of these countries, however, seem to have entered the phase of industrialisation with a short period of very rapid growth, and others much more gradually.

The periods which it does seem useful to isolate, from pre-1913 experience, are the fastest growing periods in each country—since a number of our questions are concerned with rapid rates of growth. Table 5 sets out for each country the two or three

5. For a number of countries our series start very near the time identified by Rostow as 'take-off'. See W. W. Rostow, *Stages of Economic Growth*, Cambridge University Press, 1960.

eight-year periods of most rapid growth before 1913; it also shows for how long at a stretch the various countries did in fact exceed growth rates of 2½ and 3 per cent.

CONCLUSIONS

The amount we can learn from past growth rates that is relevant to prediction about the future is limited. Our tools of measurement are crude, both because of conceptual limitations and because our figures on actual movements are still, in spite of recent improvement, subject to a wide margin of error. Most of the lessons of this study are negative—in that they suggest that some of the simple relationships that have been put forward do not hold good.

There is little evidence of a direct connection between the increase in output per man and the increase in population; and where there is an association it may be that it is the rise in the standard of living which explains the rise in population rather than the other way round. In any case, a rise in population is clearly not an essential condition of economic growth; some of the fastest growing countries have had relatively slow population growth.

There is no convincing evidence of any constancy or normality in the international pattern of growth rates (Table 6); almost any hypothesis of constancy which one tries on the figures gets a negative answer—with the one exception that Japan, in almost any period one selects, comes at the top of the table. Apart from Japan, there is no connection between the ranking of countries before and after 1913; this remains true whether or not the German and Italian figures are adjusted by excluding their early periods of slow growth. Nor is there any correlation between those countries which had the fastest spurts in the nineteenth century and those which have grown fastest since the second world war. There is some constancy in ranking if we compare 1922–1929 with either 1950–1959 or 1954–1959. The sensible explanation of this may be that in both periods the same group of countries were making rather delayed recoveries from the severe damage caused by war.

It is not safe to say—on the basis of a single comparison of pre-1913 and post-1913 averages—that growth rates are slowing down secularly. For although it is true that the post-1913 averages are lower, this can perfectly well be explained by the three cataclysms in the twentieth century. It is true that since 1950 it is the richest nations which have shown the slowest growth (Table 1): this might suggest that, after a certain point, the transfer of working population from the manufacturing sector to the service sector could have a slowing down effect. But it is far too soon, on the basis of nine years' figures, to be certain about this.

Nor can we classify countries into one group which normally grows fast and one group which normally grows slowly. Nearly all countries—again, except Japan—have had fairly long periods of both rapid growth and slow growth. At one time or another, every country except two has grown for eight years or more at a rate faster than 3 per cent a year; one of the exceptions—Britain —reached 2.7 per cent for the eight years before 1875, and 3 per cent for six of them.

These apparently negative conclusions are, in a way, encouraging: there is no suggestion of any long-term historical inevitability about growth rates. Countries which for a long time had ranked low in the list have succeeded in changing their ranking. For instance, if this article had been written ten years ago, it might have been tempting to conclude that Italy could not grow fast: before the second world war, she had never reached 2½ per cent a year for more than four years at a time.[6] Since 1950 she has ranked second, with an average growth rate of over 4½ per cent for nine years. The countries which have ranked low since 1950 have all had long periods in which they grew faster. Britain, for instance, enjoyed a continuous period of about forty-five years from 1857 in which her average growth rate was above that of 1950–1959; and the United States exceeded her post-war growth rate for forty years together.

Japan appears to be the one exception to the rule that there are no obvious rules; she is the country that has consistently grown faster than the others through nearly all the period. This may be due to a substantial extent to the fact that, in an economy starting from a very low level, the necessity of competing in foreign markets led to a higher degree of concentration of investment and the development of a small but relatively productive modern manu-

6. Except for the few years of recovery from the great depression.

facturing sector, which, owing to the particular social and institutional pattern, has continued to develop side by side with very much less productive domestic manufacture and agriculture.[7] Consequently productivity gains have been made on a much larger scale than in other countries by the transfer of workers to more productive sectors, as well as by rising productivity in each sector.[8] This process of transfer is still incomplete, and consequently rapid increases in productivity are still to be expected.[9] The Japanese long-run plan is for a growth rate in real national product per head of population of 6.9 per cent a year from 1956–58 to 1970.[10] They expect that the proportion of the labour force engaged in agriculture and other primary industry will fall from 40 to 23 per cent.

Do the historical figures throw any light on the 1950–1959 rapid rates of growth? First of all, these rapid rates are not unprecedented (Table 6). France was growing faster and Japan almost as fast in the period from 1922 to the depression. It is true that Italy had not herself previously grown as fast as 4.7 per cent a year for eight years, nor had Germany reached 4.5 per cent except in the very short period from 1925 to 1928. These two countries had no precedent in their own histories. But other countries had reached figures as high as these before—the United States and Sweden, for example. Nothing very exceptional has happened yet.

But hitherto it is true that growth rates of over 3 per cent a year for more than eight years have always been in periods when there was some special explanation—such as political integration or recovery from a war. This, together with the similarity between 1922–1929 and 1950–1959, does suggest that there may well be exceptional recovery factors in these recent rapid rates. It is noticeable that for all the fastest growing countries except

7. Kiyoshi Kojima, 'Capital Accumulation and the Course of Industrialisation, with Special Reference to Japan', *Economic Journal,* December 1960.

8. The upward bias to the figures which derives from the exclusion of the non-market product and from the underestimate of some slowly-growing sectors probably affects the Japanese figures more than those of the other countries.

9. Since, however, we expect these high rates to be due largely to an extension of the most productive sector, it does not follow that Japanese productivity within the modern factory sector will increase more rapidly than that of other countries.

10. *New Long-range Economic Plan for Japan,* Economic Planning Agency, published by Japan Times, Tokyo, 1961.

Japan the 1954–1959 rates are lower than the 1950–1959 averages.

Though nothing exceptional or unprecedented has happened yet, it will be unprecedented if the rapid post-war rates are continued for another ten or fifteen years. It would be unwise to assume, on the basis of historical experience, that this is in any way impossible. There are a large number of forces now making for higher rates of growth which did not exist before: the absence of prolonged depressions, the competition between capitalist and communist economic systems, and the development of incentives to fast growth, including techniques of planning which can be applied to predominantly free enterprise economies. Within Western Europe the economic integration now in process may be as stimulating to growth as it was when, for instance, Germany was united.

It is naive to regard a process as complex as the expansion of economic output as following some necessarily predetermined pattern; the main lesson of the historical figures is simply that no such pattern does in fact appear in them. When a farmer is estimating probable crop yields he will be wise to assume that these will be subject to the same climatic and other variations as in the past, but foolish to assume that statistical averages of past yields represent the most probable yield under improved conditions of fertilisation and irrigation.

The Pattern of U.S. Economic Growth

SIMON KUZNETS

Simon Kuznets is George F. Baker Professor of Economics at Harvard University and a pioneer in the measurement of national income and growth. This essay first appeared in 1964 and was republished in Kuznets's book, Economic Growth and Structure.

ECONOMIC GROWTH is a long-term process whose features can properly be observed only in a historical perspective. In view of the wide discussion of the country's growth (or lack of growth) during recent years, it may be helpful to take a longer look. Some of the distinctive quantitative characteristics of our economic growth over the long stretch may be useful in evaluating recent changes.

A COMPARISON OF LONG-TERM GROWTH RATES

Crude as the estimates are, we can approximate the rates of growth of the gross national product, population, and labor force in this country back to 1840, the year that may be accepted as dating the entry of this country into the period of modern industrialization. Over the one hundred and twenty years from 1840 to 1960, population grew at an average rate of about 2 percent per year; labor force, at a slightly higher rate of 2.2 percent per year; gross national product, at 3.6 percent per year; per capita product at 1.6 percent per year; and product per worker, at 1.4 percent per year (Table 1). These rates mean that in 1960 population was about 10.5 times as large as 1840; labor force, almost 13 times; per capita product and, presumably, per capita real income, over 6 times; and product per worker, over 5 times.

How does this record compare with the long-term growth of other countries? The countries of most interest to us here are those that we now consider developed: those that have managed to take advantage of the wide potentials of modern economic growth and

TABLE 1. *Rates of Growth per Year, Gross National Product, Population, and Labor Force in the United States in Successive and Overlapping Decades and Longer Periods, 1840–1960 (percent)*

	Product (1)	Popu- lation (2)	Labor force (3)	Product per capita (4)	Product per worker (5)
Successive decades					
1. 1839–49	4.24	3.11	3.57	1.10	0.64
2. 1949–59	4.95	3.09	3.18	1.80	1.71
3. 1959–69	1.99	2.39	2.07	−0.39	−0.08
4. 1869–79	4.95	2.33	3.01	2.56	1.88
Overlapping decades					
5. 1878–82–1888–92	3.73	2.26	2.70	1.44	1.00
6. 1883–87–1893–97	3.10	2.02	2.50	1.05	0.58
7. 1888–92–1898–1902	4.04	1.80	2.50	2.20	1.50
8. 1893–97–1903–07	5.03	1.78	2.60	3.19	2.36
9. 1898–1902–1908–12	3.71	1.95	2.67	1.73	1.01
10. 1903–07–1913–17	2.60	1.87	1.95	0.72	0.63
11. 1908–12–1918–22	2.60	1.50	1.05	1.08	1.53
12. 1913–17–1923–27	3.62	1.40	1.14	2.19	2.45
13. 1918–22–1929	3.99	1.47	1.35	2.49	2.61
14. 1923–27–1933–37	−0.35	0.98	1.16	−1.33	−1.49
15. 1929–1939–41	1.37	0.74	1.21	0.62	0.15
16. 1933–37–1943–47	7.02	0.96	1.84	6.00	5.09
17. 1939–41–1948–52	4.27	1.39	1.40	2.84	2.83
18. 1943–47–1953–57	2.47	1.67	0.80	0.78	1.65
19. 1948–52–1959–61	3.24	1.71	1.19	1.50	2.03
Longer periods					
20. 1840–80	4.03	2.73	2.96	1.26	1.04
21. 1880–1920	3.52	1.88	2.23	1.61	1.26
22. 1920–60	3.15	1.31	1.28	1.81	1.84
23. 1840–1960	3.56	1.97	2.15	1.56	1.38
Absolute values [1]					
24. 1959–61 [2]	509.0	179.9	69.9	2,829	7,282
25. 1959–61 as multiple of 1840 [3]	66.7	10.4	12.9	6.4	5.2
26. 1840 [4]	7.63	17.1	5.42	446	1,408

[1] Product is in billions of 1961 dollars; population and labor force, in millions; and product per capita and per worker, in 1961 dollars.

[2] Cols. 1 and 2 are the absolute values underlying line 19; col. 3 = line 25 × line 26; col. 4 = col. 1 ÷ col. 2; col. 5 = col. 1 ÷ col. 3.

[3] These figures are based on cumulated growth rates.

[4] Col. 1 = line 24 ÷ line 25; cols. 2 and 3 are the values underlying line 1; col. 4 = col. 1 ÷ col. 2; col. 5 = col. 1 ÷ col. 3.

those that are (or were) fairly large, so that their growth conditions and problems have not been too different from those of the United States.

If then we look at the long-term records of the United Kingdom, France, Germany, Russia (and the USSR), and Japan, allow for changes in boundaries, and observe long periods (ranging from 79 years for Japan to 117 years for the United Kingdom), the results of the comparison may be stated simply (Table 2). First, the annual rate of growth of population in the United States was much higher than in these other large, developed countries: compared with 2 percent in this country, the rates in the other countries ranged from 1.2 percent for Japan to 0.2 for France and, except for Japan, were half or less than half of the rate of growth of U.S. population. Second, the annual rates of growth of per capita product for the United States and for the large European countries were within a fairly narrow range: from 1.9 percent for Russia (for a period reaching back to 1860) to 1.2 percent for the United Kingdom (for a period reaching back to 1841), with 1.5 to 1.6 percent for this country. We cannot place much stress on such differences, and for practical purposes, we can assume that the U.S. rate of growth in per capita product was about the same as in the large, developed European countries. The Japanese rate, estimated for 1880–1960 at 2.8 percent, was distinctly higher. Third, the much higher rate of growth of population in the United States, combined with the same or roughly the same rate of growth of per capita product, means that there was a correspondingly higher rate of growth in aggregate product here than in the European countries. Thus, the rate of rise in gross national product in the United States was from a fifth to almost twice as high as that in the large, developed European countries.

It need hardly be mentioned that these averages are for long periods, covering subperiods that differ markedly in the rates of growth of product and population. Furthermore, for several countries, particularly Japan, the period is significantly shorter than that for the United States; and extension of the period to 1840, the initial date for this country, would only lower the averages for both the European countries and for Japan. Yet the comparison is valid and indicates the exceptional performance in the United States: high rates of growth of population and of total product, if

TABLE 2. *Rates of Growth per Year, Product, Population,
and Per Capita Product for Selected Countries over
Long Periods (percent)*

	Duration of period (1)	Product (2)	Population (3)	Product per capita (4)
Great Britain and United Kingdom				
Great Britain				
1. 1841–81	40	2.54	1.19	1.33
2. 1881–1921	40	1.77	0.91	0.86
United Kingdom				
3. 1921–1957–59	38	1.88	0.43	1.44
4. Total, 1841–1957–59	117	2.07	0.86	1.20
France				
5. 1841–50–1861–70	20	2.23	0.39	1.84
6. 1871–80–1901–10	30	2.00	0.22	1.77
7. 1901–10–1920–28	18.5	1.46	−0.13	1.60
8. 1920–28–1958–60	35	1.55	0.37	1.18
9. Total, 1841–50–1958–60	103.5	1.80	0.24	1.55
Germany				
1913 boundaries				
10. 1851–55–1871–75	20	1.63	0.74	0.89
11. 1871–75–1913	40	3.09	1.20	1.87
Interwar boundaries				
12. 1913–1935–37	23	0.57	0.53	0.04
Federal Republic				
13. 1936–1958–60	23	3.97	1.40	2.53
14. Total, 1913–1958–60	46	2.25	0.97	1.28
15. Total, 1851–55–1958–60	106	2.45	1.01	1.43
Sweden				
16. 1861–65–1881–86	20	2.88	0.72	2.15
17. 1881–85–1921–25	40	2.69	0.66	2.01
18. 1921–25–1958–60	36	3.77	0.59	3.16
19. Total, 1861–65–1958–60	96	3.13	0.64	2.47
European Russia and USSR				
European Russia				
20. 1860–1913	53	2.67	1.30	1.35
USSR				
21. 1913–28	15	0.54	0.54	0
22. 1928–58	30	4.40	0.67	3.71
23. Total, 1913–58	45	3.10	0.63	2.45
24. Total, 1860–1958	98	2.87	0.99	1.86
Japan				
25. 1878–82–1918–22	40	4.14	1.05	3.05
26. 1918–22–1958–60	39	3.97	1.36	2.57
27. Total, 1878–82–1958–60	79	4.05	1.21	2.81

not of per capita product, have existed over the long period 1840–1960. . . .

One further implication of the conclusions should be noted. We know that at present the per capita product of the United States is the highest in the world and appreciably higher than that in the developed European countries. Such comparisons are treacherous, but this statement is undeniable even if we do not accept at face value the United Nations estimates that indicate that in 1952–54 per capita income of the United States was more than double those of the United Kingdom and France and over three times that of Germany. Nor is it easy to ascribe meaning to a calculation that shows that per capita product in the United States was almost three times that of the USSR in 1958. But let us assume moderately that the advantage in recent years is, say, one-and-one-half to one. Then, if the rate of growth in per capita income in the United States is about the same as for these European countries, the implication is that in 1840 the per capita income of the United States was also at least one-and-one-half-times as high, and relatively higher if the rates of growth of per capita income in the large European countries were greater than that of the United States. A crude but suggestive calculation indicates that from the beginning of our period, the per capita income of the United States—even before its industrialization—was close to that in the most developed country, the United Kingdom, and appreciably higher than in most European countries, let alone the rest of the world (with the exception of a country like Australia in its very early period of growth). In other words, the very high per capita income of the United States compared with those of other developed countries observed today is due largely to the fact that at the beginning of its industrialization its per capita income was already relatively high, and during the 120 years following, it managed to sustain rates of growth in per capita income that were not much lower than those of the developed countries which initially had much lower per capita incomes.

THE CHARACTERISTICS OF LONG-TERM U.S. GROWTH

The high rate of population growth in the United States, higher than in other large, developed countries, was due primarily to the power of this country to attract immigrants. From 1840 to 1930, through three quarters of the long period covered here, the population of native stock grew from 14.2 to 82.7 million, less than six times the initial number; the population of foreign stock (foreign-born and native-born of foreign or mixed parentage) grew from somewhat less than 3 million to over 40 million, or over thirteen times the original number. In 1930, about a third of the country's total population was of foreign stock. Also, the rate of natural increase (the excess of births over deaths) may have been slightly higher here than in the older, developed countries, with the birth rates higher (particularly in the early nineteenth century) and the death rates somewhat lower. But the major source of the difference in the rate of growth of population and still more in that of the labor force was immigration, in ever-increasing streams and from diverse sources in Europe, although not from other continents. The importance of this stream for the economic growth of the United States is still not fully understood or completely analyzed, much of the past literature having concentrated on difficulties of adjustment and assimilation and having been biased by reformers concerned with short-term problems rather than with long-term gains. Nor have we paid sufficient attention to the effect of the decline in this source of growth in population and labor force—initiated in World War I, furthered by restrictive legislation in the 1920's, and sharply accentuated in the depression of the 1930's, never to be relaxed significantly—on the economic growth and adjustment problems of this country in recent years.

That the rate of growth in per capita product in the United States was no higher than in the large European countries (except moderately, compared with England) and in Japan, despite freedom from destructive impacts of the major wars which affected the latter countries and which are included in the averages cited above, is somewhat of a surprise. As to the comparison with Russia —where the average rate of growth of per capita product was raised largely during the costly three decades under authoritarian rule from 1928 to 1958 and where relative disregard of the more difficult problems of fitting economic growth to the needs and wishes of the population may account in good part for its high rate of measured increase—it is subject to grave doubts, but the results are hardly a puzzle. This is perhaps also true of the comparison with Japan, a country that started from initially very low levels and much later in time and in which a long-lived hierarchical social system was harnessed to the cause of rapid industrialization, while many traditional industries in the fields of consumer goods and housing were preserved. To repeat, the puzzling finding is a rate of growth of per capita product in the United States that was not significantly higher than in France and Germany, only slightly higher than in England, and significantly lower than in Sweden. Could the very rapid rate of growth of population and labor force in this country have restricted the rates of growth in per capita and per worker product? If so, what is the connection? Surely one cannot assume that the supply of natural resources had any limiting effects, insofar as most of the period of growth in the United States is concerned, compared with the conditions in the European countries. Could the limitation stem from difficulties in supplying adequate capital per worker, engendered by a rapidly growing labor force, despite the high long-term capital formation proportions in the United States, compared with the other developed countries? Or did the problems of adjustment and assimilation faced by immigrants lower average productivity, despite the fact that most immigrants were in the prime labor ages and presumably endowed with strong economic incentives? Or, finally, did the very high level of per capita income induce a lower rate of growth by permitting the exchange of work for leisure, since there was no great pressure to "catch up"? . . .

Our observation of these [long-term growth] rates should not be limited to averages over as long a period as 120 years. How have they changed *during* that period? First, has there been a long-term acceleration or retardation in the rates of growth? For population and labor force, the answer is clear: the rate of growth has declined markedly. Thus over the first forty years, from 1840 to 1880, despite the fact that the period includes the Civil War years, the population grew 2.7 percent per year; during the next forty years, the rate dropped to 1.9 percent per year; in the last forty years, from 1920 to 1960, it was only 1.3 percent per year. Likewise, the rates of growth in the labor force, through the successive forty-year periods, declined from 3.0 to 2.2 to 1.3 percent per year. To be sure, population growth has recovered since World War II; the rate of increase over the last decade (1950 to

1960) was 1.7 percent per year, but it still was lower than the rate for 1880 to 1920; ad the rate of growth of the labor force in the last decade was among the lowest, less than 1.2 percent per year (reflecting the low birth rate of the 1930's), but it may recover to higher levels in the 1960's.

The retardation in the rate of growth of population and labor force was accompanied by a decline in the rate of growth of aggregate gross national product. It was slightly over 4 percent per year from 1840 to 1880, 3.5 percent per year from 1880 to 1920, and 3.1 percent per year from 1920 to 1960 (over the last decade, it was 3.2 percent per year). It should be noted that except for the earliest period, all product rates are calculated from either five- or three-year averages at terminal points, to reduce the effects of short, cyclical disturbances.

But while the rates of growth of population and labor force declined to less than half of the early levels, the retardation in the rate of growth of gross national product was much less marked— about a quarter. This means, of course, that the rate of growth of per capita or per worker product showed a significant acceleration. The rate of growth of per capita product from 1840 to 1880 was 1.3 percent per year; from 1880 to 1920 it was 1.6 percent per year; from 1920 to 1960 it was 1.8 percent per year; and even in the last decade it was only slightly below 1.6 percent per year. The per worker product rate was slightly above 1 percent per year from 1840 to 1880; 1.3 percent per year from 1880 to 1920; and over 1.8 percent per year from 1920 to 1960. Over the last decade, from 1950 to 1960, the rate of growth of gross national product per worker was 2.0 percent per year, among the highest in the long-term record.

Two important recent monographs, John Kendrick's for the period since the 1880's and Edward Denison's for the period since 1909, show acceleration in the rate of growth of product per worker.[1] At the danger of overburdening this paper with statistical detail, I shall give the major conclusions of these studies in a brief

1. See J. W. Kendrick, *Productivity Trends in the United States* (Princeton, N.J.: National Bureau of Economic Research, 1961); and E. F. Denison, *The Sources of Economic Growth in the United States and the Alternatives before Us,* Supplementary Paper No. 13 (New York: Committee for Economic Development, 1962).

listing. The conclusions of the Kendrick study are: (1) Between 1879–1919 and 1919–53, the rate of growth of national product per unit of labor input (man-hours weighted by hourly wage rates in the base year) rose from 1.4 to 1.9 percent per year; the rate of growth of product per unit of capital input rose from 0.4 to 1.2 percent per year; and that of product per unit of combined factor input rose from 1.1 to 1.7 percent per year. (2) The measured acceleration in the rate of growth of productivity was kept down by the inclusion of the government sector and the finance and services sector, for both of which measures of productivity are quite tenuous. When these are excluded, the rise in product per unit of labor input accelerates from 0.8 percent per year in 1879–1919 to 2.4 percent in 1919–53. (3) Within the private domestic economy, excluding finance and services, the acceleration in the rate of growth of product per unit of labor input was observed in all sectors except contract construction. (4) Findings for individual sectors and for branches of manufacturing suggest that the divisions of the productive system in which the greatest acceleration in the rate of growth of product per unit of labor (or total factor) input occurred were either those in which such growth was quite low in the past (such as agriculture and woodworking manufactures) or those in which technological changes were particularly conspicuous (such as chemicals, petroleum, and electrical machinery, among manufactures).

The Denison study also shows a rise in the rate of growth of national product per unit of factor input: from 1.2 percent per year for 1909–29 to 2 percent per year for 1929–57 (per man-hour of labor, from 1.9 to 2.5). From the analysis that attempts to allocate productivity to the various components, we can gather that of the increase in the rate of growth of productivity of some 0.8 percent per year (from 1.2 to 2), greater education of the labor force accounts for 0.32 points while the major portion of the remainder is likely to be accounted for by an increased weight credited to the advance of knowledge. . . .

THE VARIABILITY OF THE U.S. GROWTH RATE

Although it is tempting to speculate on the implications of a combination of retardation in the rates of growth of the population and the labor force with acceleration in the rate of growth of product per capita and per worker, a distinctive feature of long-term growth in this country, we must turn now to a third aspect of our experience—the variability of growth. The rates of growth for each decade—calculated wherever possible from five-year averages centered on the initial and terminal years and thus largely eliminating the effects of business cycles of three to nine years in duration—fluctuate widely (Table 1). Even from the 1870's to World War I, a period unaffected by a major war, the rate of growth in per capita product varied between a low of about 1.1 percent per year (from 1883–87 to 1893–97) to a high of 3.2 percent per year (from 1893–97 to 1903–07). Swings of approximately twenty years in the growth rates of aggregate product, population, labor force, and product per capita and per worker are observable even after we cancel out as best we can the short-term business cycles.

These long swings in the rate of growth have been the subject of increasing attention in recent years in this country, and the literature dealing with them has grown markedly.[2] Their relevance to the interpretation of recent short-term changes is being examined afresh. Consideration of the technical details of the procedures for the isolation and description of these long swings and of the controversial hypotheses advanced in attempts to account for them would be out of place here. A few general comments may, however, point up the significance of these swings for the present discussion.

First, regardless of the procedure employed to eliminate the short-term business cycles or to distinguish the sustained, unidirectional long-term trends, if we limit the cancellation to cycles that are completed within a decade at most and if we stipulate that the underlying long-term trends make no more than one turn in a period of at least forty to fifty years, the resulting smoothed

2. The most convenient summary appears in Moses Abramovitz' statement in the *Hearings on Employment, Growth and Price Levels* (86th Cong., 1st sess. [1959]), Part II, pp. 411–466, and his "The Nature and Significance of Kuznets Cycles," *Economic Development and Cultural Change*, IX (April 1961), pp. 225–248. See also "Long Swings in the Growth of Population and in Related Economic Variables," pp. 328–378 below, and Simon Kuznets, *Capital in the American Economy* (Princeton, N.J.: Princeton University Press, 1961), Chs. 7 and 8, pp. 316–388.

indexes of product, population, and labor force, as well as of per capita and per worker product, would show significant variations around the underlying long-term trend. And if we describe these variations effectively, their amplitude is found to be significantly wide in relation to the average rate of growth in the underlying trend—to the point where, at the peak of a swing, the decadal rate of growth may be over twice as high as in the underlying trend, and at the trough, less than half as high. It is hardly surprising that even if we disregard periods affected by wars and revolutions and cancel out the short-term cycles, the course of economic performance is not a simple curve that can be adequately and fully described by a second-degree equation over a period of five to fifteen decades. The capacity to attain such a smooth and sustained performance would in itself be more surprising than the observed variability and would require as much explanation as the latter.

Second, granted that the long swings in product may be due in part to prolonged underutilization of economic capacity, we must not overlook the long swings in the rates of growth of population and labor force. So long as the latter are present, even the full utilization of labor and capital will not eliminate the long swings in the rate of growth of aggregate product; and if the swings in population and labor differ in timing, as they well may if they originate in processes of natural increase, there will be long swings also in the rate of growth of output per capita, even under full employment. Thus, in the United States, the rate of population growth reached a low of 0.8 percent per year in the 1930's, and while this was due to the depression following the contraction phase of a long swing, it produced a low rate of growth in labor force in the 1950's, about twenty years later. A low growth rate in the labor force leads to a low rate of aggregate growth, even under full employment, unless there is an opposite swing in the rate of growth of product per worker. (The "echo" effects of downward swings in the rates of growth of population and labor force, even if occasioned by wars, are just as marked for the Communist countries; and in addition, the errors in planning and the struggles for political succession and their associated policy choices cannot help but affect rates of growth for periods long enough to constitute phases of long swings.)

RECENT GROWTH IN THE CONTEXT OF THE SECULAR TREND

What is the relevance of the findings discussed above to the evaluation of recent growth in this country? To be sure, one may deny any relevance, either because the underlying estimates are judged to be completely unreliable or because the present is assumed to be separated from the past by a void that prohibits any inference from a long-term perspective. The first argument rests on technical grounds, and all one can say against it is that despite obvious limitations, rough estimates of the longer past are far more useful than more precise data within a short-trem span that do not permit comparisons over time. The second argument implies that we are in a completely new era, not only in the sense that conditions are new but that even our inheritance from the past has been dissipated or is irrelevant, an assumption that cannot be accepted because it disregards the many important ways in which the past has shaped this country's observable responses to new problems.

The difficulty is in formulating this evaluation, in establishing the full bearing of the past upon the present and the proximate future. And the difficulty stems from the fact that these quantitative findings on the past are relatively new, that we do not know, in an empirically testable fashion, the factors, particularly the institutional adjustments, that were involved in the growth trends and in their long swings—so that even if we could establish the current and prospective conditions under which the economy would be operating, we have no fully learned lesson of the past to apply to them. The speculations suggested above on the relation between our high rate of growth of population and labor force and our not-so-high rate of growth in product per capita and per worker, similar questions concerning the association between the marked retardation in the rates of growth of our population and labor force and the significant acceleration in the rate of growth of per capita and per worker product, and our inadequate knowledge of the mechanism that produces the long swings —all point to the meagerness of analytical understanding of these basic quantitative aspects of the country's economic growth, which are so directly relevant to the evaluation of our recent or prospective growth rates. . . .

Under the circumstances, we can only raise a few questions about the evaluation of recent changes, but even these are worthwhile if they expose the danger of easy judgments and too ready answers. The first and most obvious question is in regard to the meaning of the term "growth" when it is applied to changes over short periods, and they have to be short when we deal with current policy problems. If we say that from 1955 to 1960, the United States' gross national product grew x percent per year, and we are concerned over the low rate observed, does growth, whether of total or of per capita gross national product, mean the underlying trend *plus* the long swing around it? If so, how can we distinguish the underlying trend? How can we distinguish the factors that affect our long-term growth from those that cause the long swings and further distinguish these from the factors associated with deviations from full employment in the business cycle, so that in choosing policy actions directed at the short-term movements we do not neglect the possible effects on the rate of growth in the underlying long-term trend?

Whatever the answer to this question, and its vital importance is obvious, one clear implication of our earlier discussion is the need not only for a sharp distinction between the shorter and the longer periods when measuring the rate of economic growth but also for care in comparing these rates. The relevance of this comment can be illustrated by a citation from the January 1962 *Economic Report of the President*. Table 11 of the report contains rates of growth of gross national product per man-year for eleven countries, the United States among them, for the periods 1913–59 and 1950–59. For all the countries the rates are substantially higher for 1950–59 than for 1913–59. The accompanying text reads: "Further evidence that modern industrial economies are not helpless prisoners of past long-term trends is to be found in Table 11, which shows that the major countries of Western Europe, and Japan as well, have recently exceeded their own long-term performance" (p. 114). This statement may have been intended merely to argue against a naïve acceptance of statistically established long-term trends as true descriptions of the paths that economies had to follow and as the bases for projections into the future. But the statement can also be read as suggesting that the 1950–59 rates of change constitute a new long-term trend. Yet comparisons between rates of growth for a nine- and a forty-six-year period do not tell us that the long-term trend in the specific nine-year period was different from that in the forty-six-year period; there may have been other nine-year periods that, as phases of long swings, also greatly exceeded the average trend rate for the long period of half a century, and clearly the short-term elements in a nine-year period must be examined for their effect on the average for that period as a measure of long-term trend.[3] Since at least eight of the eleven countries were adversely affected by World War II, since the subsequent recovery processes have lasted through most of 1950–59, and also since the four countries with the highest rates of growth for 1950–59—Japan, Italy, Germany, and France—were among those most damaged by the war, such an interpretation of the differences between the rates of growth for the recent nine years and for the longer period of forty-six years would seem incautious.

Second, care must also be exercised in comparing rates of growth for short periods among countries, for they may not portray even roughly the differentials in the underlying long-term trends. In the table in the *Economic Report of the President*, already referred to, the United States, whose rate of growth in gross national product per man-year in 1950–59 was 2.2 percent per year, is eighth in rank, with six European countries and Japan all showing appreciably higher rates for the same nine-year period. But if, from the same table, we calculate the rates of growth for 1913–50, the preceding thirty-seven years, the rate of growth for the United States, 1.7 percent per year, is only slightly below that for Japan, 1.8 percent, and much above the rates for all the other nine countries, particularly the large European countries. One is tempted to argue, in line with the suggestion already made, that the high rates of growth in Europe and Japan in recent years reflect attempts to "catch up" in two ways: first, to recover from the war and, second, to take advantage of the opportunities for greater growth in productivity that were previously utilized in

3. In the original paper that contained the table discussed in the *Economic Report of the President* (January 1962), the authors note that "these rapid rates [i.e., the ones for 1950–59] are not unprecedented" and refer to past periods of growth at rates as fast. See Deborah C. Paige *et al.*, "Economic Growth: The Last Hundred Years," pp. 172–190, especially p. 180.

the United States and not for various reasons, in these other countries. This does not deny the possibility that the acceleration in
the rate of economic growth in Europe contains elements—partly
associated with the Common Market and partly caused by a shift
in public policy—that may induce persistently higher rates of
growth than were attained in the long-term pre-World War II
past. But it would require discriminating analysis to establish
these secular elements making for high growth, and no easy infer-
ences can be drawn from simple statistical comparisons for recent
short periods.

CONCLUDING REMARKS

The comments above should not be taken to mean that we need
not concern ourselves with short-term changes in the level of the
country's performance or that we can trust that even if they indicate a lag, the underlying secular trend will somehow eventually
sweep us onward to higher levels. If rates of increase in the country's performance slow down, if persistent unemployment of labor
and other resources develops, policy action must be considered—
whether or not it has been attempted in the past—for we are
continuously expanding our knowledge of methods of stimulating
and sustaining an economy's growth. But this granted, the value
of relating these short-term changes to the longer run of the
economy is undeniable, and it would be enhanced if the application of the longer perspective were based on better knowledge
and understanding of our past. Consider, for example, the finding
that in the last forty years the rate of growth of product per capita
and per worker in this country was distinctly higher than in the
past, despite the inclusion of the period of the 1930's, with the
greatest depression on record. Was this merely the result of the
retardation in the rate of growth of population and labor force?
Should we consider an entirely different hypothesis, one which
would assume that the course of technological change since the
late nineteenth century permitted increasing rates of growth of
product per worker or even per man-hour and that this country
was able to exploit this potential, unlike the countries in Europe,
which suffered devastating wars and faced other obstacles (overcome only recently)? Conversely, how much of the higher rate of

growth of product per capita or per worker in recent decades in this country has been associated with World War II and its aftermath? The implications of these different questions, in terms of the different groups of factors that would have to be examined, are obvious enough; and depending upon the answers, different interpretations of the recent past and proximate future would be suggested, and different policies would seem relevant.

It is tempting to conclude this paper with one rather general comment on the implications of our long-term pattern of economic growth. This growth occurred through decades marked by a succession of turbulent changes in this country and in the rest of the world, and these changes have been particularly rapid since World War I, the last third of the long period covered by Table 1. From a relatively small and young country, protected by what were then wide ocean distances as well as by the pax Britannica, open to immigration from the more advanced countries of the time (those in Europe), the United States has emerged to a position of leadership, of dominant size and high per capita and per worker economic performance, but vulnerable and exposed to all the dangers of leadership in a divided world in which technological advance means not only gains in peaceful productivity but also more extreme gains in destructiveness of weapons. And much of the change in the international scene was concentrated in the brief span of thirty years, from the 1930's to date.

These trite observtions suggest what may not be so obvious—that the pattern of past growth leaves its impression in the institutions that the country develops to deal with the problems generated by past growth; that these institutions may persist beyond their useful time and constitute obstacles to further growth under changed conditions; and that sustained economic growth requires continuous adjustments of social and political institutions to changed conditions—adjustments that are in good part required because the institutions that proved useful earlier and were, in fact, required in earlier economic growth are now obsolete. The impressive record of economic growth in this country was not accomplished by the repetitive application of invariant rules of economic and social behavior; it had to be a creative adjustment to changed conditions, and the cost of some of the conflicts that had developed between old and new institutions (the most striking and costly example is the Civil War) was quite high. Minimization of such costs of adjustment is as desirable today as it ever was, and the general point that economic growth almost naturally produces obsolescence and thus requires attention and drive to remove the resulting obstacles could, I believe, be illustrated today.

The following illustrations are, unfortunately, *ad hoc* examples rather than the results of thorough study. The whole system of primary and, to some extent, even secondary education in this country in the past has played a profound socializing role as an institution for the assimilation, if not so much of the foreign-born immigrants themselves, of their children, Without it, the unity and consensus so important in making the social decisions necessary to resolve possible conflicts (many of them originating from growth) would not have been secured. Yet, despite the pressure developing for higher educational standards and more advanced levels throughout the system, the tradition of the schools as a way of life rather than a way of learning is not easily overcome.

And again speculating on the influx of immigrants and the increasing proportion of foreign stock in this country, one wonders whether some of the distinctive aspects of political organization in the United States have not been, in part, a consequence. Could the resistance to reapportionment of voting power in response to greater growth of urban population be rationalized, in part, as an attempt to limit the political power of groups among whom the foreign-born and those of foreign stock are far more predominant than in the nonurban areas? Was the attainment of equality in political power by immigrants and their children delayed much beyond their attainment of economic gains and assimilation? If so, whatever elements of strength and stability were lent to the political system by such past attitudes may have been succeeded by a much more obstructive role of political traditions in dealing with current problems generated by economic growth. And, finally, one may ask whether the emphasis on limiting federal power and on the advantages of decentralized political authority, which in the past fostered so many centers of vigorous economic growth across the country, is equally valid today, when the graver problems of the international scene tend to convert economic growth into a competition rather than permit it to remain a self-determining and self-pacing process.

Perhaps the examples cited above are of dubious validity or, less likely, of small weight. But if at all pertinent, they illustrate the general point urged here, that past patterns of long-term growth leave an economic and institutional heritage which may in part be an obstacle to future growth. If so, understanding past experience may not only mean being able to evaluate properly the significance and likely persistence of current short-term changes in the level of the economy's performance. It may also help to identify those institutional obstacles to further growth that have resulted from adaptation to past growth problems. Likewise, a proper analysis of long-term trends in other countries that are sufficiently similar in organization and orientation for comparison (perhaps with some adjustments), should reveal a variety of growth experience and of feasible institutional changes which may be borrowed with some assurance of their tested contribution. Such understanding of the historical origin and of the obsolescence of institutional arrangements is no guarantee that they can, and will be, effectively modified. But one may hope that knowledge of this type contributes to general social intelligence and should at least weaken the traditional reactions that tend to sanctify, because of long usage, patterns that may have become impediments to possible growth under changed historical conditions.

Economic Possibilities
for our Grandchildren

JOHN MAYNARD KEYNES

This famous essay on the future, included in Keynes' collection
Essays in Persuasion, *appeared in 1930 when economic growth
seemed at an end to many observers. It prophesies the opportunities and problems with which continued growth will confront us
a few decades from the present.*

LET US, FOR THE SAKE OF ARGUMENT, suppose that a hundred years
hence we are all of us, on the average, eight times better off in
the economic sense than we are today. Assuredly there need be
nothing here to surprise us.

Now it is true that the needs of human beings may seem to be
insatiable. But they fall into two classes—those needs which are
absolute in the sense that we feel them whatever the situation of
our fellow human beings may be, and those which are relative in
the sense that we feel them only if their satisfaction lifts us above,
makes us feel superior to, our fellows. Needs of the second class,
those which satisfy the desire for superiority, may indeed be
insatiable; for the higher the general level, the higher still are
they. But this is not so true of the absolute needs—a point may
soon be reached, much sooner perhaps than we are all of us aware
of, when these needs are satisfied in the sense that we prefer to
devote our further energies to non-economic purposes.

Now for my conclusion, which you will find, I think, to become
more and more startling to the imagination the longer you think
about it.

I draw the conclusion that, assuming no important wars and no
important increase in population, the *economic problem* may be
solved, or be at least within sight of solution, within a hundred
years. This means that the economic problem is not—if we look
into the future—*the permanent problem of the human race.*

Why, you may ask, is this so startling? It is startling because—

if, instead of looking into the future, we look into the past—we find that the economic problem, the struggle for subsistence, always has been hitherto the primary, most pressing problem of the human race—not only of the human race, but of the whole of the biological kingdom from the beginnings of life in its most primitive forms.

Thus we have been expressly evolved by nature—with all our impulses and deepest instincts—for the purpose of solving the economic problem. If the economic problem is solved, mankind will be deprived of its traditional purpose.

Will this be a benefit? If one believes at all in the real values of life, the prospect at least opens up the possibility of benefit. Yet I think with dread of the readjustment of the habits and instincts of the ordinary man, bred into him for countless generations, which he may be asked to discard within a few decades.

To use the language of today—must we not expect a general "nervous breakdown"? We already have a little experience of what I mean—a nervous breakdown of the sort which is already common enough in England and the United States amongst the wives of the well-to-do classes, unfortunate women, many of them, who have been deprived by their wealth of their traditional tasks and occupations—who cannot find it sufficiently amusing, when deprived of the spur of economic necessity, to cook and clean and mend, yet are quite unable to find anything more amusing.

To those who sweat for their daily bread leisure is a longed-for sweet—until they get it.

There is the traditional epitaph written for herself by the old charwoman:

> Don't mourn for me, friends, don't weep for me never,
> For I'm going to do nothing for ever and ever.

This was her heaven. Like others who look forward to leisure, she conceived how nice it would be to spend her time listening-in—for there was another couplet which occurred in her poem:

> With psalms and sweet music the heavens'll be ringing,
> But I shall have nothing to do with the singing.

Yet it will only be for those who have to do with the singing that life will be tolerable—and how few of us can sing!

Thus for the first time since his creation man will be faced with his real, his permanent problem—how to use his freedom from pressing economic cares, how to occupy the leisure, which science and compound interest will have won for him, to live wisely and agreeably and well.

The strenuous purposeful money-makers may carry all of us along with them into the lap of economic abundance. But it will be those people who can keep alive, and cultivate into a fuller perfection, the art of life itself and do not sell themselves for the means of life, who will be able to enjoy the abundance when it comes.

Yet there is no country and no people, I think, who can look forward to the age of leisure and of abundance without a dread. For we have been trained too long to strive and not to enjoy. It is a fearful problem for the ordinary person, with no special talents, to occupy himself, especially if he no longer has roots in the soil or in custom or in the beloved conventions of a traditional society. To judge from the behavior and the achievements of the wealthy classes today in any quarter of the world, the outlook is very depressing! For these are, so to speak, our advance guard—those who are spying out the promised land for the rest of us and pitching their camp there. For they have most of them failed disastrously, so it seems to me—those who have an independent income but no associations or duties or ties—to solve the problem which has been set them.

I feel sure that with a little more experience we shall use the new-found bounty of nature quite differently from the way in which the rich use it today, and will map out for ourselves a plan of life quite otherwise than theirs.

For many ages to come the old Adam will be so strong in us that everybody will need to do *some* work if he is to be contented. We shall do more things for ourselves than is usual with the rich today, only too glad to have small duties and tasks and routines. But beyond this, we shall endeavor to spread the bread thin on the butter—to make what work there is still to be done to be as widely shared as possible. Three-hour shifts or a fifteen-hour week may put off the problem for a great while. For three hours a day is quite enough to satisfy the old Adam in most of us!

There are changes in other spheres too which we must expect to come. When the accumulation of wealth is no longer of high social importance, there will be great changes in the code of morals. We shall be able to rid ourselves of many of the pseudo-moral principles which have hag-ridden us for two hundred years, by which we have exalted some of the most distasteful of human qualities into the position of the highest virtues. We shall be able to afford to dare to assess the money-motive at its true value. The love of money as a possession—as distinguished from the love of money as a means to the enjoyments and realities of life—will be recognised for what it is, a somewhat disgusting morbidity, one of those semi-criminal, semi-pathological propensities which one hands over with a shudder to the specialists in mental disease. All kinds of social customs and economic practices, affecting the distribution of wealth and of economic rewards and penalties, which we now maintain at all costs, however distasteful and unjust they may be in themselves, because they are tremendously useful in promoting the accumulation of capital, we shall then be free, at last, to discard.

Of course there will still be many people with intense, unsatisfied purposiveness who will blindly pursue wealth—unless they can find some plausible substitute. But the rest of us will no longer be under any obligation to applaud and encourage them. For we shall inquire more curiously than is safe today into the true character of this "purposiveness" with which in varying degrees Nature has endowed almost all of us. For purposiveness means that we are more concerned with the remote future results of our actions than with their own quality or their immediate effects on our own environment. The "purposive" man is always trying to secure a spurious and delusive immortality for his acts by pushing his interest in them forward into time. He does not love his cat, but his cat's kittens; nor, in truth, the kittens, but only the kittens' kittens, and so on forward for ever to the end of cat-dom. For him jam is not jam unless it is a case of jam tomorrow and never jam today. Thus by pushing his jam always forward into the future, he strives to secure for his act of boiling it an immortality.

Let me remind you of the Professor in *Sylvie and Bruno*:

"Only the tailor, sir, with your little bill," said a meek voice outside the door.

"Ah, well, I can soon settle *his* business," the Professor said to the children, "if you'll just wait a minute. How much is it, this year, my man?" The tailor had come in while he was speaking.

"Well, it's been a-doubling so many years, you see," the tailor replied, a little gruffly, "and I think I'd like the money now. It's two thousand pound, it is!"

"Oh, that's nothing!" the Professor carelessly remarked, feeling in his pocket, as if he always carried at least *that* amount about him. "But wouldn't you like to wait just another year and make it *four* thousand? Just think how rich you'd be! Why, you might be a *king*, if you liked!"

"I don't know as I'd care about being a king," the man said thoughtfully. But it *dew* sound a powerful sight o' money! Well, I think I'll wait——"

"Of course you will!" said the Professor. "There's good sense in *you*, I see. Good-day to you, my man!"

"Will you ever have to pay him that four thousand pounds?" Sylvie asked as the door closed on the departing creditor.

"*Never*, my child!" the Professor replied emphatically. "He'll go on doubling it till he dies. You see, it's *always* worthwhile waiting another year to get twice as much money!"

Perhaps it is not an accident that the race which did most to bring the promise of immortality into the heart and essence of our religions has also done most for the principle of compound interest and particularly loves this most purposive of human institutions.

I see us free, therefore, to return to some of the most sure and certain principles of religion and traditional virtue—that avarice is a vice, that the exaction of usury is a misdemeanor, and the love of money is detestable, that those walk most truly in the paths of virtue and sane wisdom who take least thought for the morrow. We shall once more value ends above means and prefer the good to the useful. We shall honor those who can teach us how to pluck the hour and the day virtuously and well, the delightful people who are capable of taking direct enjoyment in things, the lilies of the field who toil not, neither do they spin.

But beware! The time for all this is not yet. For at least another hundred years we must pretend to ourselves and to every one that fair is foul and foul is fair; for foul is useful and fair is not. Avarice and usury and precaution must be our gods for a little longer still. For only they can lead us out of the tunnel of economic necessity into daylight.

I look forward, therefore, in days not so very remote, to the greatest change which has ever occurred in the material environment of life for human beings in the aggregate. But, of course, it will all happen gradually, not as a catastrophe. Indeed, it has already begun. The course of affairs will simply be that there will be ever larger and larger classes and groups of people from whom problems of economic necessity have been practically removed. The critical difference will be realized when this condition has become so general that the nature of one's duty to one's neighbor is changed. For it will remain reasonable to be economically purposive for others after it has ceased to be reasonable for oneself.

The *pace* at which we can reach our destination of economic bliss will be governed by four things—our power to control population, our determination to avoid wars and civil dissensions, our willingness to entrust to science the direction of those matters which are properly the concern of science, and the rate of accumulation as fixed by the margin between our production and our consumption; of which the last will easily look after itself, given the first three.

Meanwhile there will be no harm in making mild preparations for our destiny, in encouraging, and experimenting in, the arts of life as well as the activities of purpose.

But, chiefly, do not let us overestimate the importance of the economic problem, or sacrifice to its supposed necessities other matters of greater and more permanent significance. It should be a matter for specialists—like dentistry. If economists could manage to get themselves thought of as humble, competent people, on a level with dentists, that would be splendid!

Postindustrial America in the Year 2000

HERMAN KAHN AND ANTHONY J. WIENER

Herman Kahn, physicist, strategist and author of On Thermo-
nuclear War, *is director of the Hudson Institute. Anthony Wiener
is a sociologist with the Institute. Their book,* The Year 2000,
from which this selection was taken, was published in 1967.

THERE ARE many good reasons for trying to imagine what the
world may be like over the next thirty-three years. The most important, of couse, is to try to predict conditions in reasonable
detail and to evaluate how outcomes depend on current policy
choices. If only this were feasible, we could expect with reasonable reliability to change the future through appropriate policy
changes today. Unfortunately, the uncertainties in any study
looking more than five or ten years ahead are usually so great
that the simple chain of prediction, policy change, and new prediction is very tenuous indeed.

It is not that the period beyond the next decade is too far away
to be of interest. It is short in terms of many human concerns: a
child born this year will be only thirty-two years old on January 1,
2000, and many of today's adults will probably still be taking
active roles in the first third of the twenty-first century. Useful or
interesting as such long-range predictions would be, it is simply
too difficult to make them well, and even more difficult to estimate
how this relatively distant future depends on current policies.

Nevertheless, at the minimum, such studies, even if only partially successful, contribute to interesting lectures, provocative
teaching, and stimulating conversation, all of which can broaden
horizons and increase creativity—by no means negligible benefits.
More important, these studies can affect basic beliefs, assumptions, and emphases. Probably most important, long-range studies
provide a context in which to do five- to ten-year studies that can
and do influence policy choices. . . .

METHOD: STANDARD PROJECTIONS
AND MULTIFOLD TRENDS

In this study we have used several interrelated devices to facilitate making systematic conjectures about the future. The most important, of course, is simply to think about the problem—to seek to identify important long-term trends which seem likely to continue. These trends include the world-wide spread of a more or less secular humanism, the institutionalization of scientific and technological innovation, the expectation of continuous economic growth, and the like. For our purposes we have identified a complex, long-term "multifold trend" consisting of thirteen interrelated elements. . . .

We have attempted to construct significant baselines, statistical where possible, to project key variables in society. These include population, literacy, gross national product, energy sources, military strength, and the like; these variables and their growth rates tend both to furnish and to constrain the possibilities for any society. By selecting extrapolations of current or emerging tendencies that grow continuously out of today's world and reflect the multifold trend and our current expectations, we create a "surprise-free" projection—one that seems less surprising than any other specific possibility. Consistent with this projection, we describe a "standard world" and several "canonical variations," designed to raise certain issues.

We have used two approaches common in the study of political-military and other kinds of public policy problems—the scenario and the systematic context, or "alternative future." These methodological devices are especially valuable in the study and evaluation of the interaction of complex and/or uncertain factors. Scenarios are hypothetical sequences of events constructed for the purpose of focusing attention on causal processes and decision-points. They answer two kinds of questions: (1) Precisely how might some hypothetical situation come about, step by step? and (2) What alternatives exist, for each actor, at each step, for preventing, diverting, or facilitating the process? "Alternative futures" can be used for generating additional scenarios, for setting forth and discussing criteria, for the systematic comparison of various alternative policies (or alternative combinations of assumptions and objectives), or for the analysis and examination of specific issues. . . .

The Basic, Long-Term Multifold Trend · The basic trends of Western society, most of which can be traced back as far as the twelfth or eleventh centuries, can be seen as part of a common, complex trend of interacting elements. For analytic purposes, however, we shall separate them into thirteen rubrics, as shown in Table 1. Obviously one might wish to group these elements into fewer and more abstract categories, or to refine the analysis by identifying or distinguishing many more aspects. From the point of view of looking toward the future, the important consideration is that, as basic trends, these elements seem likely to continue at least for the next thiry-three years, though some may saturate or begin to recede beyond that point.

Having identified certain rather general trends, the question arises: How do we extrapolate from these to a point several decades ahead?

TABLE 1.

There Is a Basic, Long-Term Multifold Trend Toward:

1. Increasingly Sensate (empirical, this-wordly, secular, humanistic, pragmatic, utilitarian, contractual, epicurean or hedonistic, and the like) cultures

2. Bourgeois, bureaucratic, "meritocratic," democratic (and nationalistic?) elites

3. Accumulation of scientific and technological knowledge

4. Institutionalization of change, especially research, development, innovation, and diffusion

5. Worldwide industrialization and modernization

6. Increasing affluence and (recently) leisure

7. Population growth

8. Urbanization and (soon) the growth of megalopolises

9. Decreasing importance of primary and (recently) secondary occupations

10. Literacy and education

11. Increasing capability for mass destruction

12. Increasing tempo of change

13. Increasing universality of the multifold trend

Surprise-Free Projections and the Standard World · In projecting beyond the next decade, whether studying general trends and contexts or very specific areas, we must choose—perhaps more or less arbitrarily—among many plausible alternatives those which ought to be studied in greater detail.

One problem of long-range speculation is that the subjective curve of probabilities often seems flat. That is, no particular course of events may seem much more likely than a large range of others. In order to avoid the dilemma of Buridan's ass, who starved midway between two bales of hay because he could not decide which one he preferred, we must then make arbitrary choices among almost equally interesting, important, or plausible possibilities. That is, if we are to explore any predictions at all, we must to some extent "make them up." Clearly, the most salient of the projections we can make is one that is "surprise-free"; nevertheless it would be very surprising if in any thirty-three-year period the real world did not produce many political and technological surprises.

For the skeptical reader this "surprise-free" projection may be useful chiefly as a norm for comparison and disagreement. While the surprise-free projection is similar in spirit to the "naïve projection" of the economist, which assumes a continuation of current tendencies, it is more complex in that it also includes the implications of whatever empirical and theoretical considerations affect our expectations. (For example, a "naïve" projection of world population to 2000 would be about 7.2 billion, but our "surprise-free" projection would be 6.4 billion, and a persuasive case could be made for a somewhat lower figure.) Then while still staying within this general surprise-free projection one can specify one or more "standard" worlds for even more intensive study. . . .

Our own Standard World reflects our own expectations, of course, and we have tried to make these explicit as much as possible. . . .[1]

1. Each of the major alternatives to the Standard World can be put into one of three categories: (A) more "Integrated," (B) more "Inward-Looking," and (C) in greater "Disarray." The models in these categories envisage, respectively:
(A) a relatively peaceful, relatively prosperous, relatively arms-controlled world with a relatively high degree of consultation among nations, and the

Figure 1 shows how [according to these projections] the ten largest nations compared in GNP and population in 1965 (numerals in circles), and the points they seem most likely to reach by the year 2000 (numerals in ellipses). The numbers identifying each country are in the order of our medium or "best estimate" projections for GNP in 2000; except that the differences among Canada, India, and Italy are not significant. The elipses indicate a range of reasonable uncertainty for each year 2000 projection. In 1965, for example, the United States had a GNP of $692 billion (by United Nations definition), population of about 195 million, and per capita GNP of $3,560. By the year 2000 its GNP could be up to more than $4,500 billion (almost the top of the chart) with more than $12,000 per capita GNP; or assuming the lowest "reasonable" growth rate, GNP could be less than $1,400 billion and GNP per capita under $5,000. The range in population estimates is narrower—291 to 361 million. Our "best estimate" for the United States is for a GNP close to the top of the "reasonable range" and for a relatively moderate population growth— $3,200 billion and 318 million people. The ellipses for India and China slope backward because they are more likely to achieve relatively high GNP growth if they can limit population.

Finally we separate the 135 nations of the world into two classes —old (about 55) and new (about 80). Old nations are those that have had a relatively continuous existence at least since World War I; new nations are for the most part post-World War II creations or ancient countries recently emerged from colonial status. We consider West Germany to be an old nation; East Germany, China (newly integrated), Taiwan, India (newly independent), Egypt, and so on to be new. We also assume (again in all worlds, and for the 1967–2000 period as a whole) the fulfillment of certain widespread current expectations: that there will be more or less sustained economic growth, among all the major (and most minor) nations; and more or less sustained (but usually

---

existence of political coordination or even integration among all, or almost all, the major and/or minor powers;

(B) almost as peaceful and prosperous a world, but with little arms control or general coordination; and

(C) a relatively troubled and violent world, but one in which no large central wars have occurred.

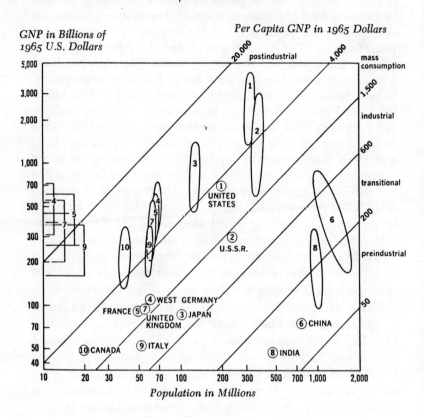

FIGURE 1. *"Surprise-Free" Projections for the Ten Major Countries*

GNP in Billions of 1965 U.S. Dollars

Per Capita GNP in 1965 Dollars

postindustrial · 20,000 · 4,000 · mass consumption

1,500

industrial

600

transitional

200

preindustrial

50

① UNITED STATES
② U.S.S.R.
④ WEST GERMANY
FRANCE ⑤ ⑦ UNITED KINGDOM ③ JAPAN
⑩ CANADA ⑨ ITALY
⑥ CHINA
⑧ INDIA

GNP axis: 5,000 · 3,000 · 2,000 · 1,000 · 700 · 500 · 300 · 200 · 100 · 70 · 50 · 40

Population axis: 10 · 20 · 30 · 50 · 70 · 100 · 200 · 300 · 500 · 700 · 1,000 · 2,000

Population in Millions

Legend (example is West Germany)

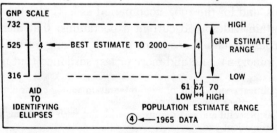

GNP SCALE
732
525 — 4 ← BEST ESTIMATE TO 2000 → 4
316

AID TO IDENTIFYING ELLIPSES

HIGH
GNP ESTIMATE RANGE
LOW

61 67 70
LOW ↔ HIGH
POPULATION ESTIMATE RANGE
④ ← 1965 DATA

tapering off) population growth; and that except in periods of actual war or great crisis there will be freedom of the seas with foreign commerce moving freely and without explicit reliance on national naval or other military power. . . .

THE LAST THIRD OF THE 20TH CENTURY
AND THE BEGINNING OF THE NEXT

Except for the possibility of the emergence of a postindustrial culture, the listing [of projections in Table 2] is "surprise-free"— it assumes the continuation of the multifold trend, but excludes precisely the kinds of dramatic and/or surprising events that dominated the first two-thirds of the century.

TABLE 2.

Final Third of the Twentieth Century (Relatively apolitical and surprise-free projection)[2]

1. Continuation of basic, long-term "multifold trend"
2. Emergence of "postindustrial" culture
3. Worldwide capability for modern technology
4. Very small world: increasing need for regional or worldwide "zoning ordinances" for control of arms, technology, pollution, trade, transportation, population, resource utilization, and the like
5. High (1 to 10 per cent) growth rates in GNP per capita
6. Increasing emphasis on "meaning and purpose"
7. Much turmoil in the "new" and possibly in the industrializing nations
8. Some possibility for sustained "nativist," messianic, or other mass movements
9. Second rise of Japan (to being potentially, nominally, or perhaps actually, the third largest power)
10. Some further rise of Europe and China
11. Emergence of new intermediate powers, such as Brazil, Mexico, Pakistan, Indonesia, East Germany, and Egypt
12. Some decline (relative) of the U.S. and the U.S.S.R.

2. More specifically, the "surprise-free" projection rules out *major changes in the old nations* that might be caused by possibilities such as the following:
1. Invasion and war; 2. Civil strife and revolution; 3. Famine; 4. Pestilence; 5. Despotism (persecution); 6. Natural disaster; 7. Depression or economic

13. A possible absence of stark "life and death" political and economic issues in the old nations.

If the basic, long-term multifold trend continues or is accelerated during the next thirty-three years, and there are no surprising but not-impossible disruptions of the sort listed above, then a "postindustrial" society seems likely to develop in affluent parts of the world.

Table 3 lists some possibilities often associated with the concept of a "postindustrial" society. This term, introduced by Daniel Bell,[3] refers to what may be as important a future change as that caused by industrialization in the eighteenth and early nineteenth centuries.

To go beyond the next thirty-three years, we can speculate briefly [in Table 4] on world society in the first third of the next century.

Increasing Affluence and (Recently) Leisure · We might conceive of nations at the end of this century as divided into five classes. The *preindustrial* countries are in the condition one might think of as historically "normal." Many people—Kenneth Boulding, Peter Drucker, J. M. Keynes, for example—have pointed out that for the last ten thousand years or so, excluding the last two or three centuries, no large human society has ever produced more than the equivalent of some $200 per capita per year, nor dropped much below about $50 per capita per year for any appreciable period of time. . . .

---

stagnation; 8. Development of "inexpensive" doomsday or near-doomsday machines; 9. Development of nuclear "six-gun" weapons technology; 10. Resurgence of Communism, or revival of Fascism; 11. A racial, North-South, rich-poor, East-West, or other disruptive polarization; 12. Economically dynamic China (∼10 percent per year growth); 13. Politically dynamic U.S., U.S.S.R., Japan, West Germany, Brazil, and other powers; 14. New religious philosophies and/or other mass movements; 15. Development of U.N. or other worldwide organizations; 16. Possible regional or other multinational organizations; 17. Psychological upsetting impact of new techniques, ideas, philosophies, and the like.

The first four of these have to do with the "four horsemen of the apocalypse" (conquest, war, famine, and death) of the sixth chapter of the Book of Revelation; the first six are associated with six seals of the book that is the subject of the Revelation. The remaining possibilities are notably modern possibilities.

3. See *The Reforming of General Education,* (New York: Columbia University Press, 1966), pp. 301 ff.; and his most recent articles on the subject, in *The Public Interest,* Nos. 6 and 7 (1967).

TABLE 3.

The Postindustrial (or Post-Mass Consumption) Society

1. Per capita income about fifty times the preindustrial

2. Most "economic" activities are tertiary and quaternary (service-oriented), rather than primary or secondary (production-oriented)

3. Business firms no longer the major source of innovation

4. There may be more "consentives" (vs. "marketives")

5. Effective floor on income and welfare

6. Efficiency no longer primary

7. Market plays diminished role compared to public sector and "social accounts"

8. Widespread "cybernation"

9. "Small world"

10. Typical "doubling time" between three and thirty years

11. Learning society

12. Rapid improvement in educational institutions and techniques

13. Erosion (in middle class) of work-oriented, achievement-oriented, advancement-oriented values

14. Erosion of "national interest" values

15. Sensate, secular, humanist, perhaps, self-indulgent criteria become central

With industrialization mankind broke out of this pattern. We shall consider *partially industrialized societies,* which we somewhat arbitrarily, but in accordance with custom, define as those with incomes between $200 and $600 per capita, as probably in a "transition" stage, without assuming that they will necessarily continue to industrialize. . . .

We call (even more arbitrarily, and certainly inaccurately as a generalization) societies with between $600 and $1500 per capita income, *industrialized.* Yet they are short of the mass consumption stage. Theirs is roughly the condition of America in the 1920's, or Europe immediately after World War II. Many preindustrial and partially industrialized societies may also, of course, have dual economies.[4] Northern and Southern Italy are examples, and this

4. If a country has large unexploited "frontier" areas as well—as many in Africa and Latin America do—we might call it a triple economy.

TABLE 4.

A Relatively "Surprise-Free" Early Twenty-First Century

1. We expect the rise of new great powers—perhaps Japan, China, a European complex, Brazil, Mexico, or India.

2. There will be new political, perhaps even "philosophical," issues.

3. There will be a leveling off or diminishing of some aspects of the basic, long-term multifold trend, such as urbanization.

4. The postindustrial and industrial worlds will have been largely realized.

5. Some success seems likely with population control, arms control, and some kind of moderately stable international security arrangements; though probably not a "world government."

6. In the industrializing world, disorder, ideology, and irrational movements will probably continue to play disruptive though geographically confined roles.

7. In the U.S. and Western Europe, there will presumably be either a return to certain Hellenic or older European concepts of the good life, or an intensified alienation and search for identity, values, meaning, and purpose, a search made necessary and facilitated by the unprecedented affluence and permissiveness of the postindustrial economy.

problem—though here defined in terms of urban-rural differences —is still worse in such areas as Latin America today, and promises to get even worse in the future. It may be worst of all by the year 2000 in the six most populous, less developed countries: China, India, Pakistan, Indonesia, Brazil, and Nigeria. These now contain, and in the future will probably continue to contain, about half the world's population, are now preindustrial, and will presumably be partially industrialized by the year 2000. The problem of relatively great development in major cities and much less in lesser cities and rural areas is already evident in these countries. . . .

Post-World War II has seen the emergence of the so-called *mass-consumption society,* first in the United States and then in Western Europe and Japan. Again arbitrarily, but reasonably, we shall define a mass-consumption society, today, as one with between $1,500 and $4,000 per capita. Japan, although it has less than $1,000 per capita, is by every superficial appearance a mass consumption society today; while the Soviet Union, with a per capita income of around $1,500, seems far short of that condition.

$4,000 per capita will probably be sufficient for transition to a *postindustrial* economy in countries like Great Britain or the Scandinavian group, while those with more ambitious goals, in terms of world power (e.g., the Soviet Union), stronger traditions of economic striving (e.g., West Germany), or higher expectations of productive affluence (e.g., the United States) would not become "postindustrial" until higher levels of affluence had been reached. Obviously these definitions cannot be taken too seriously; not only are there exceptions today, but there may be more in the future.

From our point of view, probably the most interesting classification is that of the *postindustrial* society. We shall discuss this at some length. Some other characteristics of the postindustrial society have already been noted on Table 3.

Table 5 indicates a rather impressionistic, but not wholly unreasonable, economic ranking for the nations of the world in the year 2000. The figures express national populations in millions, and the total world population is estimated at 6.4 billion. The descriptions are, on the whole, optimistic, and we would not care to defend in detail the specific rank order we have suggested. The numbers identifying each group correspond roughly to the levels of income of the previous table.

If the above scenario is realized, the year 2000 will find a rather large island of wealth surrounded by "misery," at least relative to the developed world and to "rising expectations." Even these poor countries, however, for the most part will enjoy great improvements over their traditional standards of living. The postindustrial and industrial societies will contain about 40 per cent of the world's population: more than 90 per cent of the world's population will live in nations that have broken out of the historical $50–$200 per capita range. Yet at the same time the absolute gap in living standards, between countries or sectors of countries with developed (industrial, postindustrial, mass consumption) economies and those at preindustrial levels, will have widened abysmally. . . .

TABLE 5. *Six Economic Groupings in Year 2000*
(millions of people)

(5) Visibly Postindustrial		(3) Mature Industrial	
U.S.	320	Union of South Africa	50
Japan	120	Mexico, Uruguay, Chile,	
Canada	35	Cuba, Colombia, Peru,	
Scandinavia and		Panama, Jamaica, etc.	250
Switzerland	30	N. Vietnam, S. Vietnam,	
France, W. Germany,		Thailand, the Philip-	
Benelux	160	pines, etc.	250
TOTAL	665	Turkey	75
(5) Early Postindustrial		Lebanon, Iraq, Iran, etc.	75
United Kingdom	55	TOTAL	700
Soviet Union	350	(2) Large and Partially	
Italy, Austria	70	Industrialized	
E. Germany,		Brazil	210
Czechoslovakia	35	Pakistan	250
Israel	5	China	1,300
Australia, New Zealand	25	India	950
TOTAL	540	Indonesia	240
(4) Mass Consumption		U.A.R.	70
Spain, Portugal, Poland,		Nigeria	160
Yugoslavia, Cyprus,		TOTAL	3,180
Greece, Bulgaria, Hun-		(1) Preindustrial or Small and	
gary, Ireland	180	Partially Industrialized	
Argentina, Venezuela	60	Rest of Africa	350
Taiwan, N. Korea,		Rest of Arab World	100
S. Korea, Hong Kong,		Rest of Asia	300
Malaysia, Singapore	160	Rest of Latin America	100
TOTAL	400	TOTAL	850

ALIENATION AMIDST AFFLUENCE
IN POSTINDUSTRIAL SOCIETY

We are attempting [here] to describe a plausible and culturally consistent projection of a culture, values, and style of life consistent with other features of our Standard World of the year 2000. To test whether such a projection is plausible and consistent is both naïvely simple and insolubly complicated. We can take what we now know about past and current American styles of life together with some current trends—and our knowledge of these is far from complete—and add what we believe or find plausible about the socialization of the child, the development of character, character changes in later life, ways in which social structure and culture change, and so forth, and on this basis try to assess the consequences of some simple, basic trends that are characteristic of our Standard World. These include relatively easy affluence, new technology, absence of absorbing international challenges, and considerable but not disastrous population growth. We must ask, in effect, how these trends might furnish or constrain possibilities for change in the large number of Americans already living who will probably survive into the year 2000, and in those who will be born and "socialized" in the interim.

The first salient factor seems likely to be a vastly increased availability of goods and such services as transportation and communication. A second is a likely increase in leisure and a concomitant reduction of the pressures of work. A third is the likelihood of important technological changes in such areas as psychopharmacology, with possible radical consequences for culture and styles of life. Perhaps the most important is a likely absence of stark "life and death" economic and national security issues. . . .

Economic Plausibility and Postindustrial Leisure · Let us assume, then, with expanded gross national product, greatly increased per capita income, the work week drastically reduced, retirement earlier (but active life-span longer), and vacations longer, that leisure time and recreation and the values surrounding these acquire a new emphasis. Some substantial percentage of the population is not working at all. There has been a great movement toward the welfare state, especially in the areas of medical care, housing, and subsidies for what previously would have been thought of as poor sectors of the population. Table 6 shows one possibility or "year 2000 scenario" for the distribution of work and leisure. . . .

TABLE 6. A *Leisure-Oriented "Postindustrial"* Society
(*1100 Working Hours per Year*)

7.5	Hour Working Day
4	Working Days per Week
39	Working Weeks per Year
10	Legal Holidays
3	Day Weekends
13	Weeks per Year Vacation

(Or 147 Workings Days and 218 Days Off/Year)

Thus in a leisure-oriented society one could spend

40 per cent of his days on a vocation

40 per cent of his days on an avocation

20 per cent (or more than 1 day per week) just relaxing.

A projection for a leisure-oriented society could retain the population of 318 million but cut the work year from 1600 to 1100 hours (1920 hours is now "standard" but somewhat above average) and lower the labor force participation rate to 56 per cent. Under these assumptions, and assuming that the economy has been experiencing the high rate of productivity increase, the leisure-oriented society will still provide for an increase of about 100 per cent in per capita GNP relative to 1965. Table 7 shows this.

It seems not implausible that one-half the people would work in more or less normal fashion, and that one-fifth of the people would work longer hours than normal, either for income or for compulsive or altruistic reasons. Because of the excess contribution of this group, it may be possible to maintain something close to the high GNP projected above, even though some 20 to 30 per cent of the normal labor force contribute little or no labor. The underproducers might be, in effect, hobbyists working a few days a month, or a few months a year, to acquire the income to pursue their hobbies. One can also assume that "normal" frictional unemployment will be somewhat higher than usual, and that there will also be something which might be considered "semi-frictional" unemployment (that is, people who have lost jobs but are taking some time looking for another by using their vacations, or who have unusually high or unrealistic standards of what their jobs should be or who are just lying around living on savings.) There could also be a group, assuming the above conditions, who reject any sort of gainful employment on the ground of principle or preference. And finally, there should be people who are more willing to be on relief than not, if only because they have personal

TABLE 7. *Year 2000 Economic Scenarios for U.S. Affluence and Alienation*

Population	318 million
Employed Labor Force	122 million
Leisure Oriented Society:	Work year 1100 hours
GNP	$2,321 billion
Per Capita GNP	$7,300

or family problems that make it unwise for them to work if they can survive without; or there may be some who are simply and cynically "on the dole."

The above suggests that in place of the current 20 per cent poor, we may have a similar number, but differently situated, who do not participate normally in the vocational life of the nation.

It would be possible [for the "normal" worker] to pursue an avocation as intensely as a vocation and still have a good deal of time for "third-order" pursuits. Such patterns can be consistent with continued economic growth at reasonably high rates.

Success Breeds Failure: Affluence and the Collapse of Bourgeois Value · John Maynard Keynes addressed himself to this dilemma in one of the earliest and still one of the best short discussions of some of the issues raised by the accumulation of wealth through investment.[5] As he put it,

. . . the economic problem, the struggle for subsistence, always has been hitherto the primary, most pressing problem of the human race. If the economic problem is solved, mankind will be deprived of its traditional purpose.

Will this be of a benefit? If one believes at all in the real values of life, the prospect at least opens up the possibility of benefit. Yet I think with dread of the readjustment of the habits and instincts of the ordinary man, bred ino him for countless generations, which he may be asked to discard within a few decades. . . . thus for the first time since his creation man will be faced with his real, his permanent problem—how to use his freedom from pressing economic cares, how to occupy his leisure, which science and compound interest will have won for him, to live wisely and agreeably and well.

There are those who would argue that with increased freedom from necessity men will be freed for more generous, public-spirited, and humane enterprises. It is a commonplace of the American consensus that it is poverty and ignorance that breed such evils as Communism, revolutions, bigotry, and race hatred. Yet we know better than to expect that the absence of poverty and ignorance will result in a triumph of virtue or even of the

5. "Economic Possibilities for our Grandchildren" (1930), reprinted in J. M. Keynes, *Essays in Persuasion* (New York: W. W. Norton, 1963), and in this volume, pp. 209–214.

benign. On the contrary, it is equally plausible that a decrease in the constraints formerly imposed by harsher aspects of reality will result in large numbers of "spoiled children." At the minimum many may become uninterested in the administration and politics of a society that hands out "goodies" with unfailing and seemingly effortless regularity.

One may choose almost at will from among available hypotheses that may seem to apply to the situation, and one reaches contrary conclusions depending upon the choice that is made; this indeterminancy is perhaps a measure of the inadequacy of contemporary social thought as a basis for generalization, relative to the complexity of human phenomena.

For example, one may take the Dollard et al.[6] frustration-aggression hypothesis and conclude that aggressiveness will be greatly tranquilized in a society that provides much less external and realistic frustration. This is opposed to the more complex and more psychoanalytically oriented point of view of Freud who points to the role that frustrations imposed by external reality may play in shoring up the defenses of the character structure—defenses that are crucial strengths and that were acquired through learning, with difficulty, as an infant to defer gratification and to mediate among conflicting energies of instinctual impulses, conscience, and the opportunities and dangers of the real world.[7] Research might show, if research could be done on such a subject, that many an infantile and narcissistic personality has matured only when faced with the necessity of earning a living—others only when faced with the necessity for facing up to some personal challenge, such as military service or participation in family responsibility. (The well-known finding that suicide rates drop sharply during wars and economic depressions is subject to diverse interpretation, but it may suggest that such external chal-

6. John Dollard et al., *Frustration and Aggression* (New Haven, Conn.: Yale University Press, 1939).

7. As Freud pointed out, "Laying stress upon importance of work has a greater effect than any other technique of living in the direction of binding the individual more closely to reality; in his work he is at least securely attached to a part of reality, the human community . . . and yet . . . the great majority work only when forced by necessity, and this natural human aversion to work gives rise to the most difficult social problems." *Civilization and Its Discontents* (London: Hogarth Press, 1930), p. 34. note 1.

lenges can serve crucial integrative or compensatory functions for some personalities, and, perhaps less dramatically, for many others.) This is not to say that equally effective or perhaps superior external challenges could not be found to substitute for the working role—or wartime experience—as a maturing or reality-focusing influence. If they are not found, however, while the economy and international and other threats make fewer demands, the decline of the values of work and national service may have some destructive effect.

Thus there may be a great increase in selfishness, a great decline of interest in government and society as a whole, and a rise in the more childish forms of individualism and in the more anti-social forms of concern for self and perhaps immediate family. Thus, paradoxically, the technological, highly productive society, by demanding less of the individual, may decrease his economic frustrations but increase his aggressions against the society. Certainly here would be fertile soil for what has come to be known as alienation.[8]

The alienation that we speculate may result from affluence could have little or nothing to do with whether the society is capitalist or socialist. In either case the control of the decision-making apparatus would be perceived as beyond the reach of and in fact of little interest for the average person. Thus, whatever the economic system, the politics (and even the culture) of plenty could become one not of contentment but of cynicism, emotional distance, and hostility. More and more the good life would be defined in Epicurean or materialistic, rather than Stoic, or bourgeois terms. The enhancement of private values combined with the increased sense of futility about public values would also entail a kind of despair about the long-run future of the whole

8. The word alienation has been used in many different senses, some of them well defined and some in the context of system of explanation and prescription for the ailment. The young Karl Marx, for example, followed Ludwig Feuerbach (and to some extent anticipated Freud's *Civilization and its Discontents*) in the belief that alienation resulted from civilized man's "unnatural" repression of his instinctual, especially sexual, nature. Later, however, Marx concluded that alienation resulted from the worker's relationship to labor that had to be done for the profit of another; the cure was to have the worker "own" the means of production; thus alienation could be reduced by shortening the working day, and "the worker therefore feels himself at home only during his leisure."

society. More and more people would act on the aphorism currently attributed to a leader of the new student left: "If you've booked passage on the Titanic, there's no reason to travel steerage."

Thus the classical American middle-class, work-oriented, advancement-oriented, achievement-oriented attitudes might be rejected for the following reasons:

1. Given an income per worker by the year 2000 of well over ten thousand dollars in today's dollars, it may become comparatively easy for intelligent Americans to earn ten to twenty thousand dollars a year without investing very intense energies in their jobs—in effect they will be able to "coast" at that level.

2. It may become comparatively easy for an American to obtain several thousand dollars a year from friends and relatives or other sources, and to subsist without undergoing any real hardship, other than deprivation of luxuries. (Informal polls in the Cambridge, East Village, and Haight Ashbury areas indicate that many "hippies" get along on about ten dollars per week, as do many CORE and SNCC workers.)

3. Welfare services and public facilities will generally probably put a fairly high "floor" under living standards, even in terms of luxuries such as parks, beaches, museums, and so on.

4. With money plentiful, its subjective "marginal utility" would probably tend to diminish, and there would probably be a greatly increased emphasis on things that "money cannot buy."

5. Economic and social pressures to conform may diminish as the affluent society feels increasingly that it can "afford" many kinds of slackness and deviation from the virtues that were needed in earlier times to build an industrial society.

6. If the "Puritan ethic" becomes superfluous for the functioning of the economy, the conscience-dominated character type associated with it would also tend to disappear. Parents would no longer be strongly motivated to inculcate traits such as diligence, punctuality, willingness to postpone or forego satisfaction, and similar virtues no longer relevant to the socioeconomic realities in which children are growing up.

7. Yet the need to "justify" the new patterns may remain, and to the extent that there is any residual guilt about the abandonment of the nineteenth-and early twentieth-century values, there

would be exaggerated feelings *against* vocational success and achievement. Many intellectuals and contributors to popular culture would help to make the case against "bourgeois," "managerial," "bureaucratic," "industrial," "Puritanical," and "preaffluent" values. There would then be considerable cultural support for feelings ranging from indifference to outright contempt for any sort of success or achievement that has economic relevance.

❖   ❖   ❖   ❖

ALIENATION AND THE SOCIAL STRUCTURE

Of course not everyone would suffer equally from the prevalence of affluence that we have just described. Among the voluntary poor, for example, there would be certain rock-bottom types who would insist on deprivation for reasons that have to do with personal psychopathology. Thus many skid-row derelicts, alcoholics, drug addicts, ambulatory schizophrenics, and other marginal or self-destructive personalities would insist on living at a level barely sufficient for survival. Some indeed, would insist on slow forms of suicide through starvation, exposure, or malnutrition, as with some cases of alcoholism.

Most of the relatively poor members of society would, however, be amply subsidized. They would readily accept welfare as a means of support, and the feeling that the world owes them a living would go largely unquestioned. Incentives to take unskilled jobs would be minimal, nor would holding a job—particularly a marginal one—add much to self-esteem when relief and welfare have so much group approval. Extremist movements might flourish in the general climate of alienation from the "power structure." Many whites and middle-class Negroes might view race riots and acts of destruction with indifference, or even sympathy and approval. The following statement of a well-known poet of Negritude may well come to reflect the sympathies of a larger segment of both populations:

> Mercy! mercy for our omniscient conquerors
> Hurray for those who never invented anything
> Hurray for those who never explored anything
> Hurray for those who never conquered anything

Hurray for joy
Hurray for love
Hurray for the pain of incarnate tears.[9]

At the same time, since what Oscar Lewis has described as the "culture of poverty" [10]—with its short-time perspectives and emphasis on immediate survival and pleasure, and the like—would have become, to some degree, also the culture of affluence, the assimilation of the impoverished ghetto-dweller into the larger society would pose less difficult psychological problems. The indolent spectator, the "hipster" and the "swinging cat" would have become in large degree the norm for very wide sectors of the population. Moreover, this group would be receptive to ideologies which welcome the downfall and dissolution of the American postindustrial way of life. These people would tend to be congregated in the major cities that they would probably not control politically but in which they would constitute major pressure groups and could exercise veto rights on many programs. They would probably live in rather uneasy and unstable alliance with the upper middle class, "responsible" people who would continue to control the economic structure and make use of the resources of the city. . . .

It has often been pointed out that current United States racial conflicts involving issues such as housing and education are based as much on issues of poverty and social class as on racism. Although the racism and militancy of the Black Muslims may make it difficult for whites to welcome the group, it may be the most active force since the Christian evangelists in recruiting new Negro members into the middle class.

Thus, perhaps surprisingly, this group may be the means—over one or two generations—for many who might otherwise have remained in the "culture of poverty" to acquire "father figures," motivation for striving, and ultimately typical American middle-class attitudes and occupations. When this process has been com-

9. Aimé Césaire, *Cahier D'un Retour Au Pays Natale,* as quoted in Colin Legum. *Pan-Africanism,* rev. ed. (London: Pall Mall Press Ltd.; New York: Frederick A. Praeger, 1965).

10. Oscar Lewis, *La Vida: A Puerto Rican Family in the Culture of Poverty,* San Juan and New York (New York: Random House, 1966), esp. pp. xlii-lii.

pleted, the racism of the Nation of Islam may disappear or diminish, leaving little more "unmelted" in the "pot" than in the typical "successful" American pattern, in which there ordinarily remains some ethnic self-consciousness (and some "intergroup tensions") among mostly assimilated, but still distinct, former immigrant groups.[11]

Returning to the society as a whole: The lower middle classes (who in general will be making between ten and twenty thousand 1965 dollars a year) would enjoy a greatly reduced work week with some emphasis on leisure. While their necessities and basic luxuries would be obtainable without great effort, they might still wish to increase income by moonlighting or by the wife's working. Some, of course, would have little motivation for expending extra effort and for them the problems of occupying leisure time would be a primary concern. Others would want to have money, pursue expensive hobbies, or emulate some aspect of the life patterns of the upper middle classes or even the wealthy. Both groups would provide a tremendous market for all kinds of sports and fads and particularly for various forms of mass entertainment. Year 2000 equivalents for the bowling alley, miniature slot-racing car tracks, and the outboard motor, would be everywhere. The drive-in church, the "museum-o-rama," and comparable manifestations of pressures toward a general degradation and vulgarization of culture would be a likely result of the purchasing decisions of this group. At the same time, these people might militate politically against civil rights and against the poor and relatively poor nonworking classes that they must support, and they would likely provide the primary support for both conservative national policies and political jingoism.

The upper middle class (most of whom will have annual income of perhaps twenty to sixty thousand 1965 dollars), by contrast, would, in many ways, be emulating the life style of the landed gentry of the previous century, such as emphasizing education, travel, cultural values, expensive residences, lavish entertainments, and a mannered and cultivated style of life. For some there would be much effort to amass property and money for personal and family use. Getting away from the cities and from centers of

11. See Nathan Glazer and Daniel Patrick Moynihan, *Beyond the Melting Pot* (Cambridge, Mass.: Massachusetts Institute of Technology Press, 1963).

population would be a difficult problem which only large amounts of money will solve. There would probably be some emphasis on "self-improvement," including cultural dilettantism. While among most members of this group we would expect a continuation of current well-to-do suburban patterns, in many cases patterns of life might be increasingly self-indulgent, marriages unstable, children alienated from their parents. Interest in strange and exotic political ideologies, Eastern mysticism, and the like, might flourish, as could a cult of aestheticism and a shrinking from the "grubby" or "crass" aspects of society. Effete attitudes might be combined with contempt for the lower middle class and fear of the poor and of their propensity for violence. There may also be some romanticization of the "noble savage" (or "hippy") who lives outside the values of the society, in voluntary poverty and/or minor or even major criminality.

The very wealthy would be able to buy considerable protection from these exigencies—that is, from all but the cultural confusion and normative conflicts. Because of their social power, many would have responsibility and there might be, in some groups, a sense of noblesse oblige, which would be shared by many in the upper middle class.

Youth could be especially self-indulgent or alienated, as the identity confusion typical of adolescence is exacerbated by the confusion, normlessness, and anomie of the society. Indifference to moral and ethical values and irresponsibility of personal behavior would be combined with feelings of outrage about the vast discrepancies between the wealth of the rich nations and the poor, and an especially painful situation would arise if these young people were drafted for military service in teeming, underdeveloped countries. Combined with pacifism and antipatriotic ideologies would be a strong feeling that American lives are too precious to be spent anywhere else in the world—or indeed to be wasted in America itself. Recruitment into any of the more difficult or demanding professions would be restricted to those (perhaps many) who have adopted Stoic patterns, and to the sons of fathers who are already in those professions and who identify with them. Conformers would—as always—work, aspire to comfortable sinecures, and look forward to early retirement—but now with great confidence. "Bumming around" and hip patterns of life could become increasingly common (though not the norm) in all but the lower middle-class groups. Many would live indefinitely on the resources of friends and relatives and on opportunistic sources of income without doing any sustained work, or in the upper middle-class pattern would cloak themselves in pretentions to artistic creativity. In spite of the prominence of symbols of rebellion and nonconformity, these youths, especially because of their anomie and alienation, would be subject to extreme fads of behavior and political, ethical, and religious ideas.

The lower middle class, making, say, five to twenty thousand dollars a year, are by 2000 not going to be very different from the lower middle and middle middle classes today. The upper (and middle) middle class in the year 2000 make, say, twenty to one hundred thousand dollars a year and will not necessarily feel independently wealthy. Both groups will probably continue with current work-oriented, advancement-oriented, achievement-oriented values. The extreme alienation we are talking about is restricted to minorities, which will be important in part because they are likely to be concentrated in the big cities, in part because they appeal to many of the more intellectual members of that ordinarily alienated group—adolescents—and mostly because their members will be literate and articulate and have a large impact on intellectuals and therefore on the culture generally.

Function of Work · To arrive more precisely at an answer to the question, "What are the consequences of a reduction in the amount of work that needs to be done?" one must ask, "What are the various functions for the individual of the work he performs?" It is easy to make a long list of such benefits at various levels of analysis. For example, people derive from work such benefits as role; status; sense of striving; feeling of productivity, competency, and achievement; and relationships with others and advancement in a hierarchy, whether organizational or professional.

Table 8 shows some rough characterizations and generalizations about various roles work may play for different kinds of people in the year 2000. Those whose basic attitude toward work is that it is totally abhorrent or reprehensible are not listed, since on the whole they will find it possible to avoid employment entirely.

One could easily imagine that many Americans from "normal"

TABLE 8.

Basic Attitude Toward Work As:	Basic Additional Value Fulfilled by Work
1. Interruption	Short-run income
2. Job	Long-term income—some work-oriented values (one works to live)
3. Occupation	Exercise and mastery of gratifying skills—some satisfaction of achievement-oriented values
4. Career	Participating in an important activity or program. Much satisfaction of work-oriented, achievement-oriented, advancement-oriented values
5. Vocation (calling)	Self-identification and self-fulfillment
6. Mission	Near fanatic or single-minded focus on achievement or advancement (one lives to work)

(i.e., not deprived) backgrounds will increasingly adopt the first position, that work is an interruption, while many formerly in the lower and economically depressed classes will increasingly shift to the second or third positions which reflect more work-oriented and achievement-oriented values. On the other hand, the man whose missionary zeal for work takes priority over all other values will be looked on as an unfortunate, perhaps even a harmful and destructive neurotic. Even those who find in work a "vocation" are likely to be thought of as selfish, excessively narrow, or compulsive. . . .

Other Factors in Alienation · In discussing alienation, attention ought also to be given to other aspects of cultural change that may contribute to ego-disintegration and feelings of disorientation. Here we meet the difficult problem of diagnosing the malaise of our times. What precisely causes the alienation of adolescents and many others in 1967 is a very controversial matter. Speculation about the year 2000 is, of course, many times more complicated and uncertain. If it sometimes seems to be easier this is presumably mostly because the results are less checkable—though it is possible that there will be clear and predictable tendencies in 2000 that are only ambiguously detectable today. In any case it seems plausible that the "end of ideology" and an inevitable disenchantment with the ideals and expectations of American democracy and free enterprise, coupled with a continued decline in the influence of traditional religion and the absence of any acceptable mass ideologies, have and will continue to contribute to a common spiritual and political rootlessness. As secularization, rationalization, and innovation continue to change the culture in the direction of Sensate and bourgeois norms, the influence of traditional *Weltanschauungen* seems more likely to continue to wane than to undergo any resurgence in the next thirty-three years. . . .

Technological change itself may contribute to feelings of estrangement from the new physical world and also from a society strongly affected by continual innovation and disruption. There is a long tradition in American letters of hostility to the machine,[12] and, at least since World War II, an increasing perception that the social consequences of science and technology are, at best, mixed blessings. Machines that perform some functions of the human mind far better than humans can are likely to be even more resented, in spite of their economic benefits, than machines that do the same for human muscles. The human place in the world may be most seriously disturbed by new medical technology. New drugs will raise sharply the questions, what is a real human feeling, and what is a genuine personality? Plastic replacements for hearts and other vital organs raise in new and more difficult form the old problem of defining life and death, and add a new difficulty to the old question, what is a human being?

The unconscious is, as Freud has reminded us, an inveterate punster, and it may not be accidental that phrases such as way out, far gone, out of it, and out of this world are currently used to mean strange or bizarre; and that, moreover, phrases such as way out, dropout, flip-out, freak-out, turned on, tuned in, out of my head, and cool are supposed to refer to desirable conditions.[13] Perhaps the most important alienating influence will be a purely

12. Leo Marx in *The Machine in the Garden: Technology and the Pastoral Idea in America* (New York: Oxford University Press, 1964), treats this American tradition at some length and with extreme sympathy. Lewis Mumford's *The Myth of the Machine: Technics and Human Development* (New York: Harcourt, Brace and World, 1967), is the latest in his long series of works belonging to this tradition; in particular, it represents a reinterpretation of archaeology and early history intended to show that speech, and not the ability to use tools and technics, was once, and should become again, the essential human faculty. See also Eric Hoffer, *The Temper of Our Time* (New York: Harper and Row, 1967), for some caustic comments on this idiosyncrasy of some intellectuals.

13. Freak-out can also refer to a "bad trip."

negative thing—the absence of the traditional challenge of work, community approval, and national needs.

Humanism and the Value of Time · In this "super-affluent" society of year 2000, it is not likely that efficiency (defined by the criteria of maximizing profit or income) will still be primary, though it will doubtless remain important. To some degree this has already occurred and the situation in the United States is today very different from what it was before 1929. For example, it seems to be true that when a middle-class American looked for a job in 1929, he was interested in salary and prospects for advancement. Today, however, the first questions addressed to personnel interviewers are more likely to relate the satisfaction of the applicant's family with the new neighborhood and the quality of the schools. This is, of course, particularly true of professional and managerial workers, but it seems to be more widely spread as well. It is only after the requirements of home and children have been satisfied (and sometimes considerations of pension, vacation, and insurance as well), that salary and advancement are discussed.

We could think of this phenomenon as a shift to humanistic rather than vocational or advancement-oriented values, and conjecture that this tendency will increase over the next thirty-three years. Indeed, unless there is a surprising interruption in the exponential progress of prosperity, sensate-humanist and epicurean values almost surely will come to dominate older bourgeois virtues, and may even return, in some respects, to criteria that antedated the "bourgeois" element of the multifold trend, which has been a driving force for more than five centuries.

The new values could not only be premature, they could also be wrong. The year 2000 conditions we have sketched could produce a situation in which illusion, wishful thinking, even obviously irrational behavior could exist to a degree unheard of today. Such irrational and self-indulgent behavior is quite likely in a situation in which an individual is overprotected and has no systematic or objective contact with reality. For example, there are probably many people for whom work is the primary touch with reality. If work is removed, or if important functions are taken from work, the contact these people have with reality will be to some degree impaired. The results—minor or widespread—may become apparent in forms such as political disruption, disturbed families, and personal tragedies—or in the pursuit of some "humanistic" values that many would think of as frivolous or even irrational.

Humanistic values are, of course, a question of definition. Some may judge certain ideologies that invoke humanistic language as sentimental, self-indulgent, or rationalizations of quite irrational feelings of rebelliousness and selfishness. Consider this question of humanistic versus irrational or indulgent behavior. In 1926 the British economist Arthur Redford said, in describing the adjustment of British yeomen to industrialization: "In the course of a generation or two it becomes quite 'natural' . . . for a fixed number of hours each day, regulating their exertions constantly . . . there may be some temporary restlessness among the 'hands,' but the routine soon reestablishes itself as part of the ordinary discipline of life." While this may be a rather callous observation, "progress" and other conditions predominantly made the adjustment a necessary one.

In the post affluent, seemingly very secure world of the year 2000, we will not likely, and presumably should not, be willing to ask people to make sacrifices of this order. However, new issues will arise. Consider the following two statements put forth by Berkeley students on signs they were carrying while picketing and later on a BBC television broadcast:

I am a human being; please do not fold, spindle, or mutilate.

Life here is a living hell.

One can only agree with the first, assuming we understand precisely in what way the students believe they are not treated as well as IBM cards. Thus it was widely believed, especially in the 1930's and 1940's, by people who thought they were "psychologically sophisticated," that any kind of discipline for children causes undesirable repression, inhibits creativity, and creates neuroses; that almost completely permissive upbringing is necessary for a parent not to "fold, spindle, or mutilate." Today psychoanalysts are emphasizing that a reasonable level of benevolent but firm discipline is very much needed by a child, and that excessive permissiveness is more likely to result in a child marred by guilty wilfulness, irresponsibility, and inadequacy.

Of course, the students would argue that they do not mean anything so extreme, but just that they ought to be treated better than items processed by machines. One can only sympathize with their lack of ability to communicate with a seemingly unfeeling, bureaucratic administration choosing to enforce computer decisions. But to argue that the idiosyncrasies of a computer that allows ten minutes between classes which require fifteen minutes to reach, or that assigns art classes to basements and engineering classes to top-floor rooms with windows, creates difficulties for students, is rather different from arguing that life is a "living hell."

Social Response to New Difficulties · The most serious issue raised by these speculations (in addition to their validity, of course) is whether they are not just modern manifestations of traditional "aberrant" behavior, or whether they represent a reasonable adjustment or transition state to new traditions and mores. There is also the question of to what degree society will be self-correcting and self-adjusting. Doubtless, however, there will be much room and need for improved social policies. Just as it seems likely that societies have learned to handle routine economic problems sufficiently well to avoid serious depressions, it may be that we have begun to understand social and psychological problems well enough to avoid the partial passivity and failure implicit in these speculations.

While few would now believe that the mere multiplication of productive powers is likely to bring mankind into Utopia, or into anything resembling it, it would be ironic (but not unprecedented) if this multiplication of resources were to create problems too serious for the solutions that those very resources should make feasible. Efforts will doubtlessly be needed to invent and implement ways of coping with the new and unfamiliar problems that will certainly arise. Yet, despite best efforts, social policies frequently go wrong.

Suggested Further Readings

Becker, A. S., "Comparisons of U.S. and U.S.S.R. National Output: Some Rules of the Game," *World Politics*, October 1960.

Becker, G., *Human Capital* (National Bureau of Economic Research, 1964).

Bergson, A., *Planning and Productivity under Soviet Socialism* (Columbia University Press, 1968).

Bronfenbrenner, M., "The High Cost of Economic Development," *Land Economics*, May and August, 1953.

Bruchey, S., *Roots of Economic Growth, 1607–1861* (Harper, 1965).

Campbell, R. W., *Soviet Economic Power* (Houghton Mifflin, 1960, paper).

Deane, P., "The Long Term Trends in World Economic Growth," *Malayan Economic Review*, October 1961.

de Grazia, S., *Of Time, Work and Leisure* (Twentieth Century Fund, 1962).

Denison, E. F., *The Sources of Economic Growth in the United States* (Committee for Economic Development, 1962, paper).

Denison, E. F., *Why Growth Rates Differ: Postwar Experience in Nine Western Countries* (Brookings, 1967).

Domar, E. D., *Essays in the Theory of Economic Growth* (Oxford, New York, 1957).

Easterlin, R. A., "Economic Growth: Overview" in *International Encyclopedia of the Social Sciences* (Macmillan, 1968).

Eckstein, O., "Federal Expenditure Policy for Economic Growth," *The Journal of Finance*, May 1962.

Fellner, W. J., "Rapid Growth as an Objective of Economic Policy," *Annual Proceedings of the American Economic Association*, May 1960.

Fellner, W. J., *Trends and Cycles in Economic Activity* (Holt, 1956).

Griliches, Z., "Research Costs and Social Returns: Hybrid Corn and Related Innovations," *Journal of Political Economy*, October 1958.

Hall, C. H., *Fiscal Policy for Stable Growth* (Holt, 1960).

Harrod, R. F., *Towards a Dynamic Economics* (Macmillan, London, 1948).

Hicks, J. R., "Growth and Anti-Growth," *Oxford Economic Papers*, November 1966.

International Economic Association, *The Theory of Capital*, D. C. Hague, ed. (Macmillan, 1961).

Knowles, J., *The Potential Economic Growth of the United States*, Study Paper No. 20, Joint Economic Committee, U.S. Congress (Government Printing Office, 1960, paper).

Kuznets, S., *Capital in the American Economy* (Princeton, 1962).

———, *Economic Growth and Structure* (Norton, 1965).

Levine, H. S., "The [Soviet] Economy: Hard and Soft Spots" in C. M. Foust, ed., *The Soviet World in Flux* (University of North Carolina Press, 1967).

Lewis, W. A., *The Theory of Economic Growth* (Irwin, 1955).

Machlup, F., *The Production and Distribution of Knowledge in the United States* (Princeton, 1962).

Maddison, A., *Economic Growth in the West* (Norton, 1966, paper).

Mansfield, E., *The Economics of Technological Change* (Norton, 1968).

Marglin, S. A., *Public Investment Criteria* (M.I.T. Press, 1967).

Massell, B. F., "A Disaggregated View of Technical Change," *Journal of Political Economy*, December 1961.

Meade, J. E., *A Neoclassical Theory of Economic Growth* (Oxford, New York, 1961).

National Bureau of Economic Research, *The Rate and Direction of Inventive Activity*, R. R. Nelson, ed. (Princeton, 1962).

Nelson, R. R., "The Simple Economics of Basic Scientific Research," *Journal of Political Economy*, June 1959.

Nelson, R. R., and E. S. Phelps, "Investment in Humans, Technological Diffusion and Economic Growth," *Annual Proceedings of the American Economic Association*, May 1966.

Nelson, R. R., M. J. Peck and E. D. Kalachek, *Technology, Economic Growth and Public Policy* (Brookings, 1967).

North, D. C., *The Economic Growth of the United States, 1790–1860* (Prentice-Hall, 1961; Norton, 1965, paper).

Phelps, E. S., *Fiscal Neutrality towards Economic Growth* (McGraw-Hill, 1965).

Phelps, E. S., *Golden Rules of Economic Growth* (Norton, 1966).

Phelps, E. S., "The New View of Investment," *Quarterly Journal of Economics*, November 1962.

Ramsey, F. P., "A Mathematical Theory of Saving, *Economic Journal*, September 1929.

Rockefeller Brothers Fund, *The Challenge to America: Its Economic and Social Aspects* (Doubleday, 1958, paper).

Rostow, W. W., *The Process of Economic Growth*, 2nd ed. (Norton, 1962, paper).

Rostow, W. W., *The Stages of Economic Growth* (Cambridge, 1960, paper).

Schultz, T. W., "Education and Economic Growth," *Social Forces Influencing American Education* (National Society for the Study of Education, 1961).

Slichter, S., *Economic Growth in the United States* (Louisiana State, 1961).

Solow, R. M., *Capital Theory and the Rate of Return* (Rand McNally, 1964).

Solow, R. M., "Technological Change and the Aggregate Production Function," *Review of Economics and Statistics*, August 1957.

Solow, R. M., "Technical Progress, Capital Formation and Economic Growth" *Annual Proceedings of the American Economic Association*, May 1962.

Swan, T. W., "Economic Growth and Capital Accumulation," *Economic Record*, November 1956.

Tobin, J., "Economic Growth as an Objective of Policy", *Annual Proceedings of the American Economic Association*, May 1964.

Young, A., "Increasing Returns and Economic Progress," *Economic Journal*, December 1928.